The Seductions of Quantification

THE CHICAGO SERIES IN LAW AND SOCIETY

Edited by John M. Conley and Lynn Mather

The Seductions of Quantification

MEASURING HUMAN RIGHTS, GENDER VIOLENCE, AND SEX TRAFFICKING

Sally Engle Merry

The University of Chicago Press   Chicago and London

SALLY ENGLE MERRY is the Silver Professor in the Department of Anthropology at New York University and the faculty codirector of the Center for Human Rights and Global Justice at the New York University School of Law.

The University of Chicago Press, Chicago 60637
The University of Chicago Press, Ltd., London
© 2016 by The University of Chicago
All rights reserved. Published 2016.
Printed in the United States of America

25 24 23 22 21 20 19 18 17 16   1 2 3 4 5

ISBN-13: 978-0-226-26114-0 (cloth)
ISBN-13: 978-0-226-26128-7 (paper)
ISBN-13: 978-0-226-26131-7 (e-book)
DOI: 10.7208/chicago/9780226261317.001.0001

Library of Congress Cataloging-in-Publication Data

Names: Merry, Sally Engle, 1944– author.
Title: The seductions of quantification : measuring human rights, gender violence, and sex trafficking / Sally Engle Merry.
Other titles: Chicago series in law and society.
Description: Chicago : The University of Chicago Press, 2016. | Series: Chicago series in law and society
Identifiers: LCCN 2015044525 | ISBN 9780226261140 (cloth : alk. paper) | ISBN 9780226261287 (pbk. : alk. paper) | ISBN 9780226261317 (e-book)
Subjects: LCSH: Women — Violence against — Research — United States — Methodology. | Human trafficking — Research — United States — Methodology. | Women — Violence against — Data processing. | Human trafficking — Data processing. | Quantitative research. | Social indicators. | Numerical analysis — Data processing.
Classification: LCC HV6250.4. W65 M4777 2016 | DDC 362.88082 — dc23 LC record available at http://lccn.loc.gov/2015044525

♾ This paper meets the requirements of ANSI/NISO Z39.48-1992 (Permanence of Paper).

Contents

Acknowledgments

Writing a book is always a deeply collaborative project, and I have benefited greatly from the many people I met and interviewed, the generous colleagues who read and commented on the work, graduate students who worked with me, and academic audiences who commented and provided critique. Both the National Science Foundation's Law and Social Sciences Program and the Science, Technology, and Society Program provided funding for the research. Two subsequent National Science Foundation grants to develop networks of scholars working on indicators, with Co–Principal Investigators Benedict Kingsbury and Kevin Davis, brought together scholars for conferences and edited book projects on issues of quantification. This expanded my network of scholars working on indicators and contributed greatly to my thinking about these issues. I am particularly grateful to Benedict Kingsbury, Kevin Davis, and Richard Rottenburg, colleagues with whom I have collaborated on conferences and editing books.

Many other colleagues have contributed significantly to the project by reading drafts of the book and articles I have written and by expanding my thinking with their insights and wisdom, including Philip Alston, Hilary Charlesworth, Sheila Dauer, Sakiko Fukuda-Parr, Terrence Halliday, Setha Low, Michael McCann, David Nelken, Meg Satterthwaite, Johannes Waldmueller, Emily Yates-Doerr, and many others. During the course of my research, I discussed these issues with many thoughtful people engaged in indicator work who generously took the time to talk to me and whose insights have contributed to the project — especially Yakin Erturk, Nicolas Fasel, Henriette Jansen, Srdjan

Mrkic, Eibe Riedel, Hans-Otto Sano, and Martin Scheinin. I am grateful to the UN staff who allowed me to attend meetings and understand their work. I also benefitted from the work of several wonderful graduate students at New York University in the book's research, including Amy Field, Vibhuti Ramachandran, Jessie Shimmin, and Summer Wood. Ram Natarajan generously read and commented on earlier drafts.

Audiences in many parts of the world have given me great feedback on my work. I am particularly grateful to the supportive environment of the Australian National University and its Regulatory Institutions Network, where I am an adjunct professor and have addressed many audiences thanks to Hillary Charlesworth and Margaret Jolly. My colleagues in the Department of Anthropology at New York University (NYU) and in the NYU School of Law have provided me with an intellectually stimulating and supportive environment. The Wellesley Centers for Women generously allowed me to serve as one of their representatives to the United Nations.

My husband and children have always been supportive of my research and writing, for which I am grateful. I am particularly indebted to my twin sister, Patricia Lee Engle, who got me started on this project several years ago but did not live to see it finished. She introduced me to the problem of quantification through her thoughtful and inclusive work on early child development indicators, which she did as a professor of child development at California Polytechnic State University in San Luis Obispo, and while working for UNICEF. She was a great inspiration to me, with her scholarship, activism, commitment to the global project of improving the lives of young children, and desire to incorporate the perspectives of children and their families into her measures. I dedicate this book to her memory.

A World of Quantification

Quantification is seductive. It offers concrete, numerical information that allows for easy comparison and ranking of countries, schools, job applicants, teachers, and much else. It organizes and simplifies knowledge, facilitating decision making in the absence of more detailed, contextual information. By quantification, I mean the use of numbers to describe social phenomena in countable and commensurable terms. Quantification depends on constructing universal categories that make sense across national, class, religious, and regional lines. Categorized numbers can then be bundled together into more complex representations of social phenomena, such as good governance or the rule of law. These numbers convey an aura of objective truth and scientific authority despite the extensive interpretive work that goes into their construction.

Indeed, it is the capacity of numbers to provide knowledge of a complex and murky world that renders quantification so seductive. Numerical assessments such as indicators appeal to the desire for simple, accessible knowledge and to a basic human tendency to see the world in terms of hierarchies of reputation and status. Yet the process of translating the buzzing confusion of social life into neat categories that can be tabulated risks distorting the complexity of social phenomena. Counting things requires making them comparable, which means that they are inevitably stripped of their context, history, and meaning. Numerical knowledge is essential, yet if it is not closely connected to more qualitative forms of knowledge, it leads to oversimplification, homogenization, and the neglect of the surrounding social structure. Grounding quantitative knowledge in a qualitative analysis of categories, meanings, and practices produces better indicators. The current rush to quantification risks sacrificing the insights of rich, ethnographic accounts.

A comparison of the information produced by quantitative and qualitative methods of studying battered women's treatment by the courts illustrates these differences. In 2006, I studied a nongovernmental organization (NGO) that did advocacy work with largely working-class and poor battered women, including African American, Caribbean, Latina, white, Asian, immigrant, lesbian, disabled, and formerly incarcerated women in New York City. These women became members of the organization. They carried out a human rights documentation project on the adequacy of New York City's family courts for battered women. Fourteen of the members, all domestic violence survivors, interviewed seventy-five other domestic violence survivors about their experiences in the courts and produced a report that outlined a series of abuses. The women who were interviewed talked about losing custody of their children to their batterers despite being the primary caretakers, about inadequate measures for safety in the court buildings, and about the unprofessional conduct of judges and lawyers that they experienced when they raised claims of domestic violence (Voices of Women Organizing Project 2008). The final report compared these problems to the standards articulated in human rights conventions.

In contrast, at about the same time, the UN Office of the High Commissioner for Human Rights (OHCHR) developed a set of indicators for measuring violence against women that were to be used by any country around the world (discussed in chapter 7). Some indicators assessed the adequacy of law enforcement in dealing with domestic violence, the same problem the domestic violence survivors in New York City were examining. The indicators measured the "proportion of formal investigations of law enforcement officials for cases of violence against women resulting in disciplinary action or prosecution" and the "proportion of new recruits to police, social work, psychology, health (doctors, nurses, and others), education (teachers) completing a core curriculum on all forms of violence against women" (UN Office of the High Commissioner for Human Rights 2012a: 99). Thus these indicators measured some dimensions of the legal treatment of domestic violence but not the problems raised by the formerly battered women in the New York City study.

Clearly, these two efforts to document battered women's experiences with legal institutions differ in the kinds of information they produced. While the first project was based on a particular local situation and generated its categories and questions from the experiences of those who went through it, the second did not address women's experiences at all. The first one used local knowledge to decide what to count and measure, while the second relied on global measures that had already been developed and used in many different countries. The first effort took into account the ethnicity and social class of the people interviewed as well as the history of the New York City court system, while the second did not. On the other hand, its indicators allowed comparison across cultural contexts and countries in a way that the first approach did not, and it was better able to show the global size and scope of the issue.

This book focuses on the disparity between such qualitative, locally informed systems of knowledge production and more quantified systems with global reach. It argues that despite the value of numbers for exposing problems and tracking their distribution, they provide knowledge that is decontextualized, homogenized, and remote from local systems of meaning. Indicators risk producing knowledge that is partial, distorted, and misleading. Since indicators are often used for policy formation and governance, it is important to examine how they produce knowledge.

Interest in global indicators is now booming. Efforts to measure a wide variety of social phenomena took off in the mid-1990s as scholars and organizations developed indicators for such diverse issues as failed states, transparency, poverty levels, the rule of law, good governance, and the human right to health. Although indicators were developed in the mid-twentieth century to describe economic phenomena such as gross domestic product (GDP), by the end of the century, this technology was being applied to a range of social phenomena. The use of quantitative measures by national and international governments and organizations, as well as by academics and NGOs, has continued to grow in response to the demands of policy makers and the public for information about the world and as an aid to governance.

The contemporary proliferation of indicators used as a mode of governance springs, in large part, from the desire for accountability. How can states or civil society hold governments, corporations, and individuals responsible for their actions? How can donors be sure the organizations they fund accomplish what they have promised? Accountability requires information. Quantitative data, folded into simple and accessible indicators, seem ideal. Indicators of freedom, human rights compliance, trafficking in persons, and economic development are all efforts to measure country performance against global standards and to hold states accountable for their actions. Such quantitative measures promise to provide accurate information that allows policy makers, investors, government officials, and the general public to make informed decisions. The information appears to be objective, scientific, and transparent. Indicators are appealing because they claim to stand above politics, offering rational, technical knowledge that is disinterested and the product of expertise. Once indicators are established and settled, they are typically portrayed in the media as accurate descriptions of the world. They offer forms of information that satisfy the unease and anxiety of living in a complex and ultimately unknowable world. They address a desire for unambiguous knowledge, free of political bias. Statistical information can be used to legitimate political decisions as being scientific and evidence-based in a time when politics is questioned. They are buoyed up by the rise in bureaucracy and faith in solutions to problems that rely on statistical expertise. Such technocratic knowledge seems more reliable than political perspectives in generating solutions to problems, since it appears pragmatic and instrumental rather than ideological. These are the seductions of quantification.

Knowledge Effects and Governance Effects

Numbers packaged into concepts that describe social life are now central to how many people understand the world they live in. They are also central to governance. There is currently a surge of interest in systems of performance monitoring and evaluation, for example. Holding states or corporations accountable requires information on their violations. Evidence-based decision making, experimentalism, audit mechanisms, results-based management, and new public management are emerging forms of governance that rely on measurement and counting. All these forms of governance require knowledge that is classified, categorized, and arranged into hierarchies. In other words, indicators have both a knowledge effect and a governance effect.

Despite the contemporary prominence of quantified knowledge, there has been relatively little analysis of its effects on knowledge and governance. Much of the scholarship on indicators focuses on how to develop an effective, reliable, and valid measure: how to conceptualize what is to be measured, how to operationalize broad and vague concepts, what data sets are available that can be used, how to label indicators so that they will be easy to understand and use, and how to generate buy-in from governments, donors, and other potential users of the indicator. The challenges of measurement, comparability, weighting of factors, and gathering reliable data in very different historical and cultural contexts are well known and widely discussed.

My focus, however, is not on the accuracy of indicators but on the social and political processes of indicator production and their effects on regulation and governance. My ethnographic examination of the way indicators are constructed and used shows that they reflect the social and cultural worlds of the actors and organizations that create them and the regimes of power within which they are formed. This social aspect of indicators is typically ignored in the face of trust in numbers, cultural assumptions about the objectivity of numbers, and the value of technical rationality.

Statistical knowledge is often viewed as nonpolitical by its creators and users. It flies under the radar of social and political analysis as a form of power. Yet how such numerical assessments are created, produced, cast into the world, and used has significant implications for the way the world is understood and governed. Quantitative information influences aid to developing countries, investment decisions, choices of tourist destinations, and many other decisions. A country with poor indicators for the rule of law, human rights compliance, and trafficking invites international intervention and management. Rather than objective representations of the world, such quantifications are social constructs formed through protracted social processes of consensus building and contestation. Once established and recognized, they often circulate beyond the sphere envisioned by their original creators and lose their moorings in specific methodological choices and compromises.

Beneath the "truth" of quantified knowledge, indicators are part of a regime of power based on the collection and analysis of data and their representation. It is important to see who is creating the indicators, where these people come from, and what forms of expertise they have. Rather than revealing truth, indicators create it. However, the result is not simply a fiction but a particular way of dividing up and making known one reality among many possibilities. As indicators cross the gap from social science knowledge to that used by policy makers and the public, the drawbacks and complexities recognized by their creators, such as limited data, the use of proxies, and the uncertainty of flawed or missing data, are typically stripped away. The indicators are presented as unambiguous and objective, grounded in the certainty of numbers. In this form, they act to produce a truth about the world despite the pragmatic compromises that inevitably arise in their creation. Data are never complete and may not measure exactly what the author of the indicator seeks to assess. Thus the truth of indicators can be quite misleading. For example, Morten Jerven illustrates this problem in his analysis of the flaws in information available on African economies and the impact they have on development planning (2013).

The core question of this book is how the production and use of global indicators are shaped by inequalities in power and expertise. It examines the power dimensions of indicators through an ethnographic analysis of the actors and institutions of the human rights movement engaged in the creation and use of three global indicators: indicators focused on violence against women, indicators on trafficking in persons, and indicators of human rights violations. Through a genealogical analysis of these three global indicators, I trace the gradual process of constructing indicators from the fragments of earlier ones and the cultural assumptions and theories of social change embedded in them.

The Genealogical Method

The genealogical method asks how an indicator develops, which actors and institutions promote and finance it, and how and when its features become settled (see Halliday and Shaffer 2015). It considers how the creators grapple with converting the broad terms of a standard into a series of measurable and named phenomena. Measurement generally builds on previous models and approaches, refining or expanding them or correcting their recognized problems. Adapting existing templates and forms of data analysis and presentation requires expert knowledge, producing what I call "expertise inertia." Expertise inertia means that insiders with skills and experience have a greater say in developing measurement systems than those without — a pattern that excludes the inexperienced and powerless. At the global level, experts are usually cosmopolitan elites with advanced education or people who have had previous experience in developing indicators of the same kind. They are often from the global North and trained in political science, economics, or statistics. Some are social scientists who research social phenomena such as political terror or violence against women.

Countries that have carried out relevant surveys create the models for the next set of surveys. The statisticians from these countries become global experts. In the context of global governance, this means that when experts gather to develop indicators and plan data collection, those from countries that have already tried such data gathering and analysis projects claim special knowledge and authority. For example, in an expert group meeting that I attended in Geneva in 2009, about twenty participants worked on developing measurements of violence against women. Representatives from Italy, Canada, and the United States talked about how such surveys had worked in their countries. People from poorer countries that had not yet carried out surveys of violence against women could not offer such authoritative expert knowledge. To understand how indicators are formed and developed, it is necessary to attend to the microprocesses through which surveys are created, categories defined, phenomena named, translations enacted. The microprocesses are, in turn, shaped by the actors, institutions, funding, and forms of expertise at play. This means that categories and models based on local knowledge are difficult to incorporate.

Those who create indicators grapple with the problem of finding or collecting data relevant to what they want to measure. Gathering data is expensive. Unless the sponsoring organization has funds to collect new data, it must locate existing data that can serve as proxies for the qualities being measured. This includes administrative data, regularly collected by governments (such as census data) or private organizations (such as electricity consumption), and social science data developed for research. Indicator creators with the resources to collect their own data may use population surveys targeted to the particular question they are interested in, but these are expensive. A cheaper alternative is the expert opinion survey. For example, instead of surveying those in the general population about their experiences of corruption, the organization can send questionnaires to local experts about the prevalence of corruption in their country. This is clearly less expensive, but also less comprehensive and accurate. Those without resources have to search out existing databases, which may not actually measure what the indicator seeks to count. The fact that existing data determine what an indicator can measure is what I call "data inertia." It is relatively hard to address new problems without new data collection, so the way categories are created and measured often depends on what data are available.

Both of these forms of inertia inhibit new approaches to measurement and tend to exclude inexperienced and resource-poor actors from having much influence on what is measured. They relegate those with local knowledge to the sidelines. Since those who choose the template and the modes of data collection are typically powerful individuals with experience and connections to statistically advanced countries, this means that powerful and wealthy countries are likely to set the models for less powerful ones and that weaker states and nonstate actors will have difficulty influencing the shape of the indicators.

Thus it is important to track what forms of expertise are involved in creating an indicator, who pays for the experts, who funds data collection, and which organizations develop and promote the indicator. Those with experience in developing similar indicators are more often listened to and have greater influence in designing the indicator than newcomers. Local, vernacular knowledge is typically less influential than more global, technical knowledge and, based on my attendance at meetings and reading of documents, often does not enter into the discussion at all.

Temporal Dimensions of Indicator Production

The microprocesses of indicator production take place over time. Indicators and other forms of quantitative knowledge are built up through a slow, incremental process. Many are years in the making. Some of the measures deemed most successful by the UN Statistical Commission, for example, are gross domestic product, instituted in the late 1930s, and the system of national accounts, developed first in the 1950s. Both of these measures initially required substantial theoretical work, including developing the idea that such concepts were even measurable. They also needed the creation of templates and measurement devices, mechanisms for classifying and counting, and names for the objects of measurement. They had to be presented through publicly accessible aesthetic forms and labels. Creating and maintaining indicators requires building up bodies of experts who understand them. Over time, indicators are revised as circumstances change but often remain the same in name and conception. In a few cases, indicators such as these achieve broad public acceptance. Debates continue about the details of how to measure and what to include, but the underlying concepts and measurement strategies are established.

Thus indicators gradually become more settled and less open to change. Indicator frameworks, templates, and measurements generally begin with open discussion among alternative measurement strategies and forms of data but gradually become more established and certain. This process often takes two or three decades. As the indicator crystallizes and becomes naturalized, flexible categories and proxies become fixed and unchangeable. Contestation about the indicator's underlying framework, use of data, and categories of analysis becomes more difficult over time. After a certain point, critics often succeed only in adding a variable or value. Some issues seem settled and not open to debate, while others require continuing efforts at refinement. Some of these debates concern classification and measurement, while others focus on what is to be measured and by whom. Tracing the development of indicators, their institutional basis, and the limited opportunities for their contestation and refusal reveals their quiet exercise of power.

The Ethnography of Indicators

This project is based on six years of intensive ethnographic field research that involved attending innumerable meetings and workshops, discussions with participants and others involved in global indicator projects, interviews with the major players in each of the three indicator initiatives I studied, and formal and informal meetings with activists and scholars in the United Kingdom, Europe, Australia, and India. Much of the field research depended on informal conversations with people involved in the production and use of human rights and trafficking indicators, which occurred at research meetings, academic conferences, lectures by leaders in this field in New York City and Boston, UN events in New York City and Geneva, NGO meetings, expert group meetings, workshops for academics and practitioners, and treaty body meetings and during my travels to lecture or attend conferences. I talked to academics, statisticians, human rights activists, international lawyers, and people who work for international NGOs and the UN.

In addition to ethnographic information, this book relies on the extensive documentary record available for such activities, including both the documents of meetings I was unable to attend and the records of quantification projects. UN documentation is particularly rich, and although it does not describe the informal negotiations behind the documents, it does offer a wealth of formal information, which I have supplemented by attending meetings and conferences and talking to the principal actors in these processes. My work was supplemented by fieldwork by my graduate students, Jessica Shimmin in the United States, Vibhuti Ramachandran in India, and Summer Wood in Tanzania. This is a study not of a particular place but of a global one: it traces processes that stretch across nations and continents. This is a transnational, deterritorialized social space, rich with shared meanings, practices, and technologies. I refer more specifically to these meetings and interviews in the chapters that follow as well as to the range of documentary evidence I consulted.

Governance and Indicators

THE EMERGENCE OF "INDICATOR CULTURE"

The increasing importance of quantification in governance reflects the emergence of what might be called an "indicator culture." It is a dimension of what has been labeled audit culture (Power 1999; Shore and Wright 2015; Strathern 2000). I use the concept of culture to refer to a set of techniques and practices applied within specific situations rather than as a description of a society. Thus it is a set of cultural practices, techniques, and assumptions about knowledge production embedded in particular institutional and bureaucratic settings. It is a culture in the sense of Shore and Wright's discussion of audit culture: it is not a holistic set of actions and ideas that define a society but a technology that occurs in a variety of contexts (2015). It is part of the repertoire of institutional actors seeking to persuade publics and influence governance decisions. "Indicator culture," in this sense, includes a body of technocratic expertise that places a high value on numerical data as a form of knowledge and as a basis for decision making. Its characteristics are trust in technical rationality, in the legibility of the social world through measurement and statistics, and in the capacity of numbers to render different social worlds commensurable. This perspective includes a pragmatic acceptance of imperfect measurement and skepticism about politics. It builds on social science expertise and its claims to objectivity for credibility and legitimacy. It assumes that all things can be measured and that those measures provide an ideal guide to decision making. Adherents of this approach to governance see data as the basis for policy and audit mechanisms as essential for management. The use of indicators for governance depends on the belief that experts can generate commensurable knowledge across substantial differences in language, culture, history, and place. From this perspective, indicators enable policy makers to compare freedom in Mauritius and Mauritania, poverty in Sweden and the Sudan, and human rights compliance in Russia and Rwanda despite the vast differences between these countries.

Indicators are often employed as a technology of governance in situations where lines of authority are unclear, law is soft rather than hard, jurisdiction is ambiguous, and governance requires negotiations among sovereign nation-states. They are important in regulatory situations that are governed by guidelines rather than rules. Development economics, development aid, public health, international trade and investment, global educational systems, and human rights monitoring are only a few of the areas where quantitative information is increasingly fundamental to decision making. In all these areas, universal standards have developed to which states are held accountable so that indicators can be used to make these standards more specific.

EVIDENCE-BASED GOVERNANCE

The rise of indicator culture is connected to an emerging mode of governance that is referred to as "evidence-based governance" or simply "new governance," a broad range of regulatory strategies that rely on empiricism, quantitative knowledge as the basis for decision making, and problem solving through benchmarking (de Burca 2010; Power 1999; Rittich 2014: 175). Key features are broadly framed goals, stakeholder participation, flexibility, reversibility, monitoring and peer review, transparency, a data-based approach, and learning-oriented and multilevel decision making (de Burca 2010: 235). It is related to "new public management," often referred to as "results-based management," and represents the movement of business management techniques to the public sector. It is essentially a shift from a command-and-control strategy of governance to collaborative, consensus-building discussions focused on problem solving and improvement (Simon 2004: 11–28). This model encourages learning and innovation, constant collaborative revision, and the participation of multiple stakeholders (Simon 2004; de Burca 2010; Rose 1991).

The state is no longer the only player, since nonstate actors also participate in formulating laws and policies and in the development and enforcement of norms at the international, as well as the domestic, level (Thomas in Halley et al. 2006: 385). In this regime, the use of evidence organized by guidelines, standards, metrics, and performance evaluations is essential to decision making. Audits are used to determine the quality of data. In contrast to earlier systems, which relied on rules and punishments for violations, this mode of governance works through the collaborative production of standards and the evaluation of outcomes, including the use of self-assessment and ranking techniques.

Evidence-based governance relies extensively on "soft law" in that it shapes behavior by establishing standards and requiring individuals, groups, corporations, and even nations to report on how they have met these standards (de Burca 2010; Trubek and Trubek 2005). Instead of imposing sanctions, as "hard" law does, it seeks enact change through assessment, reporting, and ranking. For example, countries that fail to meet targets or that are ranked below others on key indicators are to be "shamed" into improving their records (see also Maurer 2005; Trubek and Trubek 2005). Evidence-based governance requires information on performance assessed with reference to standards. For example, compliance with standards for the right to health is measured by maternal mortality and life expectancy. Evidence does not lead to the imposition of sanctions, but to correction and advice about how to improve performance. This approach is now widespread in such fields as development and human rights compliance as well as in many other domains of global and local governance.

Governance by indicators can increase egalitarian decision making and accountability by opening up the basis for decisions to public scrutiny. On the other hand, it can also reinforce inequality and evoke resistance among the governed. For example, Marilyn Strathern and her colleagues criticize the university evaluation program of the British government, which has introduced indicators of faculty productivity and activity as the basis for allocating revenues to academic departments (2000; Shore and Wright 1999; 2000). This mechanism creates standards that universities and professors are responsible for satisfying. These professors — the governed — argue that this regime displays a lack of trust in the faculty and leads to alienation, exhaustion, and withdrawal.

With the turn to evidence-based governance, responsibility for decision making is shifted from individual, discretionary judgment to systems of measurement established by experts. Indicators displace the capacity for judgment from those assessing performance to the creators of indicators used to assess performance. This shift reduces discretion and private decision making, opening governance up to greater public scrutiny. At the same time, it moves responsibility from judicial and political decision makers to the experts in quantification who develop and implement measurement systems. Ultimately, indicators place responsibility on the governed to conform to the indicators, regardless of who has created them.

Defining Indicators

What is an indicator? In practice, this is a very broad and vague term that refers to a wide range of quantitative and qualitative techniques for ordering knowledge. It grows out of the basic idea of signs or markers that have a particular meaning. For example, one could specify behaviors that *indicate* that a person is drunk. However, in the field of global governance, the term is used to refer to a variety of approaches to packaging knowledge. Davis, Kingsbury, and Merry (2012) define indicators as follows: "An indicator is a named collection of rank-ordered data that purports to represent the past or projected performance of different units. The data are generated through a process that simplifies raw data about a complex social phenomenon. The data, in this simplified and processed form, are capable of being used to compare particular units of analysis (such as countries or institutions or corporations), synchronically or over time, and to evaluate their performance by reference to one or more standards" (2012: 73–74).

Indicators refer to the systematic, comparative organization and presentation of information that allows for comparison among units or over time. Indicators create and define social phenomena by naming them and attaching them to data (see Davis, Kingsbury, and Merry 2012). When an indicator is labeled, it defines the phenomenon it is measuring. For example, it is hard to define intelligence, but the concept is often specified by what the IQ test measures. The process of measurement tends to produce the phenomenon it claims to measure. An indicator is labeled as measuring, for example, rule of law or corruption. It then specifies a series of measures that constitute this concept. It defines the concept by linking it to specific criteria and measurements.

Indicators are different from targets and goals, which specify objectives. Indicators provide information that can be used to assess compliance with targets and goals. They attach data to a standard in order to assess performance against that standard. For example, the Millennium Development Goals (MDGs) have goals and targets with indicators attached to each target. In reference to women's rights, Goal 3 of the MDGs specifies, "Promote gender equality and empower women." This is followed by Target 3A, "Eliminate gender disparity in primary and secondary education, preferably by 2005, and in all levels of education no later than 2015," which is measured by Indicator 3.1, "Ratios of girls to boys in primary, secondary and tertiary education," Indicator 3.2, "Share of women in wage employment in the non-agricultural sector," and Indicator 3.3, "Proportion of seats held by women in national parliament" (United Nations 2008a). Finally, a "benchmark" describes a data point that constitutes a goal to be achieved.

In practice, the term "indicator" is used for many different kinds of numerical representation with no real consistency. Meanings range from simply something that indicates or points to a fact, such as that a person has been trafficked, to an elaborate combination of data merged into a single rank or score. Todd Landman defines an indicator as "a distilled measure of a concept" (2010: 137, n. 1). He points out that an indicator may not be able to represent the totality of a concept, particularly if it has multiple elements and dimensions. It is the simplification of information, the extraction and classification of some diagnostic element out of the buzzing array of particular features of the social world, that is the hallmark of indicators.

Indicators vary in the extent to which they incorporate qualitative information, local knowledge, and contextual data. As this book indicates, there are debates about the construction and use of indicators, including the extent to which they should reflect national and local knowledge. Some indicators do a better job of representing social life than others. Those that are more accurate tend to concentrate on phenomena that are readily countable, that require less interpretation, that employ qualitative research to generate the relevant categories for counting and analysis, and that are able to gather data that are appropriate to the measure rather than relying on proxies and fillers for missing data. Indicators that offer more complex and multifaceted measures that are less superficial may suffer in the competitive marketplace of indicators, where simplicity, ranking, and conformity to popular beliefs foster indicators' acceptance.

TYPES OF INDICATORS

Indicators can be used for advocacy, monitoring, and social science scholarship. Advocates use indicators to make problems visible, social science scholars to produce scientific knowledge, and businesses and governments to monitor and control behavior. Contestation over whether statistics are to be used for advocacy, management, or scientific knowledge stretches back at least to the beginnings of government statistics in the nineteenth century and recurs in contemporary debates about indicator production. In a meeting I attended charged with developing measures of violence against women, for example, some of the participants were experts in research and statistics while others worked in UN offices or for NGOs. The group confronted the difficulty of deciding whether the goal of an indicator is to develop a scientific descriptive tool for theory development, a policy tool to assess government policies and NGO programs, or an advocacy tool to shame governments for poor performance. These are three quite different objectives. The first is to produce scientific knowledge, the second is to facilitate organizational management, and the third is to promote reform. Each suggests a somewhat different approach to formulating questions and selecting items.

Within the field of global governance, it is also possible to distinguish three types of indicators on the basis of their mode of quantification. These are based on Michael Power's analysis of first- and second-order measurements (1999), but in this context, it is necessary to add a third order. Much of the recent growth in indicators has occurred in the third order. Third-order indicators are constructs put together from other indicators, usually building on the knowledge created by first- and second-order measurements. The distinctions are not sharp; there are continuities among them.

Counts. Counts refer to numbers of people, things, events, or laws. Census data are a prime example, as are the results of many kinds of surveys, such as health and demographic surveys, crime victimization surveys, and opinion surveys. Surveys may involve a sample, or they may seek complete coverage, as a census does. Even simple counting raises three questions: (1) What is important to count? (2) What characteristics are diagnostic for identifying these countable things? (What, for example, should constitute violence against women, or how should caste identity be defined?) (3) What are the appropriate criteria for aggregation and disaggregation? Counts require cultural work: they depend on constructing categories such as gender, ethnicity, income, and employment status. Creating categories implies deciding on where to lump and split, what to include and what to leave out, how many categories to use, and what the criteria for these categories should be. The process is a deeply interpretive one, reflecting the major preoccupations of a society (Bowker and Star 1999). Countries count what they care about. For example, the US Census counts race but not religion, while Denmark does not count race; these differences reflect national histories.

There is interpretive work in determining how categories are constructed and where to disaggregate. Is average income data adequate, or is it necessary to disaggregate by race, by class, by urban versus rural residence? How are these categories to be defined across countries? Is gender a binary or a continuum? How should race be defined? Many categories must be constructed, such as those of race, unemployment, poverty, and even age. Surveys and censuses often count households, but what constitutes a household? Once these categories are created, there is a tendency for them to remain stable — the product of the pragmatics of data collection and "the inescapable inertia of categories already in use" (Bowker and Star 1999: 117). Changing categories requires a new regime of data collection and undermines comparison over time.

Ratios. Ratios, which compare two numbers, facilitate comparison among countries or organizations. Indicators of this kind evaluate one number against another. Instead of providing the number of people who are unemployed, for example, a ratio indicator describes the rate of unemployment per capita in a population. However, ratios also require the creation of categories and raise similar questions about lumping and splitting. It is also necessary to determine the baseline of the comparison. Should the rate of unemployment be calculated against employed persons? Or the total population? Or the population of working-age persons? Should they be calculated against only men or both men and women? Similarly, should the rate of domestic violence be counted against all women? Or all married women? Or all women who were ever in a partnered relationship? There are clearly many critical decisions that affect the final number. Ratios are widely used, including those of life expectancy, per-capita income, maternal mortality, and poverty. They are much more readily comparable across countries and over time than counts. Many of these ratio indicators are well established and accepted.

Composites. Composite indicators are the most widely known, persuasive, and referenced kind of indicator. Composite indicators are made up of separate systems of counts and ratios, often merged together. They combine multiple sources of data, even multiple kinds of data, converted into a single score or rank. They also merge different attributes into a single measure. They are, in effect, a basket of counts and ratios combined to define a single concept. They usually combine several measurement systems and weight the constituent parts to construct a measure of a complicated idea such as rule of law or corruption. Composites require significant interpretive work in naming, weighting, and combining elements. They may have multiple dimensions. For instance, the Human Development Index has three dimensions, the World Bank Governance Indicators have six, and the MDGs have forty-eight. They typically rely on data from other indicators. Naming a composite indicator is important, since the name defines the concept. In effect, composite indicators construct a concept by naming and measuring it.

All indicators are framed by implicit theories about what is important to count and what is not, as well how social change happens, but theoretical elaboration is greater with composite indicators than with counts or ratios. Composites crystallize complex theories such as how the rule of law works and what its constituent elements are, what constitutes a failed state, and what laws and policies promote human rights. Interpretation of composites is more extensive than that of counts or ratios because composites require merging and weighting. Composite indicators are farther from the underlying data than either counts or ratios, and it is harder to trace back the process through which behavior is converted into data and then into the indicator. They often use preexisting data sets, which serve as proxies for the variables, producing long interpretive chains. Some are presented as ranks, some as tiers, and some as scales. In a ranking system, each entity is compared to all the others in a hierarchy so that the improvement of one entity inevitably means the decline of another. Scale and tier systems lack this zero-sum quality. For example, Freedom House rates every country on a scale of "free," "partially free," or "not free." A tier system divides the population into layers or tiers based on some measurable criterion. Ranking systems tend to be the most influential indicators but also the ones that evoke the most resistance and complaint, particularly from those who are ranked poorly (see Cooley and Snyder 2015).

SUCCESSFUL INDICATORS

International organizations, governments, NGOs, academics, and UN agencies continually generate new indicators (see Davis, Fisher, Kingsbury, and Merry 2012; Merry, Davis, and Kingsbury 2015). The ecology of indicators is dense, with multiple competing measurement systems for issues such as failed states or the rule of law. A few of these become widely accepted and used, while the vast majority of indicators search in vain for global interest and influence. Successful ones are routinely cited in the media, disseminated to a wider public and gradually accepted as more or less accurate descriptions of the world. Successful indicators tend to be composites that are relatively simple in conceptualization, that are developed and promoted by powerful actors and organizations along with networks of supporters in the United Nations and governments, and that rely on academic expertise from prominent universities. Composite indicators catch the attention of the media and the public, since they summarize a large amount of information, allow for comparison and ranking of units such as colleges and countries, and offer shorthand knowledge of complex situations. Indicators have greater credibility if their rankings conform to widely accepted views of good and bad performance among countries. They usually have a long trajectory of development, often stretching over twenty or thirty years.

When an indicator is successful, the indicator and the theory embedded in it enhance each other's popularity. An index can promote a well-established idea, as in the case of Freedom House, which measures "freedom in the world" using the concept of Western liberalism (Bradley 2015), or it can introduce a new concept, as in the case of the Human Development Index (HDI), which replaced per-capita income with a broader measure of human well-being. Converting a theoretical idea, such as the nature of the rule of law or the prevalence of modern-day slavery, into an index that ranks countries aids its dissemination.

Some of the most successful versions of composite indicators seek to measure features of governance such as corruption, freedom, and the rule of law. One example is the Corruption Perceptions Index developed by a Berlin-based NGO, Transparency International. Originally designed to bring greater focus to the issue of corruption for international development, Transparency International now works through a variety of national offices to produce comparative measures of the level of perceived corruption in almost all countries of the world. One of the oldest indicators is Freedom House, a US-based NGO that began in the 1970s and now publishes an annual report, *Freedom in the World*, assessing the degree of freedom in most countries of the world (Bradley 2015). The Global Reporting Initiative, based in the Netherlands, is a multistakeholder NGO that works with businesses and civil society organizations to develop indicators for corporate social responsibility (Sarfaty 2015). A relative newcomer to the global measurement project, the privately funded World Justice Project (WJP), based in Washington, DC, publishes a Rule of Law Index assessing the extent to which countries adhere to the WJP's principles of the rule of law.

Other prominent global indicators include the Doing Business Index of the International Finance Corporation of the World Bank, the World Bank–supported Worldwide Governance Indicators, the World Bank's Country Performance Institutional Assessment (CPIA), and the United States' Millennium Challenge Corporation indicator, used to determine which countries are eligible to receive certain US aid funds (see further Merry, Davis, and Kingsbury 2015). An influential composite indicator of human trafficking is the US State Department's *Trafficking in Persons (TIP) Report*, the subject of chapters 5 and 6.

In the field of economic development, the Millennium Development Goals (MDGs) — a set of targets and goals established by the UN, based on the Millennium Declaration of 2000 — have been extremely influential. Created in the early 2000s with the goal being realized by 2015, they are now being revised for a new, post-2015 version.

Another widely accepted global indicator of economic development is the HDI. The HDI is popular because it is simple, straightforward, easy to understand, and promoted by a powerful international development organization, the UN Development Programme (UNDP). It articulates a new theory of development through its index. Developed in 1990 to replace the use of only gross national product (GNP) per capita as the measure of development, the HDI expresses the theory that social and economic development are inextricably related and need to be considered together. Instead of focusing on economic growth by itself to measure development, this indicator combines economic and social factors in what is called a "capabilities approach" that emphasizes ends, like a decent standard of living, over means, like income per capita. Following Amartya Sen's capabilities approach, it measures access to health, education, and goods that give individuals the capacity to achieve their desired state of being (Stanton 2007: 3; Sen 1999; Sen 2005). This approach constituted a new understanding of development itself. As a recent study observes, "In 1990, the United Nations Development Program (UNDP) transformed the landscape of development theory, measurement, and policy with the publication of its first annual *Human Development Report (HDR)* and the introduction of the Human Development Index" (Stanton 2007: 3).

The history of the HDI reveals several key features of a successful indicator. First, it is the product of a long period of research, analysis, and experiment. Second, it is promoted by a leading, powerful institution and formulated by development economists and international policymakers located within prominent academic and policy centers. Third, it expresses, but does not test, a theoretical position. Indicators typically embody, but do not explicitly articulate, a theory of social change. Fourth, it is recognized by its creators as a very simplified representation of a far more complex body of data but is promoted for policy makers who want a convenient and quick summary. Indicators are quite distinct from the underlying statistical data that constitute them since they are single numbers or ranks designed for ease of comprehension and use as well as accuracy. Fifth, it is politically acceptable. Although there has been considerable debate and controversy over the HDI, it has become established while other indicators developed by the UNDP, such as a political freedom index, have not.

Composite indicators that rank countries tend to be particularly influential. They often present their rankings through color-coded maps, typically coloring top countries green and bottom ones red. The HDI, the Transparency International Corruption Perceptions Index, the World Bank Institute Global Governance Indicators, the US State Department *Trafficking in Persons Reports*, and the Freedom House *Freedom in the World* report all use some form of comparison and ranking. Most present their findings using color-coded maps.

A successful indicator is built up over time and gradually acquires credibility and the appearance of objectivity and truth. To achieve public credibility, it needs strong institutional support and an appealing underling theory. Indicators that reinforce existing ideas about good and bad countries according to the relevant criteria fare better in the competition for attention and influence. If it is obvious that data collection is thin or inaccurate, it will undermine the credibility of an indicator, even though the empirical basis for the indicator is usually opaque or presented in a sketchy way.

However, even successful indicators face political challenges. Those that are the most influential, that use radical forms of simplification, and that permit scoring and ranking of countries tend to be the ones countries resist most vehemently. For example, countries resist being ranked according to their compliance with human rights standards. Many countries resent the unilateral ranking system of the US State Department's annual *Trafficking in Persons Reports* (see Gallagher and Chuang 2012). Indicator systems have to work around sovereignty concerns. Some of the most successful indicators are embroiled in battles over their data and methodologies from time to time despite widespread agreement about the general structure of the indicator. For example, although it is a prominent, widely used measure, there have been ongoing controversies over the HDI (Ward 2004: 200–203). An intense debate about the latest HDI focusing on its procedures and the data it used roiled the UN Statistical Commission in 2011. The debate also showed how important the HDI is to many countries around the world (Merry 2014).

THE MYTH OF OBJECTIVITY

Indicators promise to provide objective knowledge but sometimes fail in at least two ways. The first is creating false specificity: they appear more accurate and precise than they are. Exact rankings of countries, precise numbers of trafficked victims, and percentages of women who have experienced violence presume that these are countable phenomena that can be compared and added together. The ambiguity of the categories, errors in counting, missing data, and lack of commensurability disappear in the final presentation of the indicator to the public. In order for an indicator to succeed in policy and public domains, it must present information in a simple and unambiguous way without a great array of qualification and methodological discussion. Indicators endeavor to persuade within a rich ecology of competing indicators, in which the simplest and most coherent often prevail.

The second possible reason indicators fail to produce objective knowledge is that they camouflage the political considerations that shape the collection and presentation of data. By "political," I do not mean the kinds of pressures political leaders exert on official statistical bureaus to produce the data they wish. My analysis of the politics of indicator production refers to the ways in which indicators are subtly and even unconsciously shaped by the assumptions, motivations, and concerns of those who carry them out. Since indicators are produced by individuals, networks, and institutions with their own interests and agendas, the producers' perspectives shape the outcome. Indicators produced by advocacy organizations are more explicit in their agendas, such as showing that there is a large population of trafficking victims, but indicators that claim to produce unbiased data also reflect particular interests and perspectives. They are shaped by the disciplinary and institutional site of their creation and by the resources available to collect relevant data.

Since states and private actors often rely on indicators to make policy decisions and promote state accountability, it is urgent to examine how they are developed and how they work. By recognizing the politics of producing quantitative data, it is possible to see how particular choices about how to categorize and count shape the knowledge that is produced as well as what is missed, ignored, and not counted. For example, the US State Department's *Trafficking in Persons Reports* expose deficiencies in state efforts to prosecute traffickers, but they do not consider the failure of states to tackle rural poverty or oppressive marriage practices, even though both of these also fuel trafficking.

Indeed, despite claims to objectivity and transparency, indicators are built on a string of interpretive decisions. Although they rely on quantitative information that appears unambiguous because it is numerical, interpretations creep into the final product at each step along the way. The choice of measurement approaches, the construction of categories, the selection of data sources, the use of proxies to measure a concept when specific data are unavailable, and the label used for the phenomenon that is being measured are all matters of choice and interpretation. They define what the concept is, how it is understood, and what things can be counted to measure it.

However, this is not a simple story of a hegemonic global technology imposed on passive and helpless local communities. Any global concentration of knowledge depends on practices of counting and measuring within countries and communities around the world. International statistics are often patched together from national data sets along with those from NGO, county, city, or regional data collection systems. They rarely fit together easily but must be massaged and made to fit through statistical techniques. Classification systems often grow out of local systems of knowledge that become globalized systems into which the local systems of other countries must be squeezed. To stitch together local systems of classification, it is necessary to find ways to make different things commensurable (Bowker and Star 1999). For example, in order to measure violence against women, throwing acid in the face of one's wife in Bangladesh must be equilibrated to shooting a domestic partner in the United States. This intellectual, interpretive work is shaped by the politics of expertise and participation that determine how quantitative knowledge is developed and by whom.

In the end, those who create indicators aspire to measure the world but, in practice, create the world they are measuring. In other words, indicators do not stand outside regimes of power and governance but exist within them, both in their creation and in their ongoing functioning. They are a blending of science and politics, of technical expertise and political influence. The two work hand in hand, sometimes in overlapping or competitive ways, with considerable slippage between them. The technical is always political because there is always interpretation and judgment in systems of classification, in the choice of things to measure, in the weighting of constitutive elements, and in decisions about which denominator to use for a ratio. The political hides behind the technical. Technical knowledge may be used to avoid political discussion, to cover up or legitimate political decisions, or to displace responsibility for decisions. Indeed, technical experts typically conceive of their work as, ideally, outside the domain of the political.

Clearly, this analysis of quantification grapples with a central epistemological problem in social science: the relationship between quantitative and qualitative methodologies in producing knowledge. As generations of scholars have argued, each provides insights, but not alone. There are inevitable trade-offs. Qualitative knowledge such as a detailed ethnography of a village by itself fails to examine to what extent this village represents any larger society. Quantitative knowledge alone inevitably selects a few features for comparison, ignoring their specific histories, interconnections, and locatedness. It lacks a holistic perspective and has difficulty embedding the analysis in a social context. Both methods of research taken separately contain hazards.

22

Narratives taken out of context can be misleading, just as numbers without context are. As Haltom and McCann point out, moralistic narratives that simplify tort cases present distorted pictures of the way law works and may lead to policy changes. For example, the account of a woman burned by Mac-Donald's hot coffee in 1992 who sued the company and received a large damage award was widely circulated in the media, contributing to a myth of litigiousness and to changes in the way litigants, judges, lawyers, and the general public thought about torts and their willingness to complain about violations. Yet the media focused on the large award and dropped many of the important features of her case, such as the extent and severity of her burns and the existence of a long string of similar complaints in the past that had forced the company to acknowledge the problem. Instead, media stories focused on the litigiousness of the plaintiff (Haltom and McCann 2004: 191–226). These stories contributed to the tort reform campaign by claiming that the case was outrageous and unjustified. Haltom and McCann argue that the use of such truncated narratives by entertainment-focused media creates a public common sense about lawsuits that inhibits deeper discussions about public policy, which is ultimately undemocratic (Haltom and McCann 2004: 24). Both stripped-down narratives and stripped-down numbers can provide the basis for popular moralistic accounts that conceal and distort the dynamics of power and obstruct public debate.

Overview of the Book

This book provides a genealogy of three indicators in the context of a wider set of indicator practices and their historical origins. Each indicator has a different institutional sponsor, resource base, and form of international collaboration. They raise different issues about knowledge production and governance, translation and commensuration, and the challenges of presenting knowledge through numbers. Yet in all three cases, numbers are used to strengthen narratives and to persuade audiences of the validity of their underlying theoretical argument. In all three, the process of development is slow and builds on expertise, past experience in measurement, and social science quantification techniques. And all three resist efforts to challenge or change them.

Chapter 2 presents the theoretical framework for the project, using the power/knowledge framework and science and technology studies to examine the political dimensions of the production of quantitative knowledge. It also provides a historical context for the development of statistics, and their use in both national and colonial governance, and traces the formation and development of an international statistical body, the UN Statistical Commission. Chapter 3 describes a project to develop global indicators for violence against women by the UN Statistical Commission. A major challenge of the project was developing categories for analysis that rendered the diversity of the phenomenon commensurable. A global survey of violence against women requires shared understandings, comparable categories of measurement, and some consensus on what violence against women means. My ethnography of the process revealed several parallel initiatives to measure violence against women with different theoretical frameworks and measurement strategies. Chapter 4 discusses four of them: the gender equality approach, the human rights approach, the criminal justice approach, and the national statistical approach. Tracing the effort to produce global data on violence against women shows tensions between feminists and statisticians and global, rather than local, definitions of the problem. It also reveals the critical role played by social science expertise and institutional support.

Chapter 5 examines the US State Department's *Trafficking in Persons Reports*, published annually since 2001. They assess countries' performances in combating trafficking in persons based on a US State Department survey and assessment of antitrafficking efforts. The result is a system of ranking, carried out since 2001, that uses tiers rather than numerical scores. It ranks countries according to their compliance with a set of standards for combating trafficking, developed by the United States. It is authorized by the US Congress as a way to diminish trafficking from source countries. This indicator system is a unilateral exercise by one country that evaluates performance according to its own standards. Its intellectual groundings are largely in the field of criminal justice and prosecution, and the framework parallels an earlier ranking of countries in terms of their efforts to control narcotics. The measurement system is framed by US foreign policy, promoted by the US secretary of state, and based on data collected by US embassies around the world. Chapter 6 compares the quantitative approach to understanding and governing trafficking with the one provided by ethnographic studies.

Chapter 7 analyzes a system for measuring human rights compliance developed over seven years by the UN OHCHR. This indicator emerged out of a thirty-year effort to develop human rights indicators for social and economic rights, such as the right to health and the right to food, and to convert the broad legal obligations of human rights conventions into more specific commitments for states. The OHCHR's project generated indicators for twelve core human rights, such as the right to liberty and the right to health, and two cross-cutting rights: nondiscrimination and violence against women. These indicators are designed to support human rights monitoring by treaty bodies, the committees that oversee compliance with human rights treaties. While each human right is measured by a variety of indicators, the project does not convert these indicators into a single measure nor does it engage in ranking. This may explain its relatively slow adoption. The chapter shows how indicators serve to translate knowledge from one domain, law, to another, development economics. However, this transformation undermines the legal dimensions of human rights in order to make its ideas more accessible to wider policy and development audiences.

All three of these indicator projects confront several dilemmas. One is the need to create measures that can be compared with other countries yet are tailored to the conditions of a particular country. This is the basic dilemma of creating commensurability while maintaining flexibility. It is necessary to develop fixed categories across organizations and over time in order to compare and evaluate change, but these categories need to be defined differently to account for variations in practice, context, and history. A second dilemma is acquiring relevant data. Either data must be gathered in the categories specified by the indicator, which is a very costly process, or indicators must use existing data as proxies for what they attempt to measure. The use of proxies is problematic if they do not cover the issues the indicator seeks to measure. For example, if a study wants to assess the relative burden of water gathering on men and women, it will not be easy to use data from a household survey that simply asks if the household has access to water.

A third dilemma is promoting acceptance of indicators by policy makers and publics. Indicators that conform to existing conceptions of the world or established theories are more likely to be accepted than those that promote a new theory or provide a different way of ordering the world. Thus indicators that present new ideas may lose out in the marketplace of indicators. A fourth dilemma is the need to simplify information in order to enhance general acceptance despite the desirability of creating more complex and disaggregated categories of data and an analysis that offers a more accurate picture of social phenomena. A fifth dilemma is the tension between technical expertise and policy concerns about what, where, and how social phenomena can be measured. This dilemma pits statisticians against politicians, with politicians asking statisticians to measure phenomena that are vague, illegal, or politically motivated and statisticians insisting on their autonomy and professional judgments about what can be measured accurately.

The genealogy of these three indicators shows how the participants, organizations, and communities of expertise involved in their production and dissemination manage these dilemmas. This includes looking at the histories of each indicator and the templates and categories that they adopt. There are moments of political contestation and public debate, as well as private discussions and expert meetings, in the development of each one. Like scientific knowledge, some indicators gradually acquire certainty over time and win the support of an expanding network of experts, while others lack this support and disappear. At first, measurement systems are open and experimental, but over time, a more settled knowledge emerges about how to measure things. While tweaks to frameworks may be accepted, major shifts in frameworks and measurements are often resisted.

Conclusions

Indicators emerge through social processes shaped by power relations, expertise, and techniques of measurement. The statisticians and experts who create indicators confront challenges of missing data and unmeasurable phenomena, but through pragmatic compromises, they manage to produce quantitative knowledge that shapes public attitudes and policy decisions and responds to the human desire to know the complicated and often unknowable world. Given the increasing use of indicators, it is important to interrogate these forms of knowledge and their limitations as well as to keep open channels of contestation and resistance to their hegemony. Those who are measured typically lack a voice in the construction of the categories and measurements. Moreover, subordinated groups have difficulty resisting or changing indicators. They may be able to tweak the measurement system but rarely have the opportunity to fundamentally restructure it. Since indicators typically develop over a period of time, they become progressively harder to change. If an indicator survives competition with other indicators and is widely accepted, it comes to provide a kind of unassailable truth.

Yet indicators are not all the same. Some provide a more accurate and complex understanding of social phenomena than others. As the case studies in this book indicate, some are more superficial and simplified than others, some rely more on qualitative data in constituting their categories and analyses, and some are more attentive to local and regional conditions than others. Some are locally generated to bring attention to a problem in terms of numbers as well as stories, while others are globally produced to bring recalcitrant nations to heel. Counts and ratios stay closer to the underlying thing they are measuring, while composites have longer interpretive chains between the counting and the final presentation of information. They are more accessible and more problematic, easier to use and less transparent.

Given the power of quantitative knowledge, it is important to increase indicator literacy both to understand the strengths and the limitations of quantitative knowledge and to compare and assess different indicators. The goal of the book is to develop a more skeptical view about indicators and to provide criteria for assessing their relative merits. Like other forms of quantitative and qualitative knowledge, indicators emerge from a regime of power relations and interpretive work. Some are more transparent than others. Some rely more extensively on qualitative research to develop categories of analysis than others. There is no doubt that such forms of knowledge provide a more reliable basis for decision making than ignorance or prejudice, but it is important to balance numerical knowledge with the qualitative knowledge provided by ethnography, human rights documentation, and qualitative interview research.

By opening up the social processes by which they are formed and the underlying theoretical and political interests of those who develop them, this book seeks to make indicators' particular ideological and structural biases more visible. The case studies in the following chapters examine the complexities of this process of indicator production, the uneasy compromises that designers are forced to make, and the variety of indicators that they produce. Understanding what numbers do and do not say and the politics underlying their creation challenges the seduction of quantification: the idea that numerical data offer a particularly reliable form of truth.

CHAPTER TWO

Indicators as a Technology of Knowledge

Indicators are a technology of knowledge creation, one that depends on processes of translation and commensuration. Creating indicators requires translating social life into commensurable categories so that different events become instances of the same thing. This requires deciding how to convert the wide array of practices, structures, and political and economic systems that make up social life into commensurable categories for enumeration. As Espeland and her coauthors show, commensuration requires substantial reframing and cultural work (Espeland and Sauder 2007; Espeland and Stevens 1998; see also Comaroff and Comaroff 2006). Making things commensurable depends on identifying a core principle that they all share and that renders them various instances of the same thing. It means specifying points of similarity and ignoring other features, unbundling the whole entity under consideration into discrete, countable parts. Categories must be distinct enough that cases can relatively easily be assigned to one or another. The process of categorization inevitably constricts the way that social action is understood. For example, counts of domestic violence cannot include the kinship networks, gender norms, attitudes toward violence, or history of the relationship of a particular person. Yet it is these factors that determine the way a person experiences domestic violence. The process of translation homogenizes populations, actions, and practices and strips them of context. Sometimes this means defining an act in a way that diverges radically from the way it is experienced. For example, in order to count victims of sex trafficking, it is necessary to merge a wide variety of paths through which women become involved in sex work with various levels of coercion. Sometimes they are pressured to support themselves and their families, and sometimes they accept the work as a way of escaping a violent marriage. To count trafficking victims, it is necessary to ignore the specific features of each woman's situation, history, and agency and treat them all as the same.

Statistical measures create new categories of meaning that shape the way we experience the world (see Bowker and Star 1999). As Porter points out, although the categories of enumeration may be highly contingent at first, once they are in place, they become extremely resilient and come to take on permanent existence as a form of knowledge (Porter 1995: 42). One of the most well-known examples of this process was the introduction of the census in India by the British colonial authorities in the nineteenth and twentieth centuries (Cohn 1996; Randeria 2006). In order to generate knowledge about the population of its colony, the British initiated a large number of knowledge projects, including surveying the land and classifying and counting the population. In order to render it knowable, the population was classified by caste, religion, gender, and other criteria. The British arranged the castes in an orderly hierarchy and sought to collect "objective" information about caste identities. However, the caste categories in existence at the time were relatively fluid, situational, segmented, and local. Caste names and definitional criteria had to be standardized across India. In place of a wide range of forms of ritual and social exclusion in practice across the region, the category "untouchability" emerged as a distinct, all-India category. By about 1917, pollution by touch, for the upper castes, became the chief criterion for inclusion in the category. By redefining castes in terms of categories that applied across the subcontinent, the British rendered caste a far more fixed and intractable social entity. The new category of untouchability became a distinct, all-India caste organized around this essence (Randeria 2006). The census not only stabilized caste but also homogenized it.

Expertise is fundamental to processes of translation and commensuration. Even at the level of data collection, expertise is important in determining how data are acquired. For example, if data collectors are highly trained, they can flexibly adapt their methods to the situation, but if they are untrained and unsophisticated, they must follow rigid rules (Porter 1995: 35). As Porter notes, those who are charged with counting confront the ambiguities of classification, but once routine practices are established and compromises are reached in how the classification is done, those who use them, such as newspapers or public officials, have little opportunity to rework the numbers (Porter 1995: 42).

Thus indicators create forms of knowledge through their interpretive work. Michel Foucault's analysis of the power/knowledge relationship is useful for understanding the relationship between indicators as knowledge and as modes of power. Foucault's critique of the nonpolitical nature of knowledge and his claim that it is always embedded within frameworks of power applies to the creation of indicators as well as to other forms of knowledge. Instead of claiming that knowledge can only exist outside the sphere of power relations and its demands and interests, he argues that "we should admit rather that power produces knowledge (and not simply by encouraging it because it serves power or by applying it because it is useful); that power and knowledge directly imply one another; that there is no power relation without the correlative constitution of a field of knowledge, nor any knowledge that does not presuppose and constitute at the same time power relations" (Foucault 1979: 27). To understand the kind of knowledge that is produced by practices of measurement and quantification, it is necessary to examine the power relations within which this takes place (see Power 2004).

One effect of power is what gets measured. What is measured and counted by states and civil society organizations depends on which problems seem politically important. There is considerable interest in measuring human and drug trafficking, for example, but little in children's right to express their opinion. Moreover, since politically important issues have been measured in the past and data and templates already exist, they are easier to measure again. For example, in our study of the introduction of a manual for measuring children's rights in Tanzania, Summer Wood and I found that there was considerable data in the country on basic health issues such as the prevalence of breastfeeding, which has long been a concern of governments and donors, but little on the obligation to establish a positive agenda for children's rights or on children's right to play (Merry and Wood 2015). These issues were not as politically important as children's health and survival. Deciding to expend scarce resources to count something depends on the importance of the issue.

Indicators and Technoscience

Science and technology studies provide valuable theoretical tools for theorizing quantification and power by exploring the social processes by which scientific knowledge is made as well as its materiality: its templates, survey forms, data collection techniques, modes of analysis, and final presentation. As Asdal, Brenna, and Moser point out, "Science and technology are ordering activities that are also materially productive. They generate reality rather than discovering or revealing it. They continually bring about new, transformed material realities. In other words, they are *technoscience*" (Asdal et al. 2007: 9). Science and technology, they argue, are cultural practices, including interests, projects, meaning, and social reality, central to the construction of society. Social and political arrangements not only explain science but are themselves the effects of science (2007: 27). Indicators, the use of which is a kind of scientific practice, are similarly formed through a social and political process and, in turn, shape society and politics.

Bruno Latour's (1987) work on the social production of scientific knowledge offers a useful model for thinking about the construction of indicator knowledge. He argues that the process of producing, accepting, and supporting scientific knowledge depends on expertise, institutions, and allies. Acquiring scientific knowledge is not just a matter of discovering "truth." In order to understand this process, it is necessary to go back before a state of settled knowledge was achieved to see how it was produced and how it moved through controversies to acceptance. "To sum up, the construction of facts and machines is a *collective* process" (1987: 29). The production of scientific knowledge is a fundamentally social process that depends on networks of actors that scientists build on and cite when they make claims to knowledge.

In turn, persuasion depends on the author's capacity to create a channel that moves the reader from one established fact to another less established one, pulling the reader along until he or she accepts an idea that he or she might have found less persuasive at first. In discussing persuasion, Latour notes that "it is an easy job if you want to convince a few people of something that is almost obvious; it is much harder if you wish to convince a large number of people of something very remote from or even contrary to their current beliefs" (1987: 57–58). Authors do this by stacking up arguments, references, and "arrays of black boxes": machines or sets of commands that are too complex to explain. A technology that is depicted in a black box in a diagram is one that the reader needs to know nothing about, except its input and output; although it can be disputed in principle, it is harder to do so in practice (1987: 2, 81). The complexity of the processes described by the black box renders it far harder and more time-consuming to dispute. Thus the reader, faced with the difficulty of challenging the interior of the black box, is carried on to accept it. Moreover, as the reader examines the range of citations, actors, and organizations that support this conclusion, he or she feels that by acquiescing to this idea, he or she is not alone but in the company of many others.

Indicators similarly depend on the general social acceptance of practices of data collection and analysis, as well as assumptions about the measurability of social phenomena. They are forms of knowledge packaged and presented for nonspecialist audiences, in which the pragmatic compromises of categorization, measurement, and commensuration that form them are typically presented as black boxes. The essential quality of an indicator is that it systematizes and simplifies a complex body of knowledge. Indicators typically refer to these bodies of information and procedures by which they are produced but do not reveal the details of those procedures or the compromises necessary to produce a simple number or rank out of the available data. They are, in theory, subject to contestation at all layers, but because the knowledge base is so complex and the distance between the underlying data and the final result is so great, they are, in practice, hard to contest. Indicators also become solidified over time. It is easier to contest the names of the indicators, the categories of measurement, and the underlying data early in the process of indicator creation than it is once it has achieved widespread acceptance. The community of believers gives added credence to the indicator and renders the skeptic more isolated. For example, the idea of measuring the gross domestic product of a country now seems perfectly reasonable, even though debates remain about precisely how to do so. Thus the process of "captation," Latour's term for the channeling of readers' ideas through a series of apparently logical steps that ultimately persuade them to accept a conclusion (1987: 56), is fundamental to the production and presentation of indicators.

Latour's actor-network theory (ANT), like science and technology studies more generally (see Asdal, Brenna, and Moser 2007), emphasizes the importance of material things as well as actors in the production of knowledge (Latour 2005). The things of measurement — the survey forms, the classifications, the boxes to be checked, the continuum of possible answers, the sequence of questions, the technologies of graphic representation — are all part of the technology of statistical knowledge production, developed in a collaborative process by a series of actors, backed by institutions with incentives and money, over a long period of time. Developing indicators depends on an elaborated technical scheme of survey instruments, computer algorithms, grids for organizing information, and established practices of collecting and analyzing data. As ANT suggests, such technologies and nonhuman entities, even scallops, are creative contributors to the constitution of knowledge (Callon 1986; Latour 2005). Mastery of this technology provides the authority and expertise to construct new systems. Those who create indicators typically use existing templates for organizing information and draw on preestablished bodies of data produced by administrative agencies or state or private institutions. They build on the models and categories developed by those who have already tried to count and measure similar things. Given the costs of data collection and analysis, these people typically live in rich, industrialized countries.

Techniques such as constructing victimization surveys, counting victims of war, or assessing attitudes toward new products circulate as relatively fixed "boundary objects." Star and Griesemer define these as scientific objects that inhabit several intersecting social worlds and are able to adapt to local needs and constraints but are sturdy enough to retain a common identity in these various sites (Star and Griesemer 1999: 509). For example, a survey measuring how many women give birth with the aid of skilled attendants can be seen as a boundary object. The survey questionnaire and protocol for asking questions and filling in boxes, as well as a preset list of possible skilled attendants, such as doctors and nurses, are fixed objects, but as it is applied in various settings, new kinds of birth attendants, such as traditional healers, can be added. The term "skilled" is open to interpretation and allows adaptation to particular situations. However, the idea of needing a "skilled" attendant remains constant. In general, the templates, the categories, and the techniques of data collection constitute the technologies that shape the way indicators produce knowledge.

Indicators are constituted by knowledge that is gathered in many parts of the world and brought together in a "center," a phenomenon that Latour refers to as a "centre of calculation" (1987). Here, information is systematized and organized into a whole. Pieces that use different measurement strategies or categorizations are patched together, missing data holes are plugged, and pragmatic compromises are developed to fill in gaps. Wendy Espeland and Mitchell Stevens (2008) identify this as a potential consequence of what March and Simon refer to as "uncertainty absorption," which "takes place when inferences are drawn from a body of evidence, and the inferences instead of the evidence itself, are then communicated" (1958: 165). As Espeland and Stevens describe this process,

> "Raw" information typically is collected and compiled by workers near the bottom of organizational hierarchies; but as it is manipulated, parsed, and moved upward, it is transformed so as to make it accessible and amenable for those near the top, who make the big decision. This "editing" removes assumptions, discretion and ambiguity, a process that results in "uncertainty absorption": information appears more robust than it actually is . . . The premises behind the numbers disappear, with the consequence that decisions seem more obvious than they might otherwise have been. An often unintended effect of this phenomenon is numbers that appear more authoritative as they move up a chain of command. The authority of the information parallels the authority of its handlers in the hierarchy. (Espeland and Stevens 2008: 421–22)

In sum, indicators are a technology for producing knowledge that work within a regime of power. Thus it is critical to probe beneath the apparent truthfulness and objectivity of quantified knowledge to understand the social and political life of indicators and their histories. A key dimension of indicators is their translation of knowledge from the incredible complexity of everyday life to numbers and ranks. This book examines the translations that create and disseminate indicators by focusing on three case studies. For each case study, it examines the process of developing categories for measuring, collecting data, analyzing what data mean, generating tables and maps to present this knowledge, and finding strategies to disseminate and implement data in accessible forms. The aesthetics of presentation are an essential dimension of the translation process.

As a technology of knowledge, indicators act within the regime of global governance (see Halliday and Osinsky 2006). While we assume that they describe the world, they actually construct that world. They are neither inherently good nor inherently bad as modes of governance but contribute to the ways in which the world is understood and decisions are made in the global arena. They provide a mechanism for creating knowledge and exerting power by those who are in a position to create, disseminate, and use them. But the kinds of power they exercise depend enormously on how they are situated, where they act, and who uses them. It is the unnoticed quality of the power they exercise that renders their study critically important.

Governing the Self through Indicators

The turn to indicators is also a form of governance that engages a person in governing himself or herself in terms of standards set by others. Indicators promote self-governance among the governed by establishing standards according to which individuals, organizations, or nations should behave. This new form of governance emphasizes "responsibilization," in which individuals are induced to take responsibility for their actions (O'Malley 1999; Rose 1999). Individuals are responsibilized in terms of standards set by others. In some of the most successful examples of responsibilization, such as grades in school, the indicator comes to shape subjectivity, defining for the individual his or her degree of merit. Such indicators promote self-management — what Nikolas Rose calls "government at a distance." He argues that new systems of governance have emerged in the postwar period that seek to control individual behavior through governance of the soul (Rose 1989; 1996; 1999). Individuals come to see themselves as choice-making consumers, defining themselves through the ways in which they acquire commodities and choose spouses, children, and work (Miller and Rose 1990). Social ordering occurs through processes of choice and self-definition, while those who slip outside the bounds of appropriate behavior typically find themselves in a program or institution that encourages them to learn to manage themselves and their feelings. In the liberal democracies of the postwar period, citizens are to regulate themselves, to become active participants in the process rather than objects of domination. Thus citizen subjects are educated and solicited into an alliance between personal objectives and institutional goals, creating government at a distance. Rose dates the formation of this self-managing system of governance to the 1950s but sees a major expansion during the current era of neoliberalism and the critique of the welfare state (Rose 1989: 226–27).

On the other hand, proponents of collaborative, information-driven, consensus-based governance draw on corporate business models to argue that this form of governance produces greater levels of participation and engagement by the governed (Simon 2004: 28). Simon uses the example of the Toyota Production System — in which command-and-control management techniques are replaced by collaborative, consensus-building discussions among shop-floor workers who engage in problem solving and focus on improvement rather than assigning blame for failures — to describe this form of governance (2004: 11–28). This system encourages learning and innovation, disruptions of existing patterns of doing things, constant collaborative revision, and a prospective and collective approach to mistakes. A key strategy is benchmarking, a self-assessment process by which practices and products are compared with those of the most successful competitors. Indicators play an important role in this production process. Actors should develop their own plans with indicators and benchmarks to define successful performance with correctives if they are not achieved (Simon 2004: 29). Actors are audited to evaluate whether their plans are adequate and if they have complied.

Under conditions of self-assessment, individuals are encouraged to manage their own behavior in terms of external standards, but while Rose sees this as a form of control, Simon views it as enhancing autonomy. Rose underestimates the possibilities of resistance and noncompliance with this regime of governance, while Simon exaggerates the power of workers to determine their own actions. This discrepancy underscores a key puzzle in understanding the effects of indicators: information can enhance the monitoring of state performance and accountability, yet the way information is collected and packaged can obscure state violations. Ultimately, the difference resides in the details of how the system operates. An ethnographic, genealogical approach to particular indicators, probing how they are created and with what set of interests, constituencies, and effects, is fundamental to assessing whether governance by indicators achieves the participatory, democratic form that Simon and other advocates of experimental governance anticipate or if it is another instance of government at a distance.

A History of Indicators

Where did indicators come from? What is their genealogy? The use of quantitative measures as an aid to governance is hardly new. Historically, the creation of the modern nation-state and the project of governing colonial possessions were the two key forces driving the use of statistical data for governance. Under these pressures, the use of quantitative knowledge for policy and decision making expanded throughout the nineteenth and twentieth centuries. More recently, these technologies of knowledge and governance have been adopted by international organizations. The shift has been particularly dramatic since the mid-1990s. Great increases in the availability and transfer of data via the Internet, improvements in census and data collection efforts in countries around the world, and the expansion of measurement into new and previously uncountable spheres of social life have all produced a massive growth in the reliance on quantitative knowledge for international as well as national governance. At the same time, national and international organizations have developed new and successful indicators.

The use of numbers for financial management and population measurement began in Europe perhaps four centuries ago and has migrated across spheres of activity and nations. The use of numerical information to understand the world reflects the creation of what Mary Poovey calls "the modern fact" as a form of knowledge (Poovey 1998: xii). The modern fact is basic to the ways Westerners have come to know the world. It organizes most of the knowledge projects of the last four centuries (1998: xiii). Numbers are the epitome of the modern fact: because they are subject to the invariable rules of mathematics, they seem to be simple descriptors of phenomena and resistant to the biases of conjecture and theory. They are presented as objective, with an interpretive narrative attached to them that gives them meaning. Numbers can be assigned to observed particulars in a way that makes them amenable to statistical manipulations and to a knowledge system that privileges quantity over quality and equivalence over difference (Poovey 1998: 4).

However, Poovey shows not that numbers are noninterpretive but that they embody theoretical assumptions about what should be counted, how to understand material reality, and how quantification contributes to systematic knowledge about the world (1998: xii). Establishing the understanding of numbers as an objective description of reality outside of interpretation was a project of modernity. Although some see facts as interpreted, the idea that numbers guarantee value-free description is still pervasive (Poovey 1998: xxv). Poovey argues that the early nineteenth-century combination of numbers and analysis enabled professionals to develop systematic knowledge through non-interpretive descriptions. The nineteenth-century separation of numbers from interpretation made numbers different in kind from analytic accounts, locating them at a different stage in knowledge-producing projects. Since the numbers were different in kind from other knowledge, they could be developed by a special class of professionals who worked with them. Experts — professional knowledge producers — took responsibility for managing this kind of knowledge that existed prior to policy and could be used in neutral ways to inform it (Poovey 1998: xv).

Statistics became increasingly important as a technology of governance in nineteenth-century Europe. As scholars of the intellectual history of statistics indicate, numbers as an instrument of knowledge production were developed first for business transactions, exemplified in particular by the invention of double-entry bookkeeping, and subsequently as instruments of state governance (Poovey 1998). The use of numerical measures by states for administration and tax collection stretches back millennia, but it was only with the development of the modern state that statistics were used to describe the characteristics of populations themselves. Quantification, with its aura of objectivity, became increasingly important to a variety of government and business functions in the nineteenth century, from developing cost-benefit measures for locating transportation networks to measuring life spans by life insurance companies in the mid-nineteenth century (Porter 1995: 106–21).

The growth of nation-states in the nineteenth century depended on accurate census information about populations, seen as the source of a nation's wealth. In the early nineteenth century, nation-states began to focus on managing populations rather than securing territory. The wealth of a country depended on its workforce and population, and states required knowledge of this population in order to govern it. Knowledge of populations became ever more important with the consolidation of the modern industrial state. Colonial governance similarly required assessments of populations, their characteristics, and their capacities. As European countries expanded into new colonial domains, they developed techniques for counting and classifying these populations. Projects of surveying lands, measuring population sizes and capacities, and counting ethnic groups, castes, and races were fundamental to establishing colonial control (see Mitchell 2002). Hacking argues that in the "modern era," beginning as early as 1500, the census was an affair more of the colonies than of the homelands (1990: 17). For example, Spain, Britain, and France, as imperial states, conducted censuses in Peru in 1548, in North America in 1576, in Virginia in 1642–45, in Canada in the 1660s, and in Ireland in 1679. A census process was created by the US Constitution, and as the country expanded west as a colonial power, it took the census with it. American missionaries to Hawai'i conducted the first censuses of the Kingdom of Hawai'i in 1831–32 and 1835–36, while the Kingdom of Hawai'i initiated its own census in 1847. By 1850, the Kingdom had a complete population count disaggregated by age, sex, race, and region (Schmitt 1968: 14). The British systematically counted and classified their colonial subjects, lands, and capacities. Bernard Cohn argues that the British imperial government in India developed strategies of classification and counting that made possible the acquisition of control over the complexity of Indian society (1990; 1996). Under British influence, India evolved a great statistical bureaucracy and later became a major center for theoretical and practical statistics (Hacking 1990: 17).

Indicators have also long served as an essential technology of reform. Gathering information about violations is fundamental to creating and defining the size and scope of an issue, whether it is the ranking of students' school performance or the rate of maternal mortality, both of which usually are used to compare a country's status with global standards. In her history of the rise of statistics as a discipline in England and France in the nineteenth century, Schweber (2006) points out that statistics were fundamental not only to the new project of administering a population but also to dealing with issues such as public health, poverty, and birth and death rates. Foucault analyzes the nineteenth-century interest in population statistics as a shift toward governance designed to enhance the capacities of the nation (1991). The use of numerical measures of population by age, birth and death rates, health, poverty, and other criteria constituted the population as a measurable entity that could be known in new ways (Poovey 1998; Porter 1995; Schweber 2006). Increasingly, statistics became the basis on which governments assessed their resources, human and natural, and developed policies for promoting public health, diminishing population decline and "degeneracy," and alleviating poverty. Ian Hacking notes that nineteenth-century utilitarian reformers used statistics to improve sanitary conditions, targeting not only health but also morality (1990: 119–20). Water closets, for example, not only improved health but also increased the privacy of bodily functions, which Hacking claims was a logical extension of the demand for barriers between sleeping parents and children (1990: 120). Of course, such projects were also devices by which the rich regulated the lives of the poor in order to maintain order and morality.

During this early period of numerical governance, statistics largely consisted of counts and ratios. The unit of analysis was usually the nation or a subsection of the nation. As Ian Hacking points out, during the nineteenth century, an increasingly broad range of phenomena were subject to counting, with some states, such as Prussia, collecting data for its own sake while others, such as France, endeavored to turn this data into social laws about phenomena such as suicide (1990). Ted Porter ties the increasing focus on numbers to the needs of policy makers to make decisions among alternatives such as building railroads or canals, for which cost-benefit measures were valuable (1995). Reformers also relied on data on mortality and public health to press for improved health care and urban design (Schweber 2006).

It was not until the twentieth century that substantial efforts were made to generate comparative global statistics and composite indicators. The United Nations played a critical role in building the statistical capacities of its member nations and developing international systems of measurement that facilitated cross-national comparison (Ward 2004). The first efforts focused on counting populations and measuring economic behavior, shifting during the second half of the twentieth century to social phenomena such as well-being and quality of life (Ward 2004: 154). The social survey became increasingly well-known and used during the twentieth century in the United States, beginning with political opinions and expanding into new terrains such as sexual behavior in the *Kinsey Reports* of the 1940s and 1950s (Igo 2007). Starting in the 1930s, economists developed basic economic indicators such as gross domestic product and gross national product, while the international system of national accounts (Ward 2004: 45) was accepted by statisticians during the 1950s. With the increasing focus on measurement and governance at the global level in the late twentieth century, particularly in the sphere of economic development, scholars recognized that counting things makes them visible and that what is not or cannot be counted is made to disappear. The case of whether to include women's unpaid labor in development statistics offers a good example of this process. Current tensions around this issue and other examples of the counted and the uncounted reveal the power of numbers in governance (see Davis, Fisher, Kingsbury, and Merry 2012).

UNITED NATIONS STATISTICAL SYSTEMS

Since its formation, the United Nations has worked to develop the statistical capacities of its member nations. It has long played an important international role in fostering data collection; publishing cumulative surveys, such as the state of the world's women. The United Nations works through its member nation commission, the United Nations Statistical Commission (UNSC), and its permanent secretariat, the United Nations Statistical Division (UNSD), formerly the UN Statistical Office (UNSO). The UNSC held its first meeting in 1947. Its membership consists of twenty-four countries distributed among all the UN regions. Representatives from other countries attend the meetings as well. It meets annually in New York for four days, with at least three to four hundred people in attendance. I attended all six of these meetings between 2009 and 2014.

Initially, the United Nations focused on creating "a universally acknowl- edged statistical system and . . . a general framework guiding the collection and compilation of data" (Ward 2004: 2). One of its early missions was to fos- ter national censuses. Between 1955 and 1961, 195 national censuses were con- ducted on population, agriculture and industry, housing situations, earnings, age groups and available skills, and population densities of different areas (United Nations 1961). Another early project was developing economic statis- tics. The system of national accounts (SNA), used to measure economic activ- ity, was established in 1952 by Richard Stone at the Organization for European Economic Cooperation (OEEC) and was closely related to the widely accepted concepts of GDP and GNP (Ward 2004: 45). The goal was to provide gov- ernments with tools for their economic decision makers as they developed macroeconomic policies. Michael Ward observes that this system "set out a comprehensive framework that established the appropriate standard format for collecting and compiling all economic statistics. It created an interrelated network of concepts and definitions that remain more or less unchanged to the present day" (2004: 45). Thus the categories and framework developed in one site in Europe have shaped the way economic relationships are now ana- lyzed throughout the world. Although there are frequently debates about the details of the SNA system at UNSC meetings, the basic framework remains unchallenged.

Economic measurement remained the central concern of the UN statisti- cal system until the 1970s, when social indicators took on new importance as the movement developed outside of governments (Ward 2004: 161). During the 1980s, interest grew in gender, health, and nutrition statistics; composite social indicators; and labor participation measures, although by the end of the 1980s, social indicator work was being sidelined (Ward 2004: 163). The 1990s and 2000s added concerns about the environment; governance issues such as freedom, corruption, and human rights; and poverty and global inequality. In 2000, the UNDP promoted the Millennium Development Goals (MDGs) and their targets and indicators. Thus the UN system has expanded from its initial focus on economic measurements to a wide range of social measures that include questions of inequality, development, and the effects of globalization (Ward 2004: 15–17).

Although the UN Research Institute for Social Development (UNRISD) developed a composite social indicator, the UNSD did not. The mission of the UNSD was primarily to advise government statistical offices rather than to develop its own indicators (Ward 2004: 159). It focused on creating statistical concepts and appropriate classifications for processing the new social data that would be of use to national statistical offices. In the 1970s, the UNSO launched the National Household Survey Capability Program to help all national statistical offices develop in-house survey capabilities and ideally to put them in a routine-integrated survey program (Ward 2004: 170). The UNSD continues to produce and refine statistical systems, providing guidelines for their use and offering training sessions to national statistical offices that request them. This is the approach that the UNSD took toward the task of developing measures of violence against women, as discussed in chapter 3.

The Population Division was formed in the 1940s to estimate global population and its changing demographic composition. Although its tasks were statistically straightforward, national cultures, local laws and customs, religion, and language all affected the technical measurement of the population. As Ward notes, "Demographic statistics, however neutral they may be in any auditing or accounting sense, are invariably political in the wider meaning of the term" (2004: 192). Questions of citizenship and residence are clearly political, as are what constitutes a birth or death record in different countries (2004: 191–92). As with the rest of the UN statistical system, the Population Division has published recommendations and ideas about estimation procedures, conducting population and housing censuses, the construction of life tables, and other issues. It relies on the views of experts in demographic statistics and disseminates advice and guidelines through UN manuals and journal articles (Ward 2004: 192). The Population Division set up the UN Fund for Population Activities (UNFPA) and USAID support for the Demographic and Health Surveys under the Johnson administration. The UNFPA now focuses on women and has sought to promote women's reproductive health. The Population Division has tried to remain outside of political debates on morality and human rights, such as the right to life (Ward 2004: 193). In general, the UN stance toward producing statistical knowledge is to define it as a technical problem and not a political one, to which it brings expertise and advice that supports national initiatives.

MEASURING THE UNMEASURABLE?

However, as interest in measuring social development and the conditions leading to well-being and quality of life increased, it became clear that it was much easier to measure economic phenomena translated into real output and prices than social ones (Ward 2004: 158). This statistical uneasiness has only grown. On February 27, 2012, just before the 2012 UNSC meeting in New York City, I watched a group of high-level statistical officers and academics from the European Union, the United States, Finland, India, Japan, and Qatar discussing the issue in a panel called "Measuring the Unmeasurable: Challenging the Limits of Official Statistics." This panel focused on the problem of being asked by governments to measure the unmeasurable. Of particular concern was the difficulty of measuring nonobjective phenomena such as happiness or well-being. Speakers debated questions such as, if a statistician measures feelings, can there be a loss of credibility? How far should we go? One speaker pointed to the need for new methods and techniques to measure things like feelings in addition to facts. A speaker from Japan noted that there is a long history of developing the ability to measure the unmeasurable, as in the cases of the system of national accounts and the international comparison program that computes purchasing power parity. Some audience members commented that in the past, economists such as Keynes did not think that GDP was measurable but that we now think both GDP and national accounts can be measured. The chair of the UNSD observed that statistics are like elephants: they are very big and move very slowly, but they move. He also noted that it is this community, attending the UNSC from statistical bureaus around the world, that will decide how to move forward with these questions.

One speaker pointed out that there are things that might be unmeasurable, such as opinions, prices when there are no markets, the future, clandestine activities such as human trafficking, or fictions. The head of the Finnish statistical service asked if measuring such things "is our business" but lamented that if something is not measured by official statistics, it will be measured by someone else. "Are there limits? Are there things that our governments are asking us to do that we should not do?" she asked. Forecasting the future and measuring nonmaterial things, unobservable things, subjective things, and transnational and global phenomena are all difficult. New technologies might make things measurable in the future that currently are not, but where is the boundary? She argued that it was appropriate to produce statistics needed for national and international decision making and for monitoring national and international policies, such as MDGs, but that other needs are not the responsibility of national statistical offices. She pointed to the need to maintain credibility and the fundamental principles of statistics — such as impartiality, professionalism, scientific principles and standards, statistical relevance, reliability, quality, and transparency — despite the demands of government to measure what statisticians consider unmeasurable.

The issue of autonomy from government influence is an ongoing concern of national statistical offices. Despite the desire of statisticians to declare their work as being outside the realm of government interference, they face the constant risk that their work will be manipulated by political actors. The UNSC is guided by its statement of Fundamental Principles of Official Statistics (UN Statistical Commission 1994). These principles were adopted in 1994 to establish the independence of statistical offices from government influence at the time of the transition in Central Europe from planned to market-based economies (UN Statistics Division 2014). In 2011, UNSC members, who are typically heads of statistical offices of member nations, sought to update the Fundamental Principles of Official Statistics and strengthen their implementation. At this meeting, there were discussions of national situations in which governments had interfered in the statistical offices' production of data and analysis, as in the case of financial data from Argentina. In the 2012 meeting, country representatives discussed the need for governments to respect these statistical principles and the threats to their credibility if they did not. A UNSC committee charged with implementing the fundamental principles developed a new preamble to this document and a practical guide that is useful for countries and international organizations (UN Statistical Commission 2011a). The new draft of the preamble stated that "statistical principles in order to be effective have to be enshrined in the institutional frameworks that govern official statistical systems and be respected at all political levels and by all stakeholders in national statistical systems" (UN Statistical Commission 2012b: 3). Delegates at the 2012 meeting expressed concern about government interference with statistical offices in Argentina, Greece, Ghana, and several other countries and emphasized the importance of the independence of statistical offices. Paradoxically, it is up to governments to maintain this independence.

Thus indicators and other forms of statistical knowledge have long been central to the exercise of state power. Since the emergence of modern states, governments have recognized that controlling their populations requires knowledge of their characteristics, capacities, and performance. With the increasing role of international institutions in governance and the gradual emergence of a global structure for governance, indicators are acquiring added governmental significance in this sphere as well. The next five chapters trace how international indicators are developed, the kinds of knowledge they provide, and their impacts on modes of governance.

Measuring Violence against Women

What is violence against women, and how should we count it? This apparently simple question poses enormous challenges to measurement, particularly at the global level, where conceptions of violence and of the relationships and social structures within which it occurs are highly variable. Moreover, what constitutes violence against women is highly contested, ranging from narrow definitions of rape and intimate-partner violence to broad conceptions that include sexual slavery during wartime, female genital cutting, sex trafficking, child marriage, and violence while in police custody. Nevertheless, in the mid-2000s, the UN Statistical Commission (UNSC), at the request of the UN General Assembly, set out to develop a set of indicators and guidelines for collecting data on violence against women that could be used by countries around the world. The next two chapters track that process.

As the UNSC decided what to measure, how to categorize it, and how to gather data, it defined the phenomenon. As this chapter shows, the definition of the problem implies the way it should be handled. However, its definition was not uncontested. Although the statisticians opted for a narrow definition of violence against women, feminists and human rights organizations pressured the statisticians to take on a broader, more socially grounded conception. The feminist approach emphasized gender equality and structural violence, while the UNSC definition focused on interpersonal relationships. Although the feminists lacked the resources and institutional power to develop their own indicators, they managed to exert some influence on the final guidelines of the UNSC. Thus this case study traces the production of an indicator as well as competition over its theoretical framework, showing how quantitative knowledge develops in a competitive ecology of indicators.

Violence against women is a phenomenon that has moved from being the subject of political mobilization to a site of technical knowledge. As the global effort to diminish this violence grows, there are increasing demands to classify, measure, and count it. Assessing the size and nature of the problem is fundamental to drawing attention to the issue and holding governments accountable for their efforts. The political orientation of experts, the institutional support behind the measurement system, and the disciplinary framing of the project all shape the underlying theoretical frameworks used for quantification.

This chapter illustrates the political dimensions of technical decisions through its case study of global efforts to measure violence against women. After tracing the growing international interest in violence against women and the demand for better data from the United Nations, it focuses on the UNSC's effort to develop indicators of violence against women. It examines debates about how a measurement system should be constructed and implemented rather than how it is used. Determining how to classify forms of violence universally is a daunting project, since violence is a culturally constituted category that takes many different forms with a wide array of cultural meanings depending on context, relationships, and ideas of kinship and discipline. As experts struggle with this intractable problem, some turn to "objective" measures rather than the interpretive categories of the victims themselves. In the process, the experience of victims disappears from the measurements. Since surveys of violence against women occur more often in rich than in poor countries, the categories for counting are largely created in those wealthier, more developed countries. There is typically little opportunity for input from those who are being measured. The struggle to create categories for severe and moderate physical violence in expert group meetings, UN commissions, and UN committees illustrates how and by whom categories are formed and contested.

There are competing models for measuring violence against women now being developed by UN agencies as well as NGOs and academics. In order to show how measurement systems are distinct interpretive projects, the next chapter compares the UNSC's approach with three others based on gender equality, human rights, and criminal justice. It argues that these four approaches display significant cultural and interpretive differences in the way they conceive of, categorize, and count violence against women. They hold different underlying social theories about violence against women, but these theories are rarely made explicit. Each theory implies a particular mode of responding to the problem. And each is a product of its historical origins, the institutions that promote it, the disciplinary expertise of those who develop it, and the audience for which it is intended. As researchers, statisticians, and policy makers develop templates for surveying violence against women, they build on past work in the same theoretical framework and follow similar strategies of categorization and classification.

The UNSC's project of measuring violence against women is only one of these parallel and intersecting initiatives. Despite considerable overlap, each holds a distinct conception of what violence against women is, how broadly it should be defined, and how it should be prevented. One framework assumes that increasing gender equality is necessary to reduce violence against women while another emphasizes better policing. Which theory is used determines what questions are asked and how data are collected. Ultimately, how violence against women is understood at the global level depends on which of these frameworks prevails. The solution — whether it is criminal prosecution of batterers, equal economic opportunities, or greater respect for women — depends on how the problem is defined. Yet none of these approaches is comprehensive. Each one is insufficient without detailed qualitative studies that reveal the social and cultural context of the violence, the role of the state and structural violence, and the ways in which individuals experience and give meaning to these events to understand this violence.

The Growing Global Concern about Violence against Women

The demand for statistics on violence against women emerges from a long-term campaign to define this problem as a global issue and a human rights violation. As the national and international focus on the issue developed, it gradually expanded from a narrow concern with rape and domestic violence to a broader analysis of the way patriarchal social structure, cultural understandings of gender difference, and social and economic inequality contributed to a wide range of forms of violence. National activism in the 1980s translated into a global movement in the 1990s that defined violence against women as a human rights violation (see Dauer 2014; Merry 2006a). During the 1990s, the issue was gradually recognized as a human rights problem by many parts of the UN system. In 1990, the UN Economic and Social Council adopted a resolution recommended by the Commission on the Status of Women (CSW) stating that violence against women in the family and society derives from their unequal status in society and recommending that governments take immediate measures to establish appropriate penalties for violence against women as well as develop policies to prevent and control violence against women in the family, work place, and society (UN Commission on the Status of Women 1995: 131–32). The major UN convention on women's rights, the 1979 Convention on the Elimination of All Forms of Discrimination against Women (CEDAW), does not mention violence against women explicitly, but the committee monitoring the convention developed an initial recommendation against violence in 1989 and formulated a broader recommendation that defined gender-based violence as a form of discrimination in 1992. The 1992 statement placed violence against women squarely within the rubric of human rights and fundamental freedoms and made clear that states are obliged to eliminate violence perpetrated by public authorities and by private persons (Cook 1994b: 165; UN Commission on the Status of Women 1995: 131–32).

At the 1993 UN Conference on Human Rights in Vienna, sponsored by the UN Office of the High Commissioner for Human Rights (OHCHR), this issue became even more important (see Schuler 1992). A worldwide petition campaign gathered more than three hundred thousand signatures from 123 countries, putting the issue of violence against women at the center of the conference (Friedman 1995: 27–31). The concluding document, the Vienna Declaration and Programme of Action, formally recognized the human rights of women as "an inalienable, integral, and indivisible part of human rights" (Connors 1996: 27). The Vienna Declaration specifically called for the appointment of a special rapporteur on violence against women and the drafting of a declaration eliminating violence against women.

In 1994, the UN Commission for Human Rights condemned gender-based violence and appointed the requested rapporteur (Report of the Secretary General 1995: 132). The special rapporteur on violence against women is mandated to collect information relating to violence against women, to recommend measures to remedy it, and to work with other members of the Commission for Human Rights, the body that preceded the Human Rights Council, to investigate violations. The first special rapporteur on violence against women, Radhika Coomaraswamy, was very effective in bringing more attention to the issue. During her tenure as special rapporteur from 1994 to 2003, she prepared several substantial reports defining violence against women and investigating its various manifestations around the world. These reports helped establish violence against women as a human rights violation along with the duty of states to exercise "due diligence" in preventing violence against women in the family, the community, and public spaces. Her work expanded the definition of violence against women to incorporate a range of cultural practices and to embed the phenomenon in unequal, patriarchal social structures.

Scholars and NGOs contributed in very significant ways to defining gender violence as a human rights violation. In 1994, Rhonda Copeland, a professor of law at the City University of New York Law School, labeled domestic violence as a form of torture (1994) — a position supported by Amnesty International (Amnesty International 2001). Dorothy Thomas, head of the Women's Rights Division of Human Rights Watch in the early 1990s, worked hard to define gender violence as a human rights violation. As her colleague at the Bunting Institute at Radcliffe in 1994, I listened to her talk about getting Human Rights Watch, one of the world's largest human rights organizations, to take women's rights and gender violence seriously.

The Fourth World Conference on Women in Beijing in 1995, often called the Beijing Conference, clearly named violence against women as a violation of human rights and fundamental freedoms. Its final policy document, the Platform for Action, defined violence against women broadly as "any act of gender-based violence that results in, or is likely to result in, physical, sexual or psychological harm or suffering to women, including threats of such acts, coercion or arbitrary deprivation of liberty, whether occurring in public or private life" (United Nations 1995: sec. D, 113). It includes gender-based violence in the family and the community and acts that are perpetrated by the state, including acts of violence and sexual abuse during armed conflict, forced sterilization and abortion, and female infanticide. By declaring protection from violence for women and girls as a universal human right, the conference articulated a dramatic expansion of human rights. The platform declares, "Violence against women both violates and impairs or nullifies the enjoyment by women of their human rights and fundamental freedoms. The long-standing failure to protect and promote those rights and freedoms in the case of violence against women is a matter of concern to all States and should be addressed" (United Nations 1995: sec. D, 112). The Beijing Platform for Action flagged the need for data and invited national, regional, and international statistical services to develop improved data on the victims and perpetrators of all forms of violence against women (1995: para. 206, sec. J).

In 2003, the US division of Amnesty International, one of the oldest and most established human rights organizations, initiated a major global campaign against violence against women using a framework that defined such violence as a human rights violation whose prevention was the state's responsibility (Amnesty International 2003). As the anthropologist and director of Amnesty International's US Women's Human Rights Program from 1997 to 2008, Sheila Dauer, says, "By providing the global human rights framework for the struggle, Amnesty International will show how international human rights standards cut across national boundaries, cultures and religions and how we can hold governments accountable to meet their obligations to protect women and girls from violence regardless of who commits it or where it is committed" (quoted in Merry 2006a: 22). This campaign by one of the largest human rights organizations in the United States furthered the idea that violence against women was a human rights violation (see further Dauer 2014). In the same year, the UN Human Rights Commission passed a resolution calling on member states to develop indicators of violence against women (Erturk 2008c: 6).

In 2003, the UN General Assembly asked its secretary general to prepare an in-depth study of global violence against women, which was presented to the General Assembly in 2006 (UN General Assembly 2006). This was the first time that the General Assembly had ever discussed this issue. The report asserts that violence against women is a pressing human rights issue and highlights the ongoing persistence of the problem, describes ways for governments to respond more effectively, and stresses the need to increase governmental and international accountability. While asserting the widespread prevalence of the problem, the report argues that violence against women is influenced by factors such as ethnicity, class, age, sexual orientation, disability, nationality, and religion. It attributes violence against women to gender inequality, discrimination against women in public and private spheres, patriarchal disparities of power, and economic inequalities and claims that "violence against women is one of the key means through which male control over women's agency and sexuality is maintained" (UN General Assembly 2006: 1). Thus this important report grounds the problem in unequal social structures rather than the dynamics of interpersonal relationships (UN General Assembly 2006: 7–8; see also Bunch 1990; Schneider 2004).

Thus the 1990s and 2000s saw both a dramatic expansion of the international movement against gender violence and its redefinition as a human rights violation. The original meaning of violence against women — male violence against partners and others in the form of rape, assault, and murder — was expanded to include intimidation and psychological harm; humiliation; female genital mutilation, cutting, and excision; gender-based violence by police and military forces in armed conflict as well as everyday life; violence against refugee women and asylum seekers; trafficking in sex workers; sexual harassment; forced pregnancy, abortion, and sterilization; female feticide and infanticide; early and forced marriages; honor killings; and widowhood violations, among others (see Cook 1994a: 20; Merry 2006a; 2009). The conjoining of these disparate issues is the product of sustained activism among a transnational network of NGOs (Keck and Sikkink 1998). It was facilitated by the human rights system, and its structure, as well as its declarations and conventions, were formed by the United Nations. These formal mechanisms operate in parallel with an energetic and imaginative NGO community that pressures governments to develop global regulatory instruments to control violence against women and then to abide by them (see further Merry 2006a).

The Turn to Numbers

As global concern for violence against women increased, so did the demand for information. At each step of the United Nations' efforts to raise the profile of violence against women as a problem, it has advocated gathering more information about the extent and nature of the problem. This information is critical to pressuring states to reform. In 2003, along with the request for an in-depth study of violence against women, the General Assembly also requested that the secretary general provide "a statistical overview on all forms of violence against women, in order to evaluate better the scale of such violence, while identifying gaps in data collection and formulating proposals for assessing the extent of the problem" (UN General Assembly 2003: 1).

The secretary general's 2006 report made the need for better data and more extensive knowledge about violence against women for "policy and strategy development" one of its five major concerns. Some policy makers and activists called for "a comprehensive set of international indicators on violence against women." (UN General Assembly 2006: 56). The 2006 report describes three purposes for developing indicators on violence against women: to persuade policy makers to take action on violence against women by revealing its nature and extent, to measure programs and services for victims of violence, and to monitor states' progress in meeting their international obligations to address violence against women. It also pointed to large gaps in available data.

FORMS OF COUNTING

Information on violence against women is of two kinds: One describes state efforts to deal with violence against women, such as laws passed, shelters built, restraining orders created, and programs in operation for supporting abused women or retraining violent men. The other assesses the frequency and nature of the problem by counting the frequency with which women are victimized (prevalence) and the number of incidents of violence (incidence).

Such data can be generated by victimization surveys or by administrative data. Surveys ask individuals in a sample or a total population how often they have experienced violence or how many incidents of violence they have had.

They can be dedicated surveys that focus only on violence or modules attached to large-scale surveys, such as those on household demographic and health data or crime victimization. Surveys are the gold standard but are expensive and tend to be used infrequently. In contrast, administrative data are already collected by governments or nonprofit agencies in the course of providing services, so they do not require extra expenditures. Numbers of calls to the police for help, admissions to hospital emergency rooms for injuries, restraining orders issued for domestic violence cases, and rape prosecutions are all examples of administrative data that provide low-cost information about violence against women.

But there are limitations to administrative data for violence against women. Administrative data may be collected for purposes other than recording violence against women and not disaggregated from overall data. For example, domestic violence assaults may be buried in total assault data and not counted separately. Moreover, it is widely recognized that victims of gender violence often do not call the police and that there is a substantial "dark figure" of hidden, unreported violence. Hospitals may not ask or record whether an injured person was a victim of domestic violence. All these administrative data systems can be developed and improved, of course, but victims may still fail to report. Surveys provide superior information on the overall frequency of abuse and permit analysis of differential victimization by subgroups such as the poor, minorities, and rural women. But surveys raise new challenges. How should this broad and complex phenomenon be reduced to quantitative information? The range of violations included under the label of violence against women is extremely diverse, from domestic violence to rape during wartime to early and forced marriage. What should be counted? How should the surveys be carried out? Who will pay? How large must a survey be to be representative of a population or of subgroups within that population? How can a survey be organized so that it can be replicated? Will it be possible to assess change over time, or will the survey be only a one-time event?

One of the recurring questions is whether a survey should be a dedicated or stand-alone survey focusing only on gender violence or a module attached to an existing survey, such as a household demographic and health survey or a crime victimization survey. The latter is clearly less expensive but raises ethical issues and sampling problems. Ethically, it requires the interviewer to ask the householder he or she is interviewing whether there is a woman in the house and, if so, whether he or she can conduct a private interview with her. If there is suspicion that the topic is violence in the family, the interviewee may face reprisals or fear to report violence. From a sampling point of view, an adequate sample for a household demographic and health survey is likely to differ from that of a survey on violence against women, but the attached module will inevitably follow the sampling strategy developed for the household survey. An attached module is a second choice if funds are not available for a dedicated survey.

EXISTING DATA

According to the 2006 UN secretary general's report, at least one survey of some kind on violence against women had been conducted in seventy-one countries, and at least one national survey was available in forty-one countries, but these were generally not comparable. Many countries lacked any reliable data. Few countries collected information regularly. There were relatively few "dedicated" population-based surveys — that is, surveys focused only on violence against women. One of the first was done in 1993 by Statistics Canada, the official Canadian statistical office, followed by surveys in other countries, including Australia, Finland, France, Germany, New Zealand, Sweden, and the United States (UN General Assembly 2006: 56–57). Affluent countries can better afford to do population-based dedicated surveys than poorer ones. Some international organizations conduct surveys of poorer countries; however, these are created not by the countries themselves but by international organizations that use their own sets of questions and categories.

There were two major multicountry studies on violence against women in the early 2000s: one used a public health model; the other, a criminal justice one. The WHO Multi-Country Study on Women's Health and Domestic Violence did full-scale studies in twelve countries, most of which are resource poor: Bangladesh, Brazil, Ethiopia, Japan, Namibia, New Zealand, Peru, Samoa, Serbia and Montenegro, Tanzania, and Thailand (Erturk 2008b: 66; World Health Organization 2005). The research covered twenty-four thousand women. It focused on intimate-partner violence and health but also collected data on sexual assault, child sexual abuse, a broad range of negative health outcomes commonly associated with violence, risk and protective factors for intimate-partner violence, and strategies and services that women use to deal with this violence.

The other study, the International Violence against Women Survey (IVAWS), was designed to study the causes and consequences of violence against women and the effectiveness of preventative measures. It was carried out in eleven countries, most of which are affluent: Australia, Costa Rica, the Czech Republic, Denmark, Greece, Hong Kong, Italy, Mozambique, the Philippines, Poland, and Switzerland (Johnson, Ollus, and Nevala 2008: ix). All countries were invited to participate, but they had to raise their own funds in order to do so. All participating countries used governmental or national funds except for Mozambique, which was co-funded by three UN agencies (Johnson, Ollus, and Nevala 2008: 20). Thus this study focused on countries that could afford to carry out the survey. The IVAWS sought to extend the International Crime Victimization Survey (ICVS), a general crime survey carried out since 1989, to capture sexual and domestic violence more effectively. One of the prime concerns of the IVAWS was to examine when and how women sought help from criminal justice systems and to assess the criminal justice systems' responses (Johnson, Ollus, and Nevala 2008: 15–18). It aspired to develop and strengthen democracy "by increasing public participation in the process of formulating criminal justice policies" (Johnson, Ollus, and Nevala 2008: 17). The project was administered by the European Institute for Crime Prevention and Control (HEUNI), was linked to the United Nations Office on Drugs and Crime (UNODC) and the Interregional Crime and Justice Research Institute (UNCRI), and drew on the expertise of Statistics Canada (Erturk 2008b: 66–67). The organizers developed a questionnaire and methodology manual to be used by participating countries. In total, fifty-three thousand women were interviewed (Johnson, Ollus, and Nevala 2008: 20).

These two major multicountry studies on violence against women were done by international agencies with some national collaboration rather than by national statistical offices (Nevala 2005; World Health Organization 2005). Both have played important roles as models and templates for subsequent surveys. There are also two international household surveys of health and population in developing countries that have recently begun to include questions on violence against women. They are designed, financed, and carried out by international sponsors with some level of collaboration and choice by the countries where they take place. The Demographic and Health Surveys (DHS) are sponsored by USAID and carried out by ICF International, a large corporation in the Washington, DC, area. As of 2014, the DHS program had collected, analyzed, and disseminated data from more than three hundred surveys in over ninety countries (Demographic and Health Surveys 2014). In addition to its main health and demographic surveys, it developed optional modules for domestic violence and for female genital cutting between 2005 and 2008. An optional module is a series of questions that can be used if a country so chooses but is not a required part of the survey. The DHS optional module covers physical and sexual violence along with emotional abuse and controlling behaviors (Johnson, Ollus, and Nevala 2008: 14). The 1989 DHS of India included attitudes toward domestic violence, while the 2005–2006 DHS also used a domestic violence module to assess acts of violence (Demographic and Health

Surveys 2006; International Institute for Population Sciences and Macro International 2007).

The Multiple Indicator Cluster Surveys (MICS), sponsored by UNICEF, focus on women and children and measure health and child development. UNICEF has carried out five waves of household surveys since 1995. The website says that as of 2012, there were a total of 175 surveys in the first three waves (UNICEF 2014). In a 2013 talk in New York, the head of statistics at UNICEF said that there had been 240 of these surveys in more than one hundred countries. The MICS program tends to coordinate with governments of surveyed countries more extensively in planning and administration than the DIIS program. Questions on attitudes toward domestic violence were in an optional module in the third wave in 2005 and were moved into the main survey along with female genital cutting in the 2009 and 2012 waves (UNICEF 2015). In addition to these international surveys, there were some national surveys, even in the early period. Between 1990 and 2002, for example, data on domestic violence were collected in eleven countries (Kishor and Johnson 2004; cited in Johnson, Ollus, and Nevala 2008: 14). Thus the team preparing the secretary general's report had access to substantial survey research on violence against women, although there were many gaps.

THE UN STATISTICAL COMMISSION MANDATE

When it was presented to the General Assembly in late 2006, the secretary general's report on violence against women spurred even greater demand for statistics. The General Assembly requested more information on the extent and nature of the problem of violence against women. The 2007 General Assembly Resolution A/RES/61/143 advocated increased efforts by national statistical offices and UN agencies to develop and disseminate statistics on violence against women (UN General Assembly 2007). It recommended taking note of the WHO Multi-Country Study, which was widely viewed as an important preliminary model (UN General Assembly 2007: 6). It also asked the UNSC to develop indicators on violence against women. This General Assembly resolution set the UNSC project, which is the focus of this case study, in motion. The resolution "*requests* the Statistical Commission to develop and propose, in consultation with the Commission on the Status of Women, and building on the work of the Special Rapporteur on violence against women, its causes and consequences, a set of possible indicators on violence against women in order to assist States in assessing the scope, prevalence and incidence of violence against women" (UN General Assembly 2007: para. 18).

The UNSC was charged with developing the indicators. As the previous chapter discussed, the UNSC was established in 1946 as part of the Economic and Social Council of the United Nations to promote the development of national statistics and improve their comparability, to coordinate the statistical work of specialized agencies, to develop central statistical services, to advise UN organs on statistical matters, and generally to promote the improvement of statistics and statistical methods (UN Statistical Commission 2009). This commission includes twenty-four member countries elected for four-year terms by the UN Economic and Social Council, with membership distributed across the five UN regions (Africa, Asia, Eastern Europe, Latin America and the Caribbean, and Western Europe and other states). The UNSC has met annually for four days in New York City since 2000. Sessions are attended by observer nations, UN regional commissions, and other UN organizations and agencies, as well as other international organizations interested in international statistical work (UN Statistical Commission 2014b). I attended these sessions annually from 2009 to 2014. The UN Statistics Division (UNSD) is the secretariat for the UNSC.

The General Assembly charged the UNSC with developing indicators of violence against women in collaboration with the Commission on the Status of Women (CSW). This commission is a major organization of the United Nations, similar to the UNSC, which was also initiated in 1947, with forty-five member countries distributed across the UN's five regions following the same model as the UNSC. It meets annually in New York City for two weeks and is attended by many observer nations as well as member nations. In addition, the UNSC meetings are attended by a large number of representatives from women's NGOs around the world that hold panel discussions and events alongside the formal meetings. I have attended CSW meetings fairly regularly since 2000.

In March 2007, I attended a panel discussion at the annual CSW meeting presented jointly by the UNSC and the CSW. Both the CSW and the UNSC's vice chairpersons were present as well as other representatives from each organization. Here the UNSC took the position that it would develop the technical side of the survey while the CSW should specify its content. This is the familiar distinction between technical and substantive dimensions of indicators, yet in practice, they are hard to separate. Substantive dimensions depend on technical issues of data availability and the challenges of classification and coding. Broad concepts such as fear of violence are difficult to measure and code. At the session, the CSW distributed a background issues paper that advocated reliable statistics and sex-disaggregated data and pointed out that implementation of the Beijing Platform for Action was hindered by inadequacies in the development of statistics and indicators. It noted that the General Assembly had asked the UNSC and the special rapporteur on violence against women to develop a set of indicators on violence against women to assess its scope, prevalence, and incidence (UN Commission on the Status of Women 2007: 1–2). Thus the project was always envisioned as a collaboration between statistical experts and women's rights groups. When I interviewed the UNSD official responsible for this project, he was clear that his role was to develop the statistics and the technical side of the project and that the CSW was to determine what should be measured. He has a background in demographic and victimization surveys but not, he told me, in violence against women.

EXPERT GROUP MEETINGS

Once a policy direction is decided, a key UN mechanism is the use of experts to write reports and to develop proposals in expert group meetings. The typical process used for indicator development follows a regular sequence (see Goonesekere 2004; UN International Human Rights Instruments and Office of the High Commissioner for Human Rights 2006; Turku Report 2005). The first step is creating an expert report that looks at existing survey research; distills a set of questions, measurements, and measurement strategies; and proposes a set of standards. It is often written by an academic with experience in the area. The second step is having a set of meetings over two or three years that brings together academic experts and representatives from UN agencies, governments, and NGOs to discuss the report and individual country studies detailing work on the topic. The overarching framework is already set, but the indicator is now being groomed to travel. The third step is settling on a set of items and pilot testing them. The fourth step involves some assessment about whether the data seem to fit into other forms of knowledge about these countries and how they compare with other, similar indicators about these places (Kaufmann and Kraay 2007). If it seems quite divergent, there may be an effort to weight or adjust the findings. The goal is to produce a set of universal categories that are simple, easy to measure, and inexpensive to administer and quantify.

Thus expert group meetings are the mechanism through which educational and experiential expertise is applied to new projects and problems. Expert group meetings typically consist of academics; representatives of governments with special expertise, such as members of statistical bureaus; members of human rights treaty bodies; representatives of UN specialized agencies, such as UNIFEM or UNICEF; and UN staff who organize the meeting and produce the final report. Before the meeting, the secretariat and the participants prepare papers describing relevant research and suggestions for how to develop a survey or indicator. The UNSC survey project and the OHCHR initiative discussed in chapter 7 both followed this path.

In October 2007, an expert group meeting organized by the UN Division for the Advancement of Women (UNDAW) and the secretariat for the CSW, along with the UN Economic Commission for Europe (UNECE), the UNSC, the Conference of European Statisticians, and the UNSD met to develop indicators of violence against women. The conference, which took place over the course of three days in Geneva, included academic researchers with substantial research experience in violence against women, representatives of UN regional commissions, NGO representatives, representatives of the UNSD, and representatives of countries that had some survey experience (UN Division for the Advancement of Women 2007). The expert invited paper, written by Sylvia Walby, a sociologist from the United Kingdom with considerable experience doing domestic violence surveys in Britain, proposed a set of indicators (Walby 2007). Based on her suggestions, the group developed a limited set of measures of violence against women. This meeting proposed five global indicators covering physical violence, sexual violence, intimate-partner violence, and certain harmful practices (female genital mutilation and early marriage; UN Division for the Advancement of Women 2007: 25–27). In 2008, a second panel discussion with the CSW and the UNSC discussed the results of the 2007 expert group meeting and its proposed list of indicators (UN Commission on the Status of Women 2008a: 7).

Over the next six years, Walby's proposal from the 2007 meeting became the basis for the UNSC indicators. In 2008, the secretary general sent a report to the CSW reiterating the importance of developing indicators on violence against women and delineated a process of carrying this out in conjunction with the UNSC. Thus the secretary general also followed the model of distinguishing political work (i.e., specifying goals and monitoring), which was to be done by the CSW, from technical work (i.e., finding and analyzing data), which was to be carried out by the UNSC. According to the secretary general's report, the CSW should identify priority areas for the development of indicators, and the UNSC should provide technical expertise in identifying appropriate data and relevant sources (UN Commission on the Status of Women 2008b: 6).

The secretary general's report acknowledges that developing indicators is complex, time-consuming, and costly and should involve consultation between "users" and "producers" of statistics at all levels, starting at the global level with collaboration between the CSW and the UNSC (UN Commission on the Status of Women 2008b: 8). The recommended process is to analyze the current situation, adopt agreed-upon conclusions with regard to new policy recommendations where progress is needed, and identify one or more priority areas where indicators would be useful to the CSW in monitoring progress in conjunction with experts and consultations. After technical endorsement by the UNSC, the proposal for new indicators in the secretary general's report should be discussed at the CSW meeting. The new indicators should support further monitoring and reporting on progress by the CSW. This 2008 report notes that the CSW and UNSC collaborated in the past during the 2007 expert group meeting (UN Commission on the Status of Women 2008a: 8). The report lodged responsibility in the Statistical Commission, a body dedicated to supporting national statistical offices and producing survey models and guidelines that national statistical offices would be willing to use. Its indicators reflected this context.

The UN Statistical Commission Indicators

In order to carry forward its General Assembly mandate to develop indicators of violence against women, in 2008, the UNSC established the Friends of the Chair committee (UN Commission on the Status of Women 2008a: 7; UN Statistical Commission 2008: 39, 116) consisting of representatives of the UNSD secretariat and eight UNSC member countries, as well as representatives from regional commissions in Latin America (the UN Economic Commission for Latin America and the Caribbean [UNECLAC]), Europe (the UN Economic Commission for Europe [UNECE]), and Asia and the Pacific (the UN Economic and Social Commission for Asia and the Pacific [UNESCAP]) and from UNDAW, UNODC, WHO, and the special rapporteur on violence against women. Mexico chaired the committee. The group sought to "create a set of basic indicators with universal validity to carry out regular, precise and pertinent statistical measurements of violence against women within the framework of the national statistical systems" and to develop a set of guidelines for this project. The Mexican national statistical institute, the Instituto Nacional de Estadistica y Geographia (INEGI), was named coordinator of the Friends of the Chair group (UN Statistical Commission 2009). This group considered the recommendations of the 2007 expert group meeting for indicators of violence against women, the joint dialogue at the 2008 CSW meeting, and the 2008 report of Yakin Erturk, the special rapporteur on violence against women. Both the chair and the secretariat solicited input from all members and observers of the group and incorporated it into its report to the UNSC.

In its report to the UNSC in 2009, the Friends of the Chair proposed essentially the same set of indicators developed by the 2007 expert group meeting based on Walby's paper. The report focused on technical issues of measurement and data, including the need for internationally comparable statistical classifications for physical and sexual violence and for relationships to perpetrators and defining the terms for indicators (UN Statistical Commission 2009: 4–5).

At the February 2009 meeting of the UNSC in New York City, which I attended, the Friends of the Chair presented a list of possible indicators of violence against women for discussion (UN Statistical Commission 2009). The presentation of the report took twenty minutes and the discussion lasted twenty-five minutes more. Several countries' representatives spoke, identified only by nation per UN custom. Lebanon pointed out that some issues are sensitive and that police data are hard to use. It recommended adding someone from Arab and Muslim countries to the committee. Canada and China supported the report, but China advocated flexibility since different countries have different problems. For example, there is no female genital cutting in China, but there is a problem of mental injury, which China argued should be included. There was strong support from Japan, Lithuania, Italy, Ghana, Columbia, and Italy, with Italy calling for flexibility for different countries. Morocco pointed to conceptual issues, such as the age at which a child becomes an adult (in reference to child marriage), warning that these are very sensitive issues. The United Arab Emirates and Egypt agreed with Lebanon that it would be important to take into account the particular features of specific countries. Argentina made the same point, noting that it would be necessary to consider the cultural framework of each society. For example, early marriage is defined by the United Nations as marriage taking place before age eighteen, but in Argentina, marriage is possible at age fourteen, and it is not considered a form of violence. The UN Office of Drugs and Crime (UNODC) noted that it was developing a manual for violence against women in Europe.

The collective decision of the UNSC was to ratify the existing proposal while removing female genital cutting and early marriage. The chair of the conference welcomed the report, recognizing that it was only an interim one and that it would be important to consider national and cultural practices, making necessary the inclusion of as many countries as possible on the committee. The UNSC confirmed six of the indicators proposed by the Friends of the Chair but rejected three — female genital cutting (which the report referred to as "female genital mutilation"), child marriage, and psychological violence — that countries felt were too "sensitive," advocating the need to be "flexible." This list of approved indicators was then sent back to the Friends of the Chair committee. Since there were complaints at the UNSC meeting that the membership of the committee was not balanced and that it lacked members from the Middle East, seven new members were added. The new committee took on the project of developing guidelines for the approved indicators. The reconstituted Friends of the Chair had representatives from fifteen countries (Australia, Bangladesh, Botswana, Bulgaria, Canada, Chile, China, Costa Rica, Egypt, Ghana, Italy, Mexico, Thailand, Turkey, and the United States) and technical support from the UNSD. Its chair was still from Mexico.

Thus this indicator project did receive open, public scrutiny and was produced through a collaborative process involving representatives from several countries. However, the model it adopted was based on expertise developed through survey research in the United Kingdom and other European countries. There was not a substantive discussion of what the definition of violence against women should include beyond some limited issues of concern about "sensitivity" in particular countries. The principle of considering the perspectives of all countries was affirmed, but the core indicators were not changed, nor was the narrow definition of violence against women challenged. The UNSC approved a set of indicators that located the problem of violence against women squarely within partner and nonpartner relationships rather than in any larger set of social inequalities or structures of gender.

Mexico hosted a meeting to develop the indicators in December 2009. Representatives from eleven of the countries that were members of the committee participated along with representatives from the regional UN bodies from Europe (the UNECE) and Latin America (the UNECLAC) and observers from UNDAW and WHO. I was told it was not open to outside observers like me; however, it is extensively documented online (UN Statistical Commission 2014a). The group worked with the list of measures approved by the UNSC to develop categories for analysis and guidelines for data collection. The UNSD staff person provided an overview of existing violence-against-women surveys as the basis for discussion along with a draft set of guidelines. The committee wanted guidelines that would help national statistical offices carry out their own regular national surveys on the specific indicators that had been approved rather than developing a survey instrument. The goal of the committee, along with that of the UNSD more generally, was to support national statistical systems and to encourage countries to carry out their own surveys and administrative data collection systems.

The UNSD and the Friends of the Chair committee presented a final list of indicators and set of guidelines for national statistical offices at the February 2011 meeting of the UNSC in New York City. Even though the UNSC had rejected measuring female genital cutting, economic violence, psychological violence, and child marriage at the 2009 meeting, the Friends of the Chair reinstated the first three of these indicators, producing a total of nine indicators covering physical and sexual violence specified by severity of violence, relationship to the perpetrator, and frequency of violence for the last twelve months and during the respondent's lifetime. The report advocated a dedicated statistical survey if possible and a module attached to a health and demographic survey as a second choice (UN Statistical Commission 2009: 1–2). The formal report from the Friends of the Chair to the UNSC recommended the following indicators:

(a) Total and age specific rate of women subjected to physical violence in the last 12 months by severity of violence, relationship to the perpetrator and frequency;

(b) Total and age specific rate of women subjected to physical violence during lifetime by severity of violence, relationship to the perpetrator and frequency;

(c) Total and age specific rate of women subjected to sexual violence in the last 12 months by severity of violence, relationship to the perpetrator and frequency;

(d) Total and age specific rate of women subjected to sexual violence during lifetime by severity of violence, relationship to the perpetrator and frequency;

(e) Total and age specific rate of ever-partnered women subjected to sexual and/or physical violence by current or former intimate partner in the last 12 months by frequency;

(f) Total and age specific rate of ever-partnered women subjected to sexual and/or physical violence by current or former intimate partner during lifetime by frequency;

(g) Total and age specific rate of women subjected to psychological violence in the past 12 months by the intimate partner;

(h) Total and age specific rate of women subjected to economic violence in the past 12 months by the intimate partner;

(i) Total and age specific rate of women subjected to female genital mutilation. (UN Statistical Commission 2009: 4)

The report concluded that the Friends of the Chair would continue its work, focusing on developing administrative data sources — such as police calls and hospital data, along with a set of guidelines for producing statistics on violence against women — to be finalized and reported to the UNSC in February 2012. The report also said that the committee would explore the possibility of introducing "a worldwide homogeneous violence against women statistical data collection exercise" (UN Statistical Commission 2009: 4). The report and the proposed indicators were approved by the UNSC without discussion.

The list of core indicators approved by the UNSC defines violence against women much more narrowly than the global women's movement does. It measures the incidence of physical and sexual violence in intimate and nonintimate relationships plus female genital cutting and emotional and economic violence. It leaves out state violence by police and the military, sexual harassment, stalking, female feticide, violence against men, injury to pets and property, early and forced marriage, and many other forms of violence. It categorizes violence against women by type of relationship, type of violence, severity of violence, and frequency of violence. The complexity of relationships — their histories, the interplay of love and fear, the role of kinship, and residence patterns — disappear. Instead, a series of relatively discrete and apparently objective categories are used to measure this phenomenon across class, national, and cultural divides. In order to create internationally comparable statistical classifications, such simplification and decontextualization is, of course, essential.

The limited scope of this definition is clear when it is contrasted with the following account of a particular woman describing her experience of violence. This account from a survivor of domestic violence illustrates the gap between quantitative accounting and the experience of violence. It shows how numerical representations flatten violence and subtract history and context in comparison with narratives. It comes from a document written by a woman who had experienced violence and was seeking redress from the court. The story of Dora (a pseudonym) comes from a small town in Hawai'i during the early 1990s — the beginning of the battered women's movement. Dora is in her early twenties, a mainland white woman from a middle-class family with two years of college and an adequate family income who married a Samoan man. Like many other battered women, Dora turned to the courts only after years of violence from her husband. She wrote this account of the violence in 1992 as a request for compensation as a crime victim, although I also talked to her about her experiences:

> Sam and I have been together for almost five years. There has been abuse on and off for the first few years. This past year has been the worst; it got to the point where he would beat me at least once a day, and for about four weeks he beat me two or three times a day. It was so hard living with him. I have no family out here, only myself and our son. I lived in constant fear of Sam, never

knowing of his coming here, afraid of what he was going to be like. Sam has threatened me with guns, spear guns, a knife on one occasion. He would drag me down the hill by my hair, rip my clothes off of me, smash pans over my head. We had to replace or fix all but two doors in our house because he threw me through the other doors.

There was so much constant abuse it seemed like it would never end. Many times I thought that when I died it would be because my husband killed me. I was afraid to have him arrested because I knew he wouldn't stay in that long, and I thought that he would kill me when he got out. Finally, on May 31, 1992, I couldn't deal with it. We were driving home from Hilo; my husband was sitting in the back of our truck. I was driving because Sam was too drunk. We were driving down the road, and he reached through the back window and grabbed my face, scratching my face. Then he tried to choke me, and I felt that if he got open the door, he would kill me. I looked over at my son in his car seat. He was frightened, screaming, crying, and I knew I couldn't put up with this terror any more. I managed to drive away when he got out of the back to open my door. I just wanted the hell that my life had become to end.

As this story indicates, her experience of violence is embedded in a range of relationships, events, and meanings of masculinity and femininity, intertwined with ideas of race, class, region, and nationality. She attributed his violence to his Samoan ethnicity, for example, and felt more vulnerable because she was far away from her family. Her reaction to an incident is framed by past acts of violence. Such systems of kinship and meaning are excluded when domestic violence is counted, yet this simplification is essential to the production of comparative knowledge. The contrast between this account and the proposed indicators shows the loss of context, experience, and variation in forms of violence inherent in the use of quantitative measures. However, other efforts to develop global quantitative measures of violence against women taking place at the same time had less constricted and limited understandings of what to count than the UNSC indicators.

Alternative Approaches to Measuring Violence against Women

THE SPECIAL RAPPORTEUR ON VIOLENCE AGAINST WOMEN

While the UNSC was pursuing this approach to measurement, several other initiatives promoted quite different ideas about how to measure violence against women. One came from Yakin Erturk, the special rapporteur on violence against women. She was appointed by the Human Rights Council, formerly the Human Rights Commission, to investigate violence against women in the context of specific countries, to develop general knowledge, and to make recommendations, as did her predecessor, Radhika Coomaraswamy. In January 2008, she proposed developing violence-against-women indicators in her report to the Human Rights Council (Erturk 2008a). Her report responded to a 2004 request from the Human Rights Commission in Resolution 2004/46 on violence against women to recommend proposals for indicators on this phenomenon (2008a: 1). In the report, Erturk recommended three indicators: "grave violence," "femicide," and "social tolerance." The first refers to major forms of violence found in many countries, such as rape, serious intimate-partner violence, or sexual harassment. The second refers to the murder of women. Data on femicide are often available from criminal justice statistics. The third, social tolerance, addresses the social context of violence, focusing on the social and cultural contexts that allow it to continue (2008a: 2).

In February 2008, the special rapporteur issued a long addendum to this report: a review of existing research, current proposals in the UN system, issues of measurement, and proposals for indicators (Erturk 2008b). Liz Kelly, a prominent British sociologist and scholar of sexualized violence, contributed to this overview of existing research. As in most indicator projects, past surveys and indicators served as the models for new indicators. Since typically it is rich countries that carry out their own surveys, existing research tends to come from these countries. For example, Erturk notes that there have been previous surveys in Europe, Canada, the United States, and the United Kingdom (2008b: 47–53). These countries provide the model for the rest, a pattern of expertise inertia.

However, Erturk developed a different conceptual structure from that of other global surveys of violence against women. She wanted to measure all forms of gender-based violence, not just intimate-partner violence. This meant looking at violence in the workplace and the battlefield, as well as in the home. Since violence takes its meaning from its context, the experience of violence in intimate relationships is not the same as it is in the workplace, even if the physical act is the same (2008b: 68). She focused on the social acceptability of violence against women (Erturk 2008c: 9). While measures of social tolerance are not a good proxy for actual violence, they can be an important indicator of cultural understandings and of the extent to which there is awareness that violence is a problem and that prevention requires changes in the social acceptability of violence (Erturk 2008b: 53). Erturk's indicators offer a feminist way of thinking about violence against women, defining it in its broadest sense and

seeing it as socially embedded in structures of gender inequality and patriarchy. When I interviewed her in 2011, she stressed that this broad vision was an
important feature of her indicators.

THE UN ECONOMIC COMMISSION FOR EUROPE PROJECT

Another initiative within the UN system was a project by the UN regional
commissions to develop a survey module on violence against women. The
project was initiated by the Statistical Division of the UNECE in conjunction with the UN Economic Commission for Latin America and the Caribbean (UNECLAC) and other regional commissions. Its goal was to develop a
short survey that could be attached to an existing survey, such as the DHS. Its
leaders wanted to work with the UNSC project but introduce a more feminist
perspective. The group was better informed about gender-based violence and
more concerned with gender equality than the UNSC. It based its approach on
that of the earlier WHO Multi-Country Study, which incorporated feminist
principles and methods. In 2009, this group launched a project to develop a
survey instrument for the six indicators approved by the UNSC in February
2009 that would reshape them to be more responsive to women's experiences
and the broader definition of violence against women. Under the leadership of
the UNECE, all five regional commissions joined in the project. The initiative
was funded by a UN Development Account grant to the regional UN agencies to strengthen the capacity of countries to regularly and appropriately measure violence against women. The organizers wanted to develop a survey that
could either be attached to another household survey as a module or serve as
a stand-alone survey. The project built on the experience of the WHO Multi-
Country Study and the 2007 expert group meeting on indicators of violence
against women.

This group held an expert group meeting in Geneva in September 2009,
which I attended. It hired Henrica (Henriette) Jansen as a consultant to
develop the questionnaire and ethical guidelines for data collection. Jansen
was one of the authors of the WHO Multi-Country Study on Women's Health
and Domestic Violence and worked on it from 1999 to 2007. Her background
is in epidemiology and public health. She has considerable worldwide experience in surveying violence against women. She sometimes speaks at UN conferences, as she did in 2013, when I discussed the project and its guidelines
with her. For the 2009 UNECE meeting, she developed a draft of the survey,
which the group discussed, debating questions of wording and presentation. It
used the UNSC list of indicators but added several more. The UNECE ques-

tionnaire included measures of controlling behaviors such as isolation, intimidation, financial pressure, humiliation, and insult, as well as women's fear and the effects of the violence on their well-being. Its underlying theoretical concerns differed from those of the UNSC. It was more concerned with maximizing disclosure of violence and providing safety for women being interviewed and less concerned with national buy-in to the survey instrument. It expanded the UNSC mandate to be more compatible with the international violence-against-women movement and hoped to persuade the UNSC to adopt its questionnaire and perspective.

The UNSD official in charge of the UNSC project attended the 2009 UNECE expert group meeting along with national statistical officers from Canada, Italy, Mexico, and the United States; academic researchers and scholars who had been involved with the WHO Multi-Country Study and the International Violence against Women Survey; and representatives from UNODC, UNIFEM, and OHCHR. The author of the overview paper for the 2007 expert group meeting and one of the OHCHR experts working on human rights indicators discussed in chapter 7 also attended. The survey module was more or less finalized in 2009. In 2010, the consultant developed an interviewer's guide with carefully worked out ethical and safety recommendations to go with the module.

This initiative adopted a feminist vision of violence against women that incorporates social isolation and emotional abuse, as well as physical acts, their frequency, and injuries. It sought to maximize disclosure by posing the question of the experience of violence in a range of ways. Making sure interviews took place in a private setting where other family members could not hear the discussion was fundamental to the interviewee's safety and to persuading women to talk about their experience. In an interview in Geneva with Claudia Garcia-Moreno, the primary author of the WHO Multi-Country Study, she stressed that in that study, they were careful to make contacts with local women's centers to which they could refer any interviewee who was upset by the conversation and that they carefully trained interviewers. This included telling them not to tell other family members that they were studying violence and to change the subject instantly if a family member appeared in the interview room. These techniques were incorporated into the UNECE survey and guidelines.

In contrast, the UNSC initiative was inspired not by a concern about the issue of violence against women per se but by its overall mandate to enhance the statistical capacity of countries — particularly those with limited resources for data collection and analysis. It was also responding to the General Assembly's request for data on violence against women. Its goal was to produce a manual that national statistical offices could use to carry out surveys of violence against women. Issues of safety and disclosure were not major concerns. The UNECE initiative relied on social science scholars with extensive knowledge of gender-based violence and survey techniques developed for measuring it, while the UNSC and the UNSD experts had experience with health, housing, and victimization surveys and with developing guidelines to assist national statistical offices in carrying out surveys. The former was concerned with women who experienced violence and the latter with serving governments and national statistical offices. The first had a more feminist political stance and an interest in maximizing disclosure, while the second had a more statistical orientation and a concern with clear categories and measurable phenomena that governments were willing to count. These two groups had quite different purposes in developing their survey instruments and understood violence against women differently. This difference meant that they approached quantifying violence against women differently.

In November, 2010, a second UNECE expert group meeting was held in Geneva to discuss the pilot tests of the module, which I could not attend because of a scheduling conflict, but I discussed what happened with some of the participants. This meeting reported on four pilot surveys, each with small numbers of respondents, that had been done in Mexico, Moldova, Georgia, and Armenia. All ended up being stand-alone surveys, so that the module concept was not tested. The module concept was subsequently abandoned in favor of the stand-alone model. Participants told me that the meeting did not focus on revising the questionnaire on the basis of the pilot tests but on working on the guidelines being prepared by the UNSD.

It appears that by this time, the survey was essentially settled and the pilot tests were not used to make significant changes in its content. For example, a "training of trainers" workshop was held in Beirut in May 2010 to adapt the survey module to Arab countries (UN Economic and Social Commission for Western Asia 2010: 5–6). Organized by the UNSD and the Economic and Social Commission for Western Asia (UNESCWA), the purpose of the workshop was to teach representatives from national statistical offices how to carry out the survey with sensitivity and how to translate and adapt it to local circumstances. UNESCWA invited Henrietta Jansen to conduct the workshop. On the last day, there was an opportunity to adapt the questionnaire to Arab countries. The suggested changes were very modest, such as adding questions on polygamy, dowry, and bride price where appropriate and calculating early marriage by asking the age of one's first marriage. Honor killings were judged to be too delicate to include. Larger changes were not possible because the survey had to remain commensurable with others. As long as the questions were not changed, however, countries could add more response options by using drop-down menus. In other words, even at the regional level, adaptation meant that countries could add items or new values to variables but not fundamentally reconceptualize the survey.[1]

A HUMAN RIGHTS APPROACH

At the same time, there were efforts to develop data systems based on viewing violence against women through a human rights lens. In 2008, General Assembly Resolution 63/155 on the Intensification of Efforts to Eliminate Violence against Women asked the secretary general to ask states to provide information on their efforts to eliminate violence against women, arguing that states are obligated to promote and protect all human rights and fundamental freedoms and that all forms of violence against women, rooted in unequal gender power relations, inhibit women's ability to make use of their capabilities. The secretary general's 2010 report says that fifty-four states provided information on their laws, plans of action, availability of shelters, and supports for women (UN General Assembly 2010). This report again stresses the need for statistical data for monitoring and assessment and emphasizes the importance of developing national statistical systems (UN General Assembly 2010: 11–14). The conclusion states that despite the efforts to improve the collection of data, such as the inclusion of more population-based surveys and the creation of national databases, "the availability of more and better quality information, including statistical data, is crucial" (UN General Assembly 2010: 13). It argues that this information is essential for policy development, monitoring progress, and assessing the impact of interventions. It states that mentoring and accountability mechanisms, as well as measurable goals and timetables, should be included in national action plans. States are tasked to develop guidelines and rules for uniform data collection.

THE SECRETARY GENERAL'S DATABASE

Another simultaneous initiative was the secretary general's database, developed as part of his Unite to End Violence against Women Campaign. Announced at the 2008 CSW meeting, the campaign included data collection and analysis on the prevalence of various forms of violence against women and girls. The database was launched at the next CSW meeting in 2009, which I attended. The director of UNDAW explained that the database provides information on member states' legal strategies, policies, institutional mechanisms, training, and other measures, as well as research and statistical data. It is available online in all six UN languages and is searchable by issue and by country. It includes information on what it considers to be good or promising practices. The information in the database is based on responses to a comprehensive questionnaire sent to all UN permanent missions in September 2008. By February 2011, 106 of the 192 UN member nations had responded (UN Secretary General 2011). The database also includes information from country reports to treaty bodies, follow-up reports from the Beijing conference, and statements made at the CSW or General Assembly meetings. The audience for this database is described as government officials and decision makers, parliamentarians, representatives of national human rights institutions, civil society, members of the UN system, researchers, and academics (UN Division for the Advancement of Women 2009). Thus this database records government efforts but not the prevalence or nature of violence against women.

All these data gathering processes were aimed at governance, not theory development. Although they had different conceptual frameworks, all saw the collection of information about violence against women as a means to assess what works, to monitor efforts, and to direct policy. They developed indicators to measure policies and progress. Like the human rights indicators discussed in chapter 7, these data collection projects focus on assessing state compliance with international standards. The challenge here, as with measuring compliance with human rights laws more generally, is access to information. If the data are provided by countries themselves, it is difficult to evaluate their compliance with the standards set by the global system. There is a need for an alternative source of data. The UNSC survey of violence against women promised to provide this form of data.

THE LONG PROCESS OF INDICATOR DEVELOPMENT

This chronology shows that the process of developing the global indicators of violence against women was long and multifaceted, with many organizations and agendas. Governments, NGOs, academics, and UN agencies all participated but with quite different objectives and frameworks. Some parts of the process were open to public discussion, such as the UNSC's debate over which indicators to use, while many others took place in expert group meetings or in the offices of technical advisors. There was considerable continuity among ideas and personnel despite the separate and competing ideological streams. For example, the survey module developed at the 2009 UNECE expert group meeting drew heavily on the WHO study, including using the same consultant who worked on the WHO study. In contrast, the Friends of the Chair indicators came from the 2007 expert group meeting, not the WHO study, but the UNSC asked Holly Johnson — a criminologist who had attended the 2007 expert group meeting as well as the 2009 UNECE expert group meeting and had supervised the IVAWS study — to write the UNSC guidelines. The final guidelines were then extensively edited by Henriette Jansen, the experienced global consultant who helped develop the WHO study and drafted the survey module for the 2009 UNECE expert group meeting.

While each trajectory is relatively stable, there are clearly parallel lines, with competing ideas and overlapping memberships. Both public health and criminology experts attended the 2009 expert group meeting, as did an OHCHR expert working on human rights indicators. Many of those who came to the 2009 expert group meeting, sponsored by the UNECE, also attended the 2007 UNDAW expert group meeting. Despite this overlap of personnel, each of these initiatives is guided by different goals and employs different ways of thinking about what to measure and why it needs to be measured. In this case, the more feminist participants were clearly trying to influence the UNSD, while the UNSD staff member heading the project was skeptical about their efforts.

EXPERTISE INERTIA

Based on attending two expert group meetings and reading the extensive documents from two more, it appears to me that people from countries with experience in relevant forms of data collection exercise more influence over the shape of the survey than those who lack this experience. In expert meetings, representatives from countries that have done surveys tend to frame the issues and the questions, while those from other countries make suggestions based on their general knowledge of the situation in their own country. Those who have experience in collecting data on violence against women tend to be from countries in Europe, North America, and Latin America and from Australia and New Zealand. Living in a country that has had a DHS or MICS does not produce the authority to shape a new survey, since these are primarily planned and organized internationally. At the October 2007 expert group meeting, there were indicators and survey reports from several European countries as well as the US Centers for Disease Control and Prevention and the UN Millennium Project's Task Force on Education and Gender Equality. Although participants from Mexico, Italy, Palestine, and Korea provided reports of their surveys and indicators and Ghana discussed its use of administrative data, these were not generally surveys of violence against women. Most of the UN regional commissions presented proposals for indicators rather than using existing indicators or surveys, while the African commission focused more broadly on gender indicators (UN Division for the Advancement of Women 2007).

The expert review paper that formed the basis of the 2007 discussion examined indicators from the UN High Commissioner for Refugees, UNECLAC, UNECE, European Union, Canada, United States, United Kingdom, Italy, and Spain (Walby 2007: 5–8). Since this expert group meeting built on previous surveys and indicators and since these were largely developed in Europe, Canada, the United States, and parts of Latin America, these regions set the pattern for the rest of the world. In her report, for example, Walby used her experience working with the British Crime Survey to develop her indicator proposals. Although these meetings reach out to countries from all regions of the world, it is those that have experience developing or analyzing surveys and indicators that are the experts.

Similarly, at the 2009 Friends of the Chair meeting in Mexico, it appears that the group relied on preexisting national surveys to finalize its list of indicators. As described above, the meeting consisted of representatives from the national statistical offices of eleven of the fifteen member countries — Australia, Bangladesh, Bulgaria, Chile, China, Costa Rica, Egypt, Mexico, Thailand, Turkey, the United States, and Italy, which (while not present) participated actively — as well as observers from the UNECE, UNECLAC, UNDAW, UNSD, and WHO (UN Statistical Commission 2009: 3). The discussion in Mexico was based on a paper written by the UNSD that provided a summary of sixty-four existing national surveys of violence against women. Of these, twenty-eight were conducted by a country rather than an international agency. The vast majority of these twenty-eight were in Europe and the Americas. Sixteen were from Europe, two from North America, five from Latin America, one from Australia, and four from Asian and Pacific countries (Cambodia, Kiribati, Korea, Maldives). These surveys set the terms for the overall discussion about how to measure violence against women (UN Statistical Commission 2009).

The discussions in the 2009 UNECE expert group meeting similarly drew on past models of violence-against-women surveys as the group developed a new one. Participants at the meeting referred to the WHO Multi-Country Study and its experience with cross-national studies, the IVAWS survey, and surveys in Italy, Switzerland, Germany, Mexico, Canada, the United States, and other developed countries as they debated issues such as how to define "partners," what to use as a denominator for a prevalence measure (all women, or all married women, or all married women ages 15–49, etc.), how to phrase whether a person is in a relationship, and how to incorporate same-sex relationships. The questionnaire drew many of its questions from the WHO study as well as the DHS violence-against-women module that was itself patterned on the WHO model.

Surprisingly, at the 2009 UNECE expert group meeting, questions of cross-cultural comparison were relatively little discussed. There was considerable discussion about the cross-cultural meaning of the term "partner" and whether it implied same-sex relationships, as well as about the difficulty of defining "intimate" in intimate-partner relationships, but otherwise, there was relatively little talk about the problem of translation, linguistic or cultural, or about the difficulty of comparing violence across cultural differences in conceptions of family and households. There was also little discussion about how these differences affect who is willing to speak, about human rights issues such as state responsibility, or about the viability of using criminal justice assistance. That violence against women could be understood through surveys was not fundamentally questioned. Changes to the proposed text of the survey module were based on the past survey experiences of the experts around the table. Only the UNECE and UNECLAC representatives took active roles in the discussion; no one from the UNECA or UNESCAP attended, and the UNESCWA representative appeared only briefly. Also, no representatives from developing countries actively engaged in the discussions. Most of the conversation viewed the problems as technical ones of wording, the order of questions, and definitions of terms. Even though participants came from many countries, not all spoke equally often, and the entire conversation was in English. Experience creates expertise, which fosters influence in these global discussions. People from poorer countries, unable to conduct surveys, are squeezed out of the discussion, and their perspectives have little influence.

There was a fundamental division in this 2009 UNECE expert group meeting between the feminist activists and the statisticians. The former saw the survey as a way to expose the scope of the problem of violence against women. They wanted to add questions about state responses to encourage government action and policy change. The latter wanted to measure national populations and respect states' preferences. This meant not exposing problems that could embarrass governments. Claiming that some issues were sensitive and culturally specific served to deflect demands that they be counted. On the other hand, the feminists resisted claims that some practices they saw as violent were cultural and had to be accepted. Intriguingly, the statisticians and the feminists socialized separately. Many of the feminists had also attended the 2007 expert group meeting and had a long history of working on violence against women. They tried to persuade the statisticians to adopt their views of how to measure violence against women. In particular, they hoped that the UNSC would adopt the survey questionnaire they had carefully developed following the model of the WHO study, but based on the UNSC indicators. They worked hard to have a version available for the February 2011 UNSC meeting. However, some of the UNSD staff resisted using their approach. When I asked a key UNSD staff person if the UNSC was going to use the survey module, he said it would be included as one among several options that countries could choose. He was generally dismissive of the UNECE project and its approach.

However, when the final UNSC guidelines were published in 2013, I was surprised to find that the survey module, renamed as a "model questionnaire," was included in an annex and was the only example of a questionnaire offered (UN Statistics Division 2013: 163–96). Moreover, the text of the guidelines refers frequently to this model questionnaire as well as to the WHO study. It puts a strong emphasis on ethical and safety concerns during interviews, a core concern of the feminist activists in the UNECE project. The guidelines include examples of questions about turning to the police for help and about attitudes toward domestic violence (UN Statistics Division 2013: 224–28). Although the guidelines do not discuss violence against women in a structural sense—its connection to inequality and patriarchy—they do consider questions about controlling behavior and the experience of violence. It seems likely that this expansion in scope and the incorporation of the survey instrument are results of the work of Holly Johnson, the criminologist who wrote the guidelines in 2011 and 2012, and Henrica (Henriette) Jansen, the consultant who edited them in 2013. There was also a change in leadership of the project at the UNSD. The initial staff person, whom I interviewed several times, who said he had no expertise in gender violence, who defined his role as purely technical, and who distanced himself from substantive concerns about violence against women, was replaced before the guidelines were finished. The new staff person, whom I interviewed in 2014, was concerned with improving gender statistics at the United Nations and seemed more sensitive to women's issues. She said that ten countries had already used the model questionnaire.

This account shows how indicators take shape over time. Experts measuring new problems or places build on past experience, which is fundamental to creating expertise. Global indicators tend to build on models that were developed in more affluent and statistically advanced societies where resources are available to gather and analyze data. Thus experts from countries that have already carried out statistical data collection and analysis, often from the global North, have greater influence in shaping global indicators. When there are struggles over measurement, expertise matters as well. The shift to a more feminist set of guidelines was guided by two experts with a lot of experience in measuring violence against women. In the end, it appears that experience in measuring violence against women trumped the skepticism of the statisticians. The next chapter examines how measurement categories are created. It then turns to a comparison of four approaches to measuring violence against women, showing the differences in approach and philosophy among them, as well as their distinct organizational paths and institutional frameworks.

Categorizing Violence against Women

The Cultural Work of Commensuration

One of the critical steps in developing indicator-based knowledge is designing the categories for counting. The categories inevitably lump disparate things together under one label and separate similar things that vary along a continuum under different labels. These categories are the basis of comparison. They must all refer to the same thing, even though this thing is manifested differently in different places. For example, sexual violence takes different forms in different places. In many places, rape in marriage is not considered a violation. However, in order to compare rates of sexual violence across regions, social classes, and countries, the categories must be based on commonalities. Constructing categories is an interpretive process, with many ways of putting things together and labeling them. This chapter examines the efforts of the Friends of the Chair committee to construct the categories "severe physical violence" and "moderate physical violence" in a way that enables them to travel globally. This is an important distinction in the field of violence against women, since some critics of the movement complain that the problem is exaggerated and that most incidents are modest rather than severe. Yet there are no natural breaks along the continuum of violence: they have to be created by the engineers of the indicators. This chapter then compares the cultural dimensions of four frameworks used to measure violence against women in the measurement projects discussed in the previous chapter.

Defining Severe and Moderate Violence

Differentiating between severe and moderate physical violence might seem simple, but in order to use it in a global survey, the distinction needs to be commensurable across countries, regions, settings (i.e., rural vs. urban), and a vast array of social and cultural formations. Distinguishing between moderate and severe violence involves interpretations that are rooted in culture and context, such as the nature of one's relationship, ideas about discipline and duty, and views on the kinds of obligations wives owe their husbands. Different ways of measuring the concept produce different prevalence rates, of course. The prevailing approach to measuring the severity of violence in widely surveyed countries like the United States is to list a series of actions that increase in severity. Such a list was originally developed in the United States and has been widely used in surveys in other countries.

The Friends of the Chair committee faced the problem of developing a global measure of violence against women by severity because of the mandate they were given by the UNSC. The indicator of physical violence approved by the UNSC is the "total and age-specific rate of women subjected to physical violence in the last 12 months and during lifetime by severity of violence, relationship to perpetrator and frequency" (UN Statistical Commission 2010: 6–7). Consequently, at the Friends of the Chair meeting in 2009, the government representatives and UN agency representatives confronted the problem of differentiating between severe and moderate violence against women. They considered the three alternatives Sylvia Walby outlined in her overview paper for the 2007 expert group meeting: the nature of the act, its frequency, and its level of injury. Walby concludes that the main measure of severity should be whether an injury occurs, but responses could be differentiated into (1) fear but no physical injury, (2) minor injury, and (3) major injury or death (Walby 2007: 19, 23). However, in its final report, the 2007 expert group meeting simply said that the indicator should differentiate between severe and moderate violence without explaining how these concepts were to be defined (UN Division for the Advancement of Women 2007: 25–26).

A common strategy is to create a list of acts that are determined to be severe and a list of acts that are considered moderate. This approach defines severity as a dimension of the act itself, such that, for example, threatening someone with a gun is more serious than a slap. It ignores the fear, injury, and experience of the victim. It seems relatively objective, since it requires less interpretation by the victim. The use of a list is commonplace, with about 90 percent of the surveys in Europe collecting data on the following forms of physical violence:

pushing, grabbing, or shoving; kicking, biting, or hitting; hitting with some-thing; choking; and using, or threatening the use of, a gun or knife (UN Divi-sion for the Advancement of Women 2007: 12). The measurement of acts is based on modifications of the widely used Conflict Tactics Scale, which was developed in the United States and lists acts in ascending severity (Straus 1979). This was the approach adopted by the DHS. Its optional domestic violence module, developed in 2005, defines domestic violence according to responses to seven items that ask "whether your last husband/partner did these things to you" and how often within the last twelve months. The items are "push you," "slap you," "twist your arm or pull your hair," "punch you with his fist," "kick you," "try to choke or burn you," and "threaten or attack you with a knife or gun or other weapon." It also includes questions about controlling behavior, emo-tional abuse, and injuries (Demographic and Health Surveys 2006). The 2005–2006 DHS of India used this optional module with the same list (Demographic and Health Surveys 2006; International Institute for Population Sciences and Macro International 2007).

However, researchers working on violence against women have criticized this scale because, in the absence of considerations of frequency or fear, it indi-cates that men and women are relatively equal in their acts of violence, since it equates a single slap with a pattern of ongoing and injurious hits with one's hand. Even when men and women report the same acts, frequency and injury rates are quite disparate between genders. Moreover, this scale focuses only on domestic violence rather than a broader array of forms of gender-based vio-lence (Walby 2007: 16–19).

Nevertheless, the committee had to create aggregate categories of severe and moderate violence. It is in the acts of aggregation and categorization that power comes into play. Once decisions about categorization and aggregation are made, the categories may come to seem objective and natural, while the power exercised in creating them disappears. Consequently, it is worth consid-ering who constructs the list of actions, and on what basis, and who draws the dividing line. At the 2009 Friends of the Chair meeting, the list and the catego-ries were based on previous research. This research was done in Europe, North America, Australia, a few countries in Latin America, and in international sur-veys designed in the global North, such as the DHS and MICS.

There are, of course, national and local differences in what is interpreted as a severe act. For example, at the Friends of the Chair meeting, Bangladesh sug-gested adding the following to the list of physical violence categories: "Burn/ Acid throwing, Dropping from higher place, Smash the finger or hand, Needle the finger, Kick in the abdomen, Hit in the teeth, Murder (Femicide)." Bangladesh's proposed list of psychological violence categories similarly suggests a regionally distinctive set of categories: "Non-response to queries, Pressure for dowry, Threat of separation, To marry other women in addition to existing wife, Do not pay attention to the children, Expel from the house, Disregard the opinion of the females in household decision making, To compel to do hard work during pregnancy, To rebuke for giving birth to female child" (Ali Mollah 2009: 16–18). Several of these acts of gender-based violence are particular to Bangladesh and South Asia generally. The approach of allowing countries to add their particular forms of violence was adopted in the final report of the meeting, but only insofar as other acts of violence could be added to the list. It did not change the overarching approach of listing actions of varying levels of severity or provide for the development of new categories.

A second approach to measuring severity considers the severity of injury. This poses similar problems of condensing variety into a single category. For example, Bangladesh suggested the using the criterion of bleeding in assessing severity: "Severity in case of physical violence may be considered for those incidents, which cause injury to the victim, bleeding from any organ of the body may also be considered [a] severe type of physical violence. The other incidents may be termed as 'moderate'" (Ali Mollah 2009). Even a simple measure such as seeking medical attention varies greatly by setting (i.e., rural vs. urban) and class factors and cannot be used reliably.

A third approach to defining severity is to ask the woman about her level of fear, using her fear as a measure of severity. Australia, for example, did a survey that included questions about whether a woman changed her daily pattern of activities because of fear. Anxiety or fear was measured by its effects on activities such as work, social or leisure activities, childcare, and home security systems.

The UNSC indicators used primarily acts and the presence or absence of injuries to define severe violence. At the 2009 UNECE meeting, the UNSD official overseeing the UNSC indicator project pointed out that the biggest difficulty in classifying severity is sensitivity to cultural differences. His solution was to focus on physical acts. He planned to rely on the approaches taken by the sixty-four national surveys he had identified in the work of the Friends of the Chair. The Friends of the Chair turned to these existing surveys to develop a template for measurement in its conference report:

> Type of violence refers to violent acts experienced by women. Conducted surveys document that the most effective approach is to avoid general definitions

of violence and that the framing of the questions should concentrate on specific acts. Consequently, physical violence is an act that inflicts physical harm.

a. Moderate physical violence consists of the following categories that did not result in bruises, cuts, broken bones or need for medical treatment or hospitalization:

    i.   Hit with something

    ii.   Kicked, bit or hit

    iii.   Slapped

    iv.   Pushed, grabbed, shoved

    v.   Threatened to hit

    vi.   Other

b. Severe physical violence consist of the first four categories listed above that resulted in bruises, cuts, broken bones or need for medical treatment or hospitalization, plus several other categories:

    i.   Hit with something with aggravated consequences

    ii.   Kicked, bit or hit with aggravated consequences

    iii.   Slapped with aggravated consequences

    iv.   Pushed, grabbed, shoved with aggravated consequences

    v.   Beat

    vi.   Choked

    vii.   Threatened with knife, gun, other weapon

    viii.   Assaulted with knife, gun, other weapon

    ix.   Other

The template presented the range of acts shown in table 4.1. This table recommends assessing severity according to a scale based on acts and injuries, but when the final report was published, it recommended measuring severity not by injury or the act of violence but by assessing it separately (UN Statistics Division 2010). The final report is vague about what to include in this separate measure, beyond stating that it will consider physical and emotional consequences in determining severity (UN Statistics Division 2010: 7). This just displaces the problem, however, since a measure of consequences must then be produced, which is also likely to differ in different contexts. Given the intractable nature of this analytic problem, it is not surprising that the report does not offer a solution.

Measuring fear fared less well. The final report from the 2009 Friends of the Chair meeting expressed concern that fear is too "subjective" to measure

TABLE 4.1. *Range of violent acts against women*

	Without aggravated consequences— no bruises, cuts, broken bones, need for medical assistance or hospitalization	Aggravated consequences— bruises, cuts, broken bones, need for medical assistance or hospitalization
Hit with something	M	S
Kicked, bit or hit	M	S
Slapped	M	S
Pushed, grabbed, shoved	M	S
Threatened to hit	M	NA
Beat	S	S
Choked	S	S
Threatened with knife, gun, other weapon	S	NA
Assaulted with knife, gun, other weapon	NA	S
Other	M	S

Source: UN Statistical Commission 2009: 10–11.

M = moderate; S = severe; NA = not applicable

(UN Statistics Division 2010). Many at the meeting preferred more apparently objective data such as the nature of the act and the severity of the injury. The report concluded that fear is too labile, varying with national cultural circumstances, and therefore too subjective in the international setting. It attempted to bring the emotional consequences of violence into the analysis but did not specify how it this was to be measured. Paragraphs 18 and 19 below explain this position and why the group did not add fear to its criteria for severe violence:

17. Experience in conducting surveys on violence against women points to the need to list different acts of violence rather than attempting to develop a general and generic definition of physical violence, which is dependent on national circumstances, cultural background, tradition, subjective perception and so forth. Consequently, the preliminary classification of individual acts of physical violence presented in the draft outline of the *Guidelines for Producing Statistics on Violence against Women, Volume I: Statistical Survey* is an adequate basis for further elaboration. The list should not be exhaustive or closed-ended, as country specific types of violence need to be incorporated as distinct modalities. In that context, the wording of the modalities requires

careful consideration due to linguistic and substantial peculiarities. In addition, the meeting agreed that it was convenient to develop an aggregated list of acts consisting of groupings of individual acts, to allow for national specificities and, at the same time, for international comparisons.

18. As the severity of a given violent act can be perceived differently by victims depending on the perpetrator, it is not recommended to assign a severity level to individual acts of violence. It would be preferable to assess the topic of severity independently of the list of acts of violence, by developing a scale based on consequences suffered by the victim.

19. The Friends of the Chair group discussed at length having "fear" taken into account to define categories of severity and even acts of violence. For example, if the victim is incapable to lead her daily life as a result of violence, the event should be considered as "severe," even if no physical damage has been done. However, national cultural circumstances have different social views of "fear," making it a subjective term that loses meaning in international settings. Consequently, the meeting decided that due consideration must be given to both physical and emotional consequences when determining severity. (UN Statistics Division 2010: 7)

Clearly the committee struggled with how to incorporate injuries, fear, and the perspective of the victim into the distinction between severe and moderate violence, recognizing the broad cultural variation of a global sample. Relying on measures of acts or injuries rather than a person's fear displaces the decision about whether the violence is severe from the person experiencing it to the experts who decide which acts are severe. It moves the locus of the judgment of severity away from the person who has experienced violence to the expert who is developing objective measures. In this case, these experts tended to speak from their experience carrying out surveys in Europe, North America, and more affluent parts of Latin America. National differences were accommodated by adding local options for severe acts of violence.

The report was scheduled for discussion at the UNSC in February 2011, which I attended. The content of the report itself was neither presented nor discussed, although the document was available to all the attendees. It was therefore approved as presented. It is interesting that the resistance to measuring female genital cutting and emotional and economic violence mentioned in the previous discussion was not raised, even though the Friends of the Chair had put these measures back into the report. The dilemma of how to measure severe physical violence was passed on to the consultant writing the guidelines.

The UNECE meeting, in contrast, concluded that severity of physical violence should be measured by three criteria — the nature of the act, the level of injury, and the level of fear — thus adopting a broader definition that takes greater account of the perception of the victim. Severity is measured by the form of the violence perpetrated, divided into moderate and severe, and/or whether any injury has occurred, with injury grouped into three levels and options such as "internal injuries" and "miscarriages" added. They also included the impact of violence on mental well-being in the survey (UN Economic Commission for Europe 2009: 6).

The consultant writing the guidelines for the UNSC, an experienced researcher on violence against women in criminology, told me that she found the simple list of acts inadequate as a measure of severity and planned to include measures of frequency, injury, and whether the abused person experienced the violence as being severe. The importance of the emphasis on experience is supported by my ethnographic observations of women's domestic violence support groups in a small US town, suggesting that perceptions of severity depend on the history of the relationship and a long series of events, both violent and nonviolent, that humiliate, frighten, and injure the individual in a wide variety of ways. I found that the act of physical violence was less important to these women than the violations of a sense of self, repeated insults and humiliations, threats to children and pets, and excessive demands for money that they experienced (Merry 1995; 2009). It was events like these that concerned the battered women I spoke to and was the focus of their conversation in support groups, not the specific acts of violence they endured. Such nuanced and contextualized understandings of violation cannot be revealed by a list of acts, nor are they amenable to study through a cross-national survey.

The final guidelines for the UNSC indicators, published in 2013, expanded the definition of severity to a concept more like the one adopted by the UNECE project. The guidelines note that it is difficult to measure severity by asking women directly because of the multidimensional nature of violence. They offer a concise definition of severity as being measured by the nature of acts and their consequences, similar to table 4.1 of the Friends of the Chair committee (UN Statistics Division 2013: 74). But then the guidelines expand this core definition by stretching the categories of acts and consequences. They point out that it is also necessary to measure impacts on a woman's daily activities as well as her past experiences of violence and the level of risk of injuries she faces. Consequences include injuries, mental health repercussions, miscarriage, violence during pregnancy, and fear of the perpetrator. Moderate physical violence refers to acts that do not result in bruises, cuts, broken bones, miscarriage, or other consequences. According to the guidelines, when a woman is not pregnant and the violence does not lead to fear of her part-ner or for her life, it is also considered moderate. Severe violence refers to acts that produce injuries, cause fear of a partner or for a woman's life, and acts that occurred while she was pregnant. Some acts, such as hitting with a fist, choking, or threatening with a knife or gun, are considered severe, regard-less of the consequences (UN Statistics Division 2013: 23–24, 74). Thus the UNSC guidelines began from the basic definition proposed by the Friends of the Chair committee but were expanded in ways advocated by the UNECE group to include fear, mental health consequences, pregnancy, and the victim's history with violence. They also suggested that these indicators could be used separately or in combination. Such struggles over categorization clearly have important consequences for creating definitions and, ultimately, assessing the size and scope of the problem.

Other surveys of violence against women that confronted the challenge of defining severe and moderate violence developed different categories. In com-parison to the UNSC's focus on objective measures, the more feminist special rapporteur on violence against women emphasized continuity of violence over time. Erturk's report to the Human Rights Council proposed developing an indicator for "grave" violence against women with international agreement on its definition (Erturk 2008c: 17). She advocated including a combination of spe-cific acts, such as rape, serious sexual assault, sexual coercion during childhood or adulthood, female genital mutilation, child/forced marriage, and trafficking and sexual exploitation, as well as actions that follow a pattern over time, a "course of conduct" in intimate-partner violence, including stalking and sexual harassment. She considered a series of incidents to be generally far more seri-ous than a single event, regardless of the particular act (Erturk 2008b: 112, 132).

The International Violence against Women Survey (IVAWS), a criminal-justice-focused survey of violence against women in eleven countries discussed in chapter 3, not only based its assessments of severity on the nature of the acts themselves but also measured several other dimensions of severity. Severity of physical violence was assessed according to the familiar list of six specific acts of increasing severity plus a seventh category for anything else. This list begins with "threatened to hurt you physically in a way that frightened you" and ends with the two most severe, "tried to strangle or suffocate you, burn or scald you on purpose" and "used or threatened to use a knife or gun on you" (Johnson, Ollus, and Nevala 2008: 29). The questionnaire also asks about perceptions of seriousness, injury, the need for medical care, fear for one's life, using alcohol or medication to cope with the effects of the violence, reporting to police and other agencies, whether the incident was a crime, and frequency. To understand when women seek help or report an incident to the police, the survey used a broad definition of seriousness, including whether the woman thought her life was in danger, whether she was injured, whether she viewed the incident as serious, and whether she thought it was a crime (Johnson, Ollus, and Nevala 2008: 133–66). Thus the survey assessed seriousness based on perceptions, fear, and injury in addition to the act itself. Although all these questions provide information on severity, the format of the questionnaire and the small sample sizes precluded incorporating these criteria into overall measurements of severity (Johnson, Ollus, and Nevala 2008: 27, 52). The project was carried out within severe financial constraints, making larger sample sizes and further analysis difficult.

Nevertheless, the research did suggest that acts themselves are not necessarily adequate guides to determine severity (Johnson, Ollus, and Nevala 2008: 55, 58). For example, women were more likely to view acts by previous partners as serious than they were to view acts by present partners as serious (Johnson, Ollus, and Nevala 2008: 60). The data also indicate that seriousness differed from "actual" violence. For example, not all of those who were victimized violently considered the experience to be serious, and many said it was not a crime (Johnson, Ollus, and Nevala 2008: 72). However, when women said that they feared for their lives in cases of intimate-partner violence, 90 percent also said that they perceived the situation to be serious. Indeed, the authors of the survey argue that fearing for one's life is a very important indicator of severity, but it is not necessarily connected to rates of physical injury (Johnson, Ollus, and Nevala 2008: 71).

The survey module developed by those at the more feminist 2009 UNECE meeting listed six actions with increasing severity, from "slapped and thrown something at you that could hurt you" to "pushed you or shoved you or pulled your hair," "hit you with his fist or with something else that could hurt you," "kicked you, dragged you or beat you up," "choked or burnt you on purpose," and "threatened with or actually used a gun, knife, or other weapon against you." The author of the questionnaire, Henriette Jansen, labeled the first two — slapped and pushed — as "moderate violence" and the last four as "severe." Although the list was roughly the same as that used by the IVAWS, it clustered the elements into two categories while the IVAWS left them as a ranked series. Thus what constitutes severe physical violence in the two questionnaires differs somewhat, with the UNECE questionnaire adopting a slightly broader definition of severe physical violence by including four of the six types. This means that it would find a higher prevalence of severe physical violence.

The UNECE questionnaire also included questions about controlling behavior such as isolation (e.g., "does your partner/husband try to keep you from seeing your friends, does he try to restrict contact with your family of birth") and emotional abuse such as insults, humiliation, threats, and inju- ries. Its conception of violence incorporates social isolation and emotional abuse as well as acts, their frequency, and the level of injury they cause. Like the IVAWS survey, this questionnaire enables a definition of severity viewed through a broader lens than simply that of acts; however, in none of these studies was there an effective joining of questions of perception, fear, injuries, and consequences in defining severe violence. Instead, the category was almost always pegged to a list of specific acts derived from substantial research in a few wealthy countries, along with assumptions about the nature of each act and the addition of injuries and, in the UNECE's case, fear. The complexity of women's perceptions and fears were relatively little measured.

Through this process of deciding how to measure something like severe physical violence, the concept is established and defined. Over time, as Latour (1987) points out for the development of scientific knowledge in general, such a categorization gradually becomes an accepted "black box" that no longer needs to be explained or justified. Surveys on violence against women are relatively new, but through this process and others, the categories of analysis are becoming more fixed, following the process by which the successful indicators discussed in chapter 1, such as the Human Development Index (HDI), were established. When the HDI was first proposed in 1990, there was considerable debate even in the popular press about what it meant and how it was to be used. Gradually, such discussions disappeared; now media reports tend to view the HDI as a fact about a country without further debate or deliberation. Poverty has the same status despite the enormous difficulties of determining what poverty is and how it should be measured. Indeed, when the indicators of violence against women were introduced to the UNSC in 2009, the chair of the Friends of the Chair committee said that although measuring violence against women now seems very complex, poverty, too, was thought difficult to measure twenty years ago.

The Cultural Dimensions of Indicators: A Comparison

Although there is overlap between the personnel and approaches of these initiatives, it is possible to distinguish four separate theoretical frameworks among them: gender equality, human rights, criminal justice, and statistical capacity. These four frameworks differ in how violence against women is defined, the size of the problem, and its relationship to larger structures of inequality. They take different approaches to gathering and analyzing information and constructing indicators, and they produce different kinds of knowledge. The differences are institutional as well as theoretical. Each comes from a particular UN organization and academic discipline. I will compare five features of each approach: (1) its theory about the nature and causes of violence against women, (2) its institutional support, (3) its models and practices for gathering and classifying data, (4) its prevailing form of expertise, and (5) its strategies for change. These five features produce subtle but important differences in the way information is gathered, categorized, and interpreted.

These four frameworks have significantly different resources available to them for gathering and analyzing data and creating indicators. Both criminal justice and national statistical offices are better funded to collect and analyze data than advocates of gender equality or human rights. Consequently, these conceptions provide the bulk of the information available on violence against women. It seems likely that their narrower, more individualistic definitions of violence against women will prevail over the broader, more structurally embedded ones.

GENDER EQUALITY

Theoretical Framework. The underlying theoretical framework for the battered women's movement links violence to inequality between men and women. In the 1970s, feminists saw violence as a key mechanism for maintaining gender subordination. This perspective was developed through a series of global conferences on women from 1975 to 1995, culminating in the Beijing Platform for Action of 1995, which identified violence against women as one of twelve major issues for women. In the 1970s and 1980s, ending women's subordination required ending gender-based violence, but since the 1990s, the focus has flipped so that reducing violence against women is thought to depend on diminishing gender inequality. Feminists working on violence against women tend to advocate gender equality as a solution.

Gender equality models see violence against women as the product of entrenched patterns of gender inequality and social tolerance of violence (see Merry 2009). This contrasts with the view that violence against women is a product of particular kinds of interpersonal relationships—especially intimate ones. Even when analyzing intimate-partner violence, however, the gender equality approach emphasizes emotional, psychological, economic, and sexual abuse and controlling behaviors, as well as physical violence.

Institutional Support. The gender equality approach to measuring violence against women is institutionally supported within the UN system by the CSW, CEDAW, women's secretariat, UNDAW, special rapporteur on violence against women, UNECE, and UNECLAC, among others. Since the 1990s, the CEDAW committee has queried countries about their work on violence against women and advocated gender equality. Europe has already developed considerable statistical capacity in the area of measuring violence against women, and the UNECE is a leader in gender statistics while in 2005 the Conference of European Statisticians set up a Steering Group in Gender Statistics and a Task Force on Gender-based Violence. In 2005, the ECE Statistical Journal of the United Nations published a special issue on the measurement of violence against women (Special Issue on "Violence Against Women" 2005: 189). The gender equality framework was also promoted by the UNDAW expert group meeting in 2007, the UNECE expert group meeting of 2009, and the special rapporteur's 2008 report on indicators on violence against women, all discussed above. The 2006 secretary general's in-depth report on violence against women took a gender equality approach as well, possibly due to influence by its advisory board of prominent, international feminist activists in the field of violence against women: Charlotte Bunch, Susana Chiarotti, Radhika Coomaraswamy, Yakin Erturk, Alda Facio, Asmer Khader, Irene Khan, Widney Brown, and Heisoo Shin.

Models and Practices. Surveys produced within this framework address social tolerance of violence against women by asking about attitudes toward this violence as well as a wide range of other dimensions of violence, such as stalking, controlling behaviors, intimidation, and isolation. There is considerable emphasis on ethical and safety issues in conducting surveys, including elaborate guidelines and extensive training programs for interviewers. From this perspective, violence-against-women surveys should be stand-alone surveys focused only on that issue, rather than attached to a household or victimization survey, in order to maximize the safety of the interviewee. Administrative data by themselves are considered inadequate, given the widely recognized pattern of underreporting of many forms of violence against women.

Expertise. The experts who promote a gender equality perspective tend to be social scientists and public health experts, who are predominantly sociologists and epidemiologists. They build on a substantial body of academic research on violence against women carried out at national and local levels, mostly in relatively wealthy, industrialized countries. At the UNDAW expert group meeting of 2007, for example, the expert Sylvia Walby was a professor of sociology and gender at the University of Lancaster and had done considerable research in Britain. In her report to the meeting, she advocated a broad and nuanced approach to surveying women's experiences of violence (Walby 2007). The UNECE survey module follows this model, measuring controlling behaviors, emotional abuse, fear, and their effects on everyday activities, in addition to physical and sexual violence. The WHO's study of Domestic Violence and Women's Health (2005) was another important model for the UNECE survey instrument. The core research team for the WHO study included experts in epidemiology, public health, and gender violence: Claudia Garcia-Moreno and Henriette Jansen from the WHO, Charlotte Watts from the London School of Hygiene and Tropical Medicine, and Mary Ellsberg and Lori Heise from PATH (Washington, DC). Henriette Jansen, who worked on the WHO study from 1999 to 2007, served as the consultant for the UNECE survey module. She relied on this model and her experience in using it in developing the UNECE survey instrument. In discussions at the 2009 UNECE expert group meeting, the WHO Multi-Country Study was often cited as a precursor to the project. The UNECE survey incorporated a public health perspective in its focus on psychological harm and family relationships and in its use of prevalence measures, meaning the number of women of a given age who had experienced violence of various kinds during the previous year and during their lifetimes (UN Economic Commission for Europe 2009).

Researchers working in the gender equality framework recognize the problem of underreporting violence and seek to develop measurement techniques to encourage disclosure of violent incidents. Without attention to this problem, surveys risk severely underestimating the number of victims — a worry for advocates for battered women. Underreporting is an ongoing challenge because victims are often reluctant to disclose incidents of violence in interviews or fail to seek help from official agencies that might count them. In the 2009 UNECE meeting, as in the 2008 report by Erturk, there was considerable discussion about how to encourage disclosure. The survey writers tried to find many ways of asking questions about violence in safe environments in order to increase disclosure. Experience with survey research showed that asking only once produces lower rates of disclosure than asking multiple times in different ways and about specific acts of violence. Women often fear anger and reprisals from family members for talking about violence within their family, so they feel that the subject of the survey should be concealed and the interview held in private.

Moreover, in many situations women see violence as normal or disciplinary rather than as unpermitted, so they may not mention it in an interview. The battered women's movement has encouraged women to redefine the violence they experience as abusive and criminal rather than as disciplinary, but without this shift, it may not be reported. When gendered violence is not named or recognized, it is hard to survey. Asking about specific acts is one way of dealing with this conundrum, but this misses cultural context and meaning. Violence against women is itself an interpretive category. Since the gender equality approach takes a contextual view of violence against women and sees the behavior in the context of relationships and wider attitudes of social tolerance, counting acts of violence alone provides inadequate information. The special rapporteur advocates measuring social tolerance as well as the prevalence of violence, and the UNECE survey module explores the relationships within which the violence occurs. There is no easy answer to this measurement challenge.

Strategies for Change. The strategy for change underlying the gender equality measurement approach is that increasing gender equality and empowering women will diminish violence. Advocates for this position support women's empowerment and social changes that diminish patriarchal values and social structures (Erturk 2008b: 27). Thus effective strategies must tackle prevailing forms of gender inequality and the cultural attitudes defining it. "Improvement" is defined as diminished violence. Of course, these changes can also produce higher rates of reporting to administrative agencies and more frequent disclosure in surveys as women come to see violence as a crime rather than as discipline. Simple outcome numbers are clearly inadequate.

The larger goal is to foster a society in which women are not subordinated on the basis of their gender. As Erturk said in her report to the Human Rights Council, her goal is to promote a major social transformation. Society needs to shift its attitudes of indifference toward gender violence and to rethink gender roles in order for these changes to take place (2008c). Erturk thinks that general attitudes, awareness of violence, and efforts toward prevention are keys to reform. Measuring the extent of the forms of violence against women is a strategy for promoting such a social transformation that should include measurements of social tolerance of violence, attitudes toward violence against women, and ideas of gender inequality. The Commission on the Status of Women and the CEDAW and its committee promote a similar perspective. Yet neither of these bodies nor the special rapporteur can engage in data collection. Despite the expertise and expansive aspirations promoted by this perspective, it lacks the resources and administrative capacity to carry forward global measurements. Consequently, key actors and organizations can only endeavor to persuade others to engage in data collection and analysis compatible with this perspective. The gender equality advocates worked hard to bring their perspective to the UNSC indicator project and, as the discussion of the final guidelines indicated, succeeded in expanding the UNSC's initial narrow view of violence against women. Their more expansive questionnaire and detailed ethical and safety recommendations were incorporated into the guidelines, facilitating greater disclosure of the scope of the problem.

HUMAN RIGHTS

Theoretical Framework. Efforts to measure violence against women from a human rights perspective are closely related to those focused on gender equality, but they begin from the premise that violence against women violates women's fundamental freedoms and human rights and that it is the responsibility of the state to protect these rights. This framework focuses on determining who is responsible for protecting and fulfilling these rights and increasing state accountability. It identifies duty bearers for the rights it articulates and seeks to hold these actors accountable for performing their duties. This framework emphasizes violations that occur in the public sphere rather than domestic violence. While the gender equality perspective views victims of violence as being embedded in unequal social structures, the human rights approach sees victims as individuals in relation to the state. It advocates dealing with apparently disparate issues, such as domestic and family violence and trafficking, through an integrated approach (Erturk 2008b: 15). States are responsible for exercising due diligence to prevent violations, even by nonstate actors. The human rights approach requires attention to how well national and international actors have fulfilled their obligations and the use of disaggregated data to expose patterns of discrimination (Erturk 2008b: 26). In her report on indicators of violence against women to the Human Rights Council, the special rapporteur recommended indicators of state action, as well as prevalence and social tolerance, measuring, for example, the ratification of relevant international and regional laws, the criminalization of perpetrators, awareness raising, prevention, support services, action plans, access to justice, reporting, and training (Erturk 2008c).

In general, the human rights system focuses on individual rights and the protection of the body, as well as discrimination and the plight of vulnerable populations such as women and children. Human rights work takes a broad and inclusive definition of violence against women in a variety of contexts that includes both state and nonstate actors' violence. The secretary general's 2006 report takes this position, as do the indicators of violence against women developed by the special rapporteur and those of the Office of the High Commissioner for Human Rights (OHCHR). The struggle to define violence against women as a human rights violation was a long and difficult one, as discussed earlier, but the secretary general's report was a major milestone.

The human rights approach incorporates many forms of violence against women and is not restricted to intimate-partner violence. It joins civil and political rights with social, economic, and cultural rights. Violations include a wide range of behaviors, encompassing female genital cutting, killings in the name of honor, rape during wartime, sexual violence against women in prisons and by police, and domestic violence. Moreover, violence against women is located in a variety of contexts. In its project to develop indicators for major human rights, discussed in chapter 7, the OHCHR developed an indicator for violence against women that offered a broad conceptual map of a range of forms of violence. In addition to domestic violence, it includes "sexual and reproductive health and harmful traditional practices," "violence at work," "forced labor and trafficking," "community violence and abuse by law enforcement officials," and "violence and (post-)conflict and emergency situations" (see table 4.2). These attributes are divided into specific indicators, such as "proportion of women/men who report feeling unsafe in public places or limiting their activities because of safety or harassment" as an outcome measure of community violence and "proportion of women who have experienced physical or sexual violence by current or former partner during the last year [life time]" as an outcome measure for domestic violence (UN Office of the High Commissioner for Human Rights 2012a: 99). These indicators include both public and private settings for violence against women. They take into account the political context in a way that the UNSC indicators do not.

Human rights indicators start from a set of standards, as indicators typically do, but in this case, they are the agreed-upon universal standards of the human rights system. Grounding measurement in such universal standards facilitates developing comparable units of measurement. It also suggests that it is important to measure whether human rights treaties have been ratified and relevant laws passed in assessing state action, in addition to looking at programs, implementation, and outcomes. Human rights indicators are grounded in human rights commitments and cross-cutting principles: nondiscrimination, progress, participation, and remedies. There is a particular concern with violence experienced by vulnerable populations such as women, children, migrants, refugees, and trafficked persons. Consequently, human rights indicators stress disaggregating data by gender, race, disability, and other protected categories.

The special rapporteur on violence against women's major report on indicators of violence against women, prepared in 2008, combined the human rights framework with a gender equality one (Erturk 2008b: 90). This report was prepared by the Child and Woman Abuse Studies Unit of London Metropolitan University, a center for the study of all forms of violence against women and

TABLE 4.2. *Illustrative indicators on violence against women (Universal Declaration of Human Rights, arts. 1–5 and 16)*

	Sexual and reproductive health and harmful traditional practices	Domestic violence	Violence at work, forced labour and trafficking	Community violence and abuse by law enforcement officials	Violence and (post-)conflict and emergency situations
Structural	• International human rights treaties relevant to the elimination of discrimination against women, including all forms of violence against women, ratified by the State without reservations				
	• Date of entry into force and coverage of the principle of non-discrimination between men and women and prohibition of all forms of violence against women in the constitution or other forms of superior law				
	• Date of entry into force and coverage of domestic law(s) criminalizing violence against women, including rape, domestic violence, trafficking, traditional harmful practices, stalking and sexual abuse of children				
	• Date of entry into force and coverage of legal act instituting an independent oversight body with specific mandate to protect women against violence (e.g., accredited NHRI)				
	• Time frame and coverage of policy or action plan for the elimination of discrimination and all forms of violence against women and including data collection and dissemination programme				
	• Number of registered or active NGOs and full-time equivalent employment (per 100,000 persons) involved in the protection of women against violence				
	• Time frame and coverage of policy to eliminate harmful traditional practices, including female genital mutilation, early or forced marriage, honour killing or maiming and foetal sex determination • Legally stipulated minimum age for marriage	• Date of entry into force and coverage of legislation criminalizing marital rape and incest • Date of entry into force and coverage of legislation protecting gender equality and women's ability to leave abusive relationships (e.g, equal inheritance, asset ownership, divorce)	• Time frame and coverage of policy or programme against sexual harassment in the workplace • Time frame and coverage of policy to combat trafficking, sexual exploitation and forced labour and provide protection and access to remedy for victims	• Date of entry into force and coverage of legislation defining rape in relation to a lack of consent rather than use of force • Time frame and coverage of policy to combat community violence and abuse by police forces	• Time frame and coverage of policy or programme to prevent or address sexual violence in conflict, post-conflict or emergency situations • Time frame and coverage of special measures for participation of women in peace processes

Process					
• Proportion of received complaints on all forms of violence against women investigated and adjudicated by the national human rights institution, human rights ombudsperson or other mechanisms and the proportion of these responded to effectively by the Government					
• Proportion of public social sector expenditure on national awareness-raising campaign on all forms of violence against women (including harmful traditional practices) and on national prevention programme integrated into school curriculum					
• Number of perpetrators of violence against women (including harmful traditional practices, domestic violence, trafficking, sexual exploitation and forced labour) arrested, adjudicated, convicted and serving sentences (by type of sentence)					
• Proportion of women of reproductive age using or whose partner is using contraception and effective preventive measures against sexually transmitted diseases (e.g., HIV/AIDS)* • Unmet need for family planning* • Number of safe and unsafe abortions per 1,000 women of reproductive age • Proportion of women whose age at marriage is below 18 years** • Proportion of managerial and other leader positions (e.g., religious leader) occupied by women	• Proportion of women reporting forms of domestic violence to law enforcement officials or initiating legal action • Number of available places in shelters and refuges per 1,000 population (urban and rural) • Number of adopted restraining orders • Proportion of men and women who think that abuse or violence against women is acceptable or tolerable	• Proportion of and frequency of business organizations inspected for conformity with labour standards • Proportion of migrants working in the sex industry • Proportion of informal sector workers (e.g., domestic workers) shifted to formal sector employment	• Proportion of new recruits to police, social work, psychology, health (doctors, nurses and others), education (teachers) completing a core curriculum on all forms of violence against women • Proportion of victims of rape who had access to emergency contraception or safe abortion, prophylaxis for sexually transmitted infections/HIV • Proportion of sexual crimes (e.g., rape) reported to the police (population survey) • Proportion of formal investigations of law enforcement officials for cases of violence against women resulting in disciplinary action or prosecution	• Proportion of health staff trained in medical management and support for victims of sexual and other violence • Proportion of victims of sexual and other violence accessing appropriate medical, psychosocial and legal services • Proportion of reported cases of sexual or other violence where victims (or related third parties) initiated legal action • Proportion of expenditure on relief and emergency assistance devoted to women and child welfare

continued

TABLE 4.2. *Continued*

	Sexual and reproductive health and harmful traditional practices	Domestic violence	Violence at work, forced labour and trafficking	Community violence and abuse by law enforcement officials	Violence and (post-)conflict and emergency situations
Outcome	• Proportion of women subjected to female genital mutilation** • Sex ratio at birth and age 5–9 years • Maternal mortality ratio* and proportion of deaths due to unsafe abortions	• Proportion of women who have experienced physical and/or sexual violence by current or former partner in the past 12 months / during lifetime** • Proportion of women subjected to psychological and/or economic violence by their intimate partner**	• Reported cases of women/men victims of trafficking (within and across countries), sexual exploitation or forced labour • Proportion of working women who have been victims of sexual abuse / harassment in the workplace	• Proportion of women / men who report feeling unsafe in public places or limiting their activities because of safety or harassment • Proportion of women who have experienced physical violence or rape / sexual assault during the past year [lifetime]**	• Reported cases of death, rape (attempted or completed) and other incidents of violence against women that occurred in conflict, post-conflict or emergency situations

• Femicide rates (e.g., murder by intimate partner, sexual murder, killing of prostitutes, honour killing, female infanticide, dowry deaths)

• Proportion of women who have experienced physical, sexual and psychological violence during the past year [lifetime], by severity of violence, relationship to the perpetrator and frequency**

• Proportion of victim-survivors of physical, sexual or mental violence, included trafficking and forced labour, who received assistance, compensation and rehabilitation services

• Suicide rates by sex

Source: UN Office of the High Commissioner for Human Rights 2012a: 99. http://www.ohchr.org/Documents/Publications/Human_rights_indicators_en.pdf.

All indicators should be disaggregated by prohibited grounds of discrimination, as applicable and reflected in metadata sheets.

* MDG-related indicators; ** UNECE indicator

child abuse from a feminist perspective. Among its distinctive features were incorporating many forms of violence against women in addition to intimate-partner violence, connecting measurements to human rights principles and international law, and acting as a steering instrument in global efforts to end violence against women. The consultants for this report recognized that countries start at very different places in terms of resources and experience (2008b: 11). The study began by surveying states about their plans of action, the forms of violence against women each covers, and the mechanisms, indicators, and the surveys of violence they have worked on in the last decade, among other issues. Of the sixty-three countries who responded, over half (57 percent) came from Europe (twenty-three) and the Americas (thirteen; Erturk 2008b: 12–14). The report used the structure-process-outcome template developed by the OHCHR to organize its indicators. According to the report, indicators must address ratification of CEDAW and other human rights instruments, constitutional guarantees of gender equality, plans of action on violence that are implemented, a legal framework that is nondiscriminatory and effective, awareness of officials, resources for support and advocacy services, awareness-raising and prevention programs, and collection and publication of data, including evaluations of new policies. However, the report recognizes that it may be impractical to address all these issues and that they will need some adaptation to become indicators (Erturk 2008b: 90–91).

In general, the more inclusive the definition of violence against women and the broader the array of legal and programmatic state responses that are assessed, the more difficult it is to convert this information into simple, measurable indicators. There is a trade-off between producing simple, workable indicators and incorporating context, political and social structure, and varieties of violence. The use of indicators presses toward simpler, noncontextual definitions that are less integrated with other social processes such as discrimination, inequality, and lack of legal intervention or social services. The proposed indicators in the special rapporteur's report are comprehensive. They specify five levels of compliance depending on state resources. They also emphasize measuring social tolerance, recognizing its importance in promoting the kinds of social transformation that the special rapporteur considers necessary to eliminate violence against women (Erturk 2008b: 138). Thus the models for this report are both national studies and the OHCHR indicator project, but together, they produce a complicated set of indicators.

Institutional Support. The institutional supports for the human rights approach are international, national, and regional human rights institutions, including the Human Rights Council and its special rapporteur and the

OHCHR, which developed the human rights indicators on violence against women. A representative of the OHCHR indicator project attended the 2007 and 2009 expert group meetings. The secretary general's report also takes a strong human rights position and has fostered new initiatives, such as the UNITE campaign. The CEDAW and its monitoring committee have also supported the human rights approach to violence against women.

Models and Expertise. The disciplinary basis of the human rights approach is human rights law. The experts designing and leading this approach are predominantly human rights lawyers, assisted to some extent by social scientists who study domestic violence. Consistent with legal expertise, there is an emphasis on state actions and laws and monitoring state effort and accountability. This approach views indicators within the context of judicial processes of assessment and evaluation of state performance, such as treaty body deliberations about compliance with human rights obligations (see Merry 2015).

Strategies for Social Change. The embedded theory of social change is that if states adopt effective laws, policies, and programs, violence against women will diminish. Improvement is primarily the result of improving state programs and generating good practices. The human rights approach to indicators offers a comprehensive, holistic picture of violence against women that links respect for individual autonomy to structural factors that limit autonomy and agency. However, one consequence of this inclusive, holistic framework is that it is not amenable to simple numerical measurement, and many of the variables it wishes to measure lack empirical data. Moreover, the human rights system lacks the resources and expertise to engage in its own data collection. In 2011, when I interviewed Yakin Erturk about the proposed indicators, she said that the Human Rights Council had listened to her report and passed her suggestions on to the UNSC. As far as she knew, it had done nothing further about them. The UNSD leader of the indicators project said that defining violence against women is difficult because human rights advocates want it defined very broadly, while countries want something narrower. Broad conceptions require more expensive data collection, which is one reason why countries may choose not to adopt them. Here the costs of data collection and analysis drive theory.

CRIMINAL JUSTICE

Theoretical Framework. Measuring gender-based violence through crime victimization surveys has a long history. In the United States in the late 1960s, victimization studies for all crimes became an important complement to police-incident data, which were increasingly recognized as missing substantial amounts of information. In the 1980s, victimization studies became generally popular in society as a way of assessing crimes and providing victims' perspectives on them. In 1989, the International Crime Victimization Survey began to collect data every few years on eleven forms of crime in over sixty countries. However, this general victimization survey did not adequately measure crimes of violence against women. National surveys were redesigned to collect information on women's experiences of sexual and domestic violence by the early 1990s. A 1992 survey redesign in the United States resulted in significant increases in data on the prevalence of sexual and domestic violence (Johnson, Ollus, and Nevala 2008: 12). The British Crime Survey was remodeled in 1996 to incorporate domestic violence. Statistics Canada was the first national statistical agency to overhaul its approach by adding a dedicated survey of women's experiences of violent victimization. It used the basic crime victimization survey as a starting point (Johnson, Ollus, and Nevala 2008: 11–13). However, criminal justice surveys confront questions about what violence against women includes, since it is not "self-defined" as a criminal act. Some commonly referenced forms of violence against women, such as sexual harassment, sex trafficking, and marital rape, are not crimes everywhere. Some forms of violence are condoned or perpetrated by states, such as forced sterilization or the violence of police or prison guards. Thus deciding what counts as violence against women is difficult. The criminal justice approach favors focusing on those behaviors defined as crimes and allowing state institutions to draw their own definitions, but in this case, recourse to the legal definition of each country is inadequate.

Institutional Support. One of the important institutional supports for this approach is the UN Office of Drugs and Crime (UNODC). This office views violence against women as a crime but recognizes that unlike most crimes, it lacks a clear definition in the law. The genealogy of the contemporary international criminal justice approach includes a series of UN conferences and resolutions since the mid-1980s that have addressed violence against women. For example, UN Congresses on Crime Prevention and the Treatment of Offenders in 1985, 1990, and 1995 adopted resolutions on violence against women. In 1997, the UN Commission on Crime Prevention and Criminal Justice approved a resolution on the elimination of violence against women. The General Assembly approved a resolution on crime prevention and criminal justice measures to eliminate violence against women in 1997, and the 1998 Rome Statute of the International Criminal Court codified rape, sexual slavery, forced prostitution, forced pregnancy, forced sterilization, and any other form of sexual violence during armed conflict as crimes against humanity and war crimes (Johnson,

Ollus, and Nevala 2008: 7). By the end of the 1990s, the problem was moving into the mainstream of criminal justice concerns.

98

Models and Practices. At the 2007 expert group meeting that came out of the secretary general's report, a proposal from the UNODC advocated strengthening the links between indicators for violence against women and work in crime-trend assessment and monitoring (Malby and Alvazzi del Frate 2007: 1). It suggested two linkages: one with conventional crime indicators, such as the periodic UN Survey of Crime Trends and Operations of Criminal Justice Systems (CTS), and the other with crime victimization surveys. The first one is based on administrative data on recognized crime. The UN Surveys on Crime Trends and the Operation of Criminal Justice were authorized in 1984 and have been carried out regularly since then. The twelfth wave of these surveys is now taking place. For these surveys, the UNODC sends questionnaires to member states to gather their information. The other linkage between violence against women and crime studies are victimization surveys, such as the International Crime Victim Survey (ICVS). This survey measures both prevalence (proportion who have suffered a crime during a particular period) and incidence (number of criminal acts experienced by victims during the same time period; Malby and Alvazzi del Frate 2007: 2). It is often funded by international agencies or aid funds when countries lack the resources for their own surveys.

The UNODC proposal to the 2007 meeting notes that since not all forms of gender-based violence included in the secretary general's report are crimes, neither of these approaches alone is adequate. Specialized surveys such as the WHO Multi-Country Study and the IVAWS are useful. But it argues that there is also a place for general victim surveys and administrative statistics. Using definitions of forms of violence consistent with those of the CTS allows for greater comparability with existing crime data. For example, physical assault should be distinguished from indecent and/or sexual assault, and the definition of physical assault should make clear which actions, such as slapping, are included (Malby and Alvazzi del Frate 2007: 6). It is also important to separate the nature of the action from its effect. The proposal suggests using the following categories based on a review of the CTS, CVS, and existing specialized surveys on violence against women:

- homicide
- rape
- major assault
- assault
- sexual assault

- harassment
- female genital mutilation/cutting
- trafficking in persons

While these categories might have subcategories, such as honor killings as a percentage of homicides, they could be effective as global indicators as a compromise between detail and ease of measurement and presentation (Malby and Alvazzi del Frate 2007: 6). The UNODC proposal also suggested adding questions about the frequency of violence to the prevalence measures, using a one-year time frame to be compatible with most recorded crime statistics. Thus the criminal justice approach uses existing categories of criminal behavior and approaches to measuring crime to organize the diffuse field of forms of violence against women.

Criminal justice approaches are particularly concerned with measuring the criminal justice system's response. It is important to ask the victim if she reported the violence to the police in order to assess the size of the "dark figure": the number of unreported crimes. The UNODC proposal sought to identify gaps or flaws in the criminal justice system, so it chose indicators that reflected criminal justice system responses and crime trend assessment and monitoring. Questions assessed the adequacy of police responses and whether the problem was resolved by the police. The latter question is also in the CTS. The basic argument of this UNODC proposal was that indicators of violence against women should be designed to follow, as much as possible, the model of crime trends surveys and crime victimization surveys in order to develop comparable data for international comparisons. For example, one of the indicators would be the number of women, per one hundred thousand, experiencing at least one of the eight offenses listed above during the previous year. This proposal would also use administrative data for homicides of women (Malby and Alvazzi del Frate 2007: 10).

Expertise. This approach is clearly framed by criminal justice work on measuring crime. It does not focus on gender equality or on women's human rights. It employs categories that parallel existing criminal justice categories in police reports and victimization surveys. It measures severity by the act, not its impact on the victim, although the authors of the survey recognize that impact is an important factor. Both the UNODC proposal and the IVAWS, discussed above, ask about victims' recourse to the criminal justice system and its adequacy. This approach clearly has a different orientation, considers different kinds of information valuable, and assumes a different idea of improvement for the problem than the others do.

Strategies for Change. The underlying social change theory of the criminal justice indicators is that a stronger criminal justice intervention is necessary to control violence against women. Measurements include assessments of the use of the criminal justice system by victims and the adequacy of its response — issues largely ignored in the other approaches. The criminal justice approach seeks to harmonize categories of counting violence against women with other crime data rather than with forms of human rights violations or gender discrimination. It is much less concerned with measuring gender inequality or non-criminal actions such as abusive or controlling behavior within relationships.

COMPARING GENDER EQUALITY, HUMAN RIGHTS, AND CRIMINAL JUSTICE APPROACHES

The number of violations produced by a criminal-justice-focused survey is likely to be smaller than those produced by a gender equality or human rights survey. A crime survey uses a narrower definition of the phenomenon, particularly when it focuses on criminal events such as rape and assault. The scope is especially limited when it documents only those forms of victimization defined as crimes in national legal frameworks. Criminal justice surveys may be limited to the last twelve to eighteen months and therefore may undercount events further in the past. Like crime victimization statistics, they are interested in counting the number of incidents in a short time period rather than the entire experience of a person's life. Crime victimization studies take this approach because of recognized inaccuracies in the recall of remote events. In contrast, surveys in the areas of gender equality and health tend to use a lifetime measure. Moreover, gender equality approaches make multiple efforts to ask about violent encounters in order to encourage disclosure. Nondisclosure is considered a serious problem to be tackled. While the criminal justice approach recognizes the inadequacy of police or court statistics, given the tendency of victims to underreport, it appears to make less effort to overcome nondisclosure. The human rights approach could potentially generate the largest number of victimizations, since its definition of violence against women is the broadest, including behaviors such as fear of walking at night and being trafficked, but it includes many forms of violence against women for which there is limited or no information available.

The trajectory of the criminal justice approach is as long as the others but draws on different institutions and forms of expertise. It builds on a long tradition of measuring crimes, including violence against women, through police statistics and crime victimization surveys. The genealogy includes a series of conferences, some organized by the UNODC, that focus on measuring and monitoring crime, a set of resolutions about crime and gender violence, and important developments such as the naming of sexual violence during wartime as a crime against humanity in the Rome Statute that created the International Criminal Court. Those who work in this field typically have a background in criminology and statistics. For example, one of the authors of the IVAWS was Holly Johnson, a criminologist and statistician.

There are overlaps between this and other approaches, of course. The IVAWS, for example, shared with the gender equality approach concerns with gender inequality and violence and sought to assess a range of negative impacts of violence. Its measures incorporated information on the experiences and fear of victims and their perceptions of acts' seriousness — more of a gender equality approach. On the other hand, a significant part of the study examined recourse to the police and perceptions of the adequacy of the criminal justice system's response. It was concerned with how the criminal justice system was understood and used by victims and whether they found it effective. It examined, in particular, the effects of problems such as the attrition of cases by criminal justice systems that drop cases rather than prosecuting them. It also asked if respondents viewed the incidents as crimes. One example of the overlap between approaches is the fact that Holly Johnson, the lead author of the IVAWS, attended the 2009 UNECE expert group meeting, although she was unable to attend the 2010 meeting, and she wrote the guidelines for the UNSC indicators.

However, there are also significant differences between these approaches. The gender equality approach imagines the solution to violence against women as creating gender equality and ending gender discrimination, while the human rights approach advocates a broad range of state interventions through the passage of relevant laws, policies, and programs; awareness raising; and ongoing monitoring of state accomplishments. The criminal justice field advocates a more effective criminal justice response along with a better and more responsive array of services.

NATIONAL STATISTICAL CAPACITY

Theoretical Framework. The national statistical approach encourages national statistical offices to develop routine approaches to measuring violence against women. It offers training and support to national statistical offices and develops guidelines for these offices to use in carrying out surveys. The major concern of this approach is persuading states to carry out surveys on violence against women regularly, to develop administrative statistics, and to foster as much comparability among nations in their measurement strategies as possible. The goal is to establish consistent measurement systems that will enable countries to assess their policies and their accomplishments. In order to support and facilitate work done by national statistical offices and to foster comparability among national statistical surveys and administrative data collection, the UNSD creates consistent and coherent guidelines for data collection.

Its strategy is to develop a common definition across countries and get national buy-in so that national offices will carry out the data collection. For example, the representative of the UNSD told the Friends of the Chair group at its 2009 meeting that the main objective of the meeting was "to institute a universal methodology on statistics of violence against women. The meeting would therefore produce a proposal for a set of *Guidelines for Producing Statistics on Violence against Women* in terms of classifications, topics, data, outputs and other pertinent issues" (2009: 4). The Friends of the Chair committee and the UNSD are primarily interested in providing technical assistance to national statistical bureaus. At the 2009 UNECE meeting, the UNSD representative emphasized that in developing these guidelines, he balances what is possible against costs and then makes recommendations to national statistical offices. After the UNSC's proposed guidelines were drafted, they were circulated among the members of the Friends of the Chair committee, most of whom came from national statistical offices, to be sure they were workable.

Expertise. In my several interviews with this key UNSD staff person, he told me it was very important to get national support for the survey and to establish a system that countries could replicate over time. Repeated surveys are essential for assessing improvement. It is also important to have a large enough sample size, and one that covers the whole country, to follow patterns, which usually requires a national effort. His core concerns were not feminism or gender-based violence but good statistical practice and clear and unambiguous guidelines. His goal is to strengthen statistical capacity in national statistical offices. For the indicators of violence against women, he wanted to develop an effective set of guidelines so that countries could carry out the survey. He has a background in victimization surveys and works extensively on housing and demographic surveys.

When I asked him in February 2011 about how he proposed to handle the challenges of defining severe physical violence, he replied that he was a statistician, not a sociologist or anthropologist, and would leave that up to them. In 2013, as the guidelines were being finalized, he said that there was too much variation and that it was not possible to settle on a conception of severe physical violence; instead, it would now be an option, and countries would have to decide for themselves. When I asked again about comparison, he said it was possible to develop comparable data on physical acts, but countries had to decide for themselves on definitions of severity. From a statistical point of view, he had given up on defining a universal category of severe physical violence. By 2013, he had moved to a different division of the UNSD and was finishing up the project while a new staff person took over his position.

When one of the experts at the 2009 UNECE meeting asked him if the UNSD would like more input from individual experts in this process, he replied that the UN was an intergovernmental body and did not generally rely on experts. This statement clearly differentiates the way the UNSC uses expertise from the way other initiatives use it. It values statistical expertise and tends to put greater emphasis on the input of governments, particularly national statistical offices, than on academic expertise. In contrast to nongovernmental measurement projects that can move forward despite government resistance, UNSC work is constrained by government preferences and concerns. For example, in order to develop indicators for violence against women, it was necessary for the UNSC member governments to approve them.

Institutional Support. The national statistical capacity approach is supported by the UNSC and the UNSD, which worked on the indicators in conjunction with the CSW and the special rapporteur at the General Assembly's request. Previously, these groups had collaborated on developing indicators to measure progress on implementation of the Beijing Platform for Action. However, there was a clear division of labor between the statisticians and the gender policy group. At a joint session with the UNSC and the CSW in 2007, the CSW was asked to identify priority areas for which the UN Statistical Commission would provide technical expertise in identifying appropriate data and sources (UN Commission on the Status of Women 2008b: 6, para. 19). One result was the 2007 meeting organized by the UNDAW, the secretariat for UN Women to support the work of the CSW and the UNSC in developing indicators on violence against women (UN Commission on the Status of Women 2008b: 7, para. 21). Subsequently, the UNSC held joint meetings with the CSW in 2008, 2009, and 2011, of which I attended the latter two. At the 2011 CSW meeting in New York City, the Friends of the Chair committee's chair from Mexico presented a progress report that included pilot surveys in four countries and mentioned his aspiration to develop a universal indicator for violence against women. He also claimed that the UNECE indicators were part of his project rather than a rival effort. There was no discussion of the substance of the indicators or their methodology, nor were any details of the questionnaire or its contents made available to the audience of national representatives of women's ministries and NGOs. The purpose of this and the previous joint meetings I attended was to inform both groups about the initiative, not to gather advice or input.

Models and Practices. The UNSC has expanded from its initial work on economic and social behavior to new issues, such as women, the environment, and civil society (Ward 2004: 15–17, 21, 53), but it still focuses on technical assistance, developing guidelines, promoting international comparability, and developing national statistical systems. It is primarily concerned with methods of data collection and analysis rather than developing new ideas, which tend to come from outside (Ward 2004: 46, 30). The UNSD provides technical assistance and training for national statistical bureaus, some of which are very small. Some even close down between censuses and may have to start from scratch each time (see Jerven 2013). Technical assistance includes being sure costs of data collection are not too high. Thus the Friends of the Chair recommended developing administrative statistics, which are less costly than specialized surveys, in case surveys proved to be too expensive. The bulk of the important 2009 report to the UNSC by the Friends of the Chair discussed the technical issues of doing surveys on this topic, such as defining terms and collecting relevant data (UN Statistical Commission 2009).

Expertise. The national statistical approach emphasizes using techniques of statistical data collection and analysis with integrity and professionalism, which means without politics (Ward 2004: 12). The 2014 UNSC meeting approved, to much fanfare and drinking of champagne, a twenty-year revision of the 1994 Fundamental Principles of Statistics (UN Statistical Commission 2012b; UN Statistics Division 2014). As discussed in chapter 2, these principles were first drafted in the early 1990s in response to the distrust of statistics that developed in Eastern Europe and the former Soviet states. In a press release marking the first World Statistics Day in 2010, the director of the UNSD celebrated the achievements of official statistics and their core values of "Service, Integrity, and Professionalism." He noted that statisticians have "worked hard over many decades to define and implement global statistical standards which have resulted in high quality, comparable statistics." The adoption of the shared professional values enshrined in the Fundamental Principles of Official Statistics "has further crystallized [the UNSD's] professional responsibility; this is a major achievement of the global statistical community" (UN Statistical Commission 2011b). In February 2011, the UNSC devoted two hours of its short, four-day meeting time to discussing these principles (UN Statistical Commission 2011a). These principles include data "being made available on an impartial basis by official statistical agencies" (principle 1) and deciding according to strictly professional, scientific, and ethical considerations on the methods of collecting, processing, storing, and presenting statistical data (principle 2). Thus these principles emphasize the independence of statistics from politics and the professional responsibility of statisticians to provide valid and reliable information, regardless of the wishes of politician. Politics are a threat.

For example, in the long discussion at the 2011 UNSC meeting about the alleged flaws in the 2010 report of the UNDP's Human Development Office and its HDI, the countries that complained typically referred to violations of the fundamental principles of statistics as they charged the UNDP with failing to use official national statistics and to resolve discrepancies between international and national data (UN Statistical Commission 2011c; 2011d). Clearly, there is a professional culture of statisticians that sees political pressure as a threat to trust in official statistics. It seems that statisticians themselves played an important role in constructing statistics as a sphere of technical knowledge separate from politics. Asserting professional standards such as integrity and insisting that statistics are separate from policy both contribute to establishing the autonomy of statistics from politics.

Strategies for Change. The national statistical approach to measuring violence against women defines it relatively narrowly as physical or sexual violence against a woman by another person — either an intimate partner or someone else. Thus all the indicators except female genital cutting are described only by their frequency, the characteristics of the violent acts, and the nature of the relationship between the perpetrator and the victim. The goal of the national statistical approach is to produce internationally comparable data that states will collect regularly to enable the monitoring of improvements over time. It focuses on more tangible, measurable phenomena.

The experts are statisticians, who often have experience in victimization or demographic surveys at the national as well as international level. They are particularly concerned with developing reliable statistics through providing manuals, guidelines, and training sessions. When new manuals and guidelines are produced, the UNSD will send experts to countries that request help and organize a five-day training session at the national or regional level, including role plays and instructions on data analysis. These efforts will facilitate producing comparable data. They are concerned about statistical rigor and clarity. For example, some statisticians were concerned about the categories developed for the indicators of violence against women in the Friends of the Chair process, since they were not mutually exclusive. All questions about physical and sexual violence overlapped with questions about physical and sexual violence in intimate-partner relationships. It would make more sense to ask about each form of violence and the relationship within which it occurred, but as one statistician said, the activists insisted on separating the two sets of questions. While the majority who come to the UNSC meetings are men, many women participate as well.

Institutional Support. This approach to measurement is far more influenced by government concerns and interests than the other three. The very narrow definition of violence against women the UNSC developed is the product of national concerns about measuring "sensitive" and "cultural" issues. Many of those who attend UNSC meetings and participate in the Friends of the Chair are statistical experts who work for their governments. New initiatives build on official statistical strategies rather than the work of academic researchers, international organizations, or nongovernmental organizations. They rely on past models of research and surveys, particularly by national governments, as well as the work of statistical experts. In contrast to the other initiatives, these indicators are shaped by open international debate. But this also serves to reduce them to the least common denominator on which most can agree.

Thus this is an initiative that relies largely on governments. The secretariat sees its role as supporting government efforts, as providing technical assistance for whatever standards on which governments decide. Governments tend to resist creating indicators that show them performing poorly. Because of its connection to governments, the UNSC has access to resources to carry out surveys but can do so only as long as governments are interested in doing so. In interviews with staff from the UNSD, I was told that there is ample funding to support this initiative and that governments are eager to find ways of measuring violence against women, since there is a great deal of international pressure to do so.

The underlying theory of this approach is that measuring the problem will facilitate monitoring the effectiveness of various policies and programs. It supports the general UN focus on generating statistics to monitor government progress in implementing measures to diminish violence against women. The goal of the surveys is to examine the same place over time rather than to compare countries against each other. Its purpose is to provide quantitative information about progress within a country. Rather than enhancing gender equality or human rights, the goal of this initiative is to foster responsible and accountable government that has reliable information on which to base reform policies. These measurement projects promise to provide widespread, regular, and population-based information about violence against women.

However, what the UNSC is measuring is far narrower than what is proposed by the gender equality and human rights approaches. It does not deal with state violence, the need for broader social transformation in gender inequality patterns, state responsibility for mitigating the problem, or even the adequacy of the criminal justice system. Forms of structural violence that facilitate gender violence are off the table. There is no reference to war, refugees, patriarchy, or the political or economic exclusion of women. Thus the UNSC, the organization that has the best resources and capacity to measure violence against women, also takes the narrowest and least transformative approach to measurement.

Conclusions

Clearly, this massive effort to quantify violence against women has brought greater visibility to a problem that has long remained hidden and unspoken. Counting is important to raise awareness and to discourage the idea that violence is only a problem for the unruly few. These efforts at quantification clearly help bring the issue of violence against women to visibility, whatever their interpretive frameworks. But this comparison shows that even the apparently simple question of what to count is a fundamental dimension of the power of quantification to shape public knowledge. Discussions about creating indicators often focused on the clarity of the concept and the measurability of the behavior, but there were also important political considerations about what was included and what was left out. Although the four approaches claim to be measuring the same thing, they are clearly using different categories and counting different things. In practice, they are not measuring the same thing, even though they are calling it by the same name.

One way of understanding these differences is by analyzing the genealogy of a system of measurement. The four frameworks described here have distinct historical trajectories, institutional supporters, experts and expertise, and templates for counting and analysis. Each values different issues, chooses to ask somewhat different questions, and is motivated by different theories about how to diminish violence against women. Each has developed over a period of years, building on past measurements and theories.

Consequently, each will find something different. The first two, which take a broader definition of violence against women, are likely to produce higher numbers of victims than the criminal justice or national statistical approaches. These two approaches include a wider range of situations and activities. The gender equality approach includes public attitudes toward violence against women. The human rights framework examines a wider range of contexts and adds a focus on state violence. Forms of counting that use the criminal justice framework focus primarily on domestic violence and rape. They do not count the wider array of forms of violence understood within their social contexts that are incorporated in the human rights model and the gender equality framework, such as police violence, sexual harassment in the workplace, sex trafficking, sexual slavery during armed conflict, or fear of walking at night, to list a few. Female genital cutting, honor killings, religious prostitution, early marriage, and an array of other practices of violence not defined as criminal in a particular society will not be counted. Social tolerance for violence against women, including within the family, is not part of this system of enumeration.

Moreover, some of these approaches focus on the act of violence rather than the experience of the victim. Consequently, victims are less able to define the problem in their own terms. Fear, changes in the victim's way of life, and perhaps other emotional, psychological, and financial dimensions of violence are less likely to be counted. Finally, a narrower definition of violence against women contributes to the fragmentation of the issue, which separates violence in the family from trafficking, for example, or the sexual violence of war from the sexual violence of the home. Thus the choice of paradigm for measuring violence against women has major implications for how the phenomenon is ultimately counted and understood.

Which of these approaches will come to dominate the field of international violence against women? This is hard to predict, of course, but it is telling that these approaches vary significantly in their institutional and financial support. Neither the gender equality approach nor the human rights approach has the resources for major global surveys. Moreover, their broad categories and complex measures are not readily amenable to quantification. The health sector might have the resources if the problem were defined as a public health issue as it was in the WHO study, but otherwise, the gender equality and human rights constituencies lack the funding for major survey research. Both the criminal justice and national statistical approaches have more resources, so their approaches are more likely to prevail. Criminal victimization surveys often have international support in developing countries and are domestically financed in wealthier countries. Thus it seems likely that the institutional support and trajectory of development is such that the criminal justice and national statistical approaches will come to predominate in measurement efforts, while the gender equality and human rights approaches will not. The result is a smaller number of victims counted and a narrower definition of the phenomenon — either as domestic violence and rape or as physical and sexual violence within intimate and stranger relationships. The narrower definition of violence against women, which does not include structural violence, state violence, or social attitudes that tolerate or even support violence, will become the basis for survey data. This concept does not focus on state responsibility or the impact of social attitudes toward violence such as indifference or support for some forms of violence defined as discipline.

This prediction reveals how important the supporters of any approach are in creating a dominant public understanding. The process of creating and then accepting an indicator as a relatively reliable form of knowledge takes years. Tracing back the process by which it was originally formed and who was able to influence its shape and measures is therefore a critical way of understanding what is included and what is neglected in the final formulation. It also reveals the cultural, class, and national frameworks that determine what is measured and how it is interpreted. This trajectory determines how an issue is defined and how information is gathered. The indicator promoted by the organization with the greatest resources will probably determine the public understanding of an issue. In the case of violence against women, whether the problem is seen as one of male-female relationships or as a problem of state indifference and social and political tolerance of violence against women depends on whether the data collection and analysis is done by national statistical offices, criminal justice agencies, human rights commissions, or feminist NGOs. Who creates and authors the data also determines whether the problem appears to be widespread and severe, which in turn shapes policy decisions. Inequalities in these institutional, political, and theoretical domains have enormous consequences for the way in which violence against women is understood and made known.

Those engaging in measuring a phenomenon like violence against women are aware of these struggles over the shape and content of measurement systems. In this case, the gender equality and human rights activists were eager to shape the UNSC indicators to be more compatible with their perspective. An influential member of UNECLAC told me she was very pleased that the UNSD was working on an indicator on violence against women, since that meant that gathering statistical information on violence against women was more likely to happen. She said that the indicator was less attuned to issues of gender equality than she would like, but this was a pragmatic compromise. The special rapporteur on violence against women told me that she hoped her broad perspective on violence against women as a structural problem of patriarchy would counter the fragmentation of the issue she had seen, with the focus on a lot of specific issues, such as sexual violence during wartime, domestic violence, and honor killing. Seeing them as a series of problems does not acknowledge how they are all connected and run through society as a whole. She is concerned that people do not see the issue in context or make connections between its various forms.

However, she could only recommend this perspective to the Human Rights Council, not develop and deploy her own measurement system.

In the end, the more feminist perspective did have an influence on the UNSC indicators. Even though a contact at the UNSD told me that there would be many examples of questionnaires in the final report, when it was published, the UNECE survey module was the only model questionnaire included. The guidelines referred to it frequently as an example of how to do surveys of violence against women (UN Statistics Division 2013: 196–221). The guidelines included a range of experiential measures of violence against women and controlling behavior, along with a list of physical injuries. The final guidelines include measures of attitudes toward domestic violence and requests for help from the police or others (UN Statistical Commission 2013: 224–28). These guidelines were substantially edited just before publication by Henriette Jansen, the consultant who wrote the UNECE model questionnaire, which may have made it possible for her to incorporate some of her perspectives into the guidelines. A change of leadership for the project in the UNSD probably contributed to this turn toward a more feminist, human rights framework. Through the 2009 UNECE expert group meetings and the work of Johnson and Jansen, among many others, the gender equality focus influenced the UNSC indicators. This example underscores the importance of a genealogical analysis that follows the people, the ideas, and the money as the project to develop indicators moves forward.

To claim that indicators reveal objective truth is to ignore these complex social processes through which they are constructed, the trajectories of their development over time, and the competing ideologies about what causes violence against women. Clearly, there are major differences in how violence against women is defined and how it can be diminished that channel the very conceptualization of the problem and the way it is categorized, counted, analyzed, and represented. Since each approach is based on past experience, which is unequally distributed among rich nations and poor nations, there is a bias toward establishing the norms and measurements based on the experiences of wealthy countries.

Finally, the paradigm that is created internationally differs from the way violence against women is understood in the vernacular. International categories and conceptions are often quite different from the way violence is experienced in the everyday lives of ordinary women. Vernacularization refers to a process by which global ideas, such as those of human rights or a right to live free of violence, enter into local situations and are refashioned in local contexts (Levitt and Merry 2009; Merry 2006b). In the process of vernacularization, global ideas such as women's right not to be hit may be reinterpreted, redefined, and relocated in a different context. In Levitt and my work with women's NGOs in India, for example, the NGO leaders said they took a human rights approach to violence against women, but in practice, they simply encouraged women to stand up for themselves. There is a mismatch between the way violence against women is understood in the vernacular and the kinds of measurements that take place at the global and even national levels (see Merry and Coutin 2014). Vernacular understandings rarely travel to the expert group meetings, the consultations among those with experience, or the heads of national statistical offices. There are certainly research studies, NGOs, and international organizations that develop a far more interpretative and participatory practice of measurement than others, of course, but they may not be included in global systems of measurement.

In sum, apparently small decisions about how to categorize severity, how to select models for the next study, how to decide which experts to consult, and what theory of violence and its solution to employ have major impacts on the kind of data that are generated and the picture they paint of the world. There are not "objective" numbers: these numbers are clearly interpreted at every step of the way. What appears to be an objective, scientific process of data collection and analysis has important political dimensions and consequences but works largely outside the sphere of political debate and contestation. As such, it constitutes a key dimension of power in the new global governance.

Measuring the Unmeasurable

The US Trafficking in Persons Reports

Human trafficking is virtually impossible to measure. The definition is murky, the process is shadowy and illegal, and its operation varies in different parts of the world. Trafficking victims are very hard to find and count. Because it is illegal, those involved in networks of organized crime clearly seek to evade detection. There is ambiguity about who has actually been trafficked. How does the enumerator know when a person has been coerced into sex work? If a woman who has been rescued from a brothel escapes from protective custody and returns to sex work, does this mean she consented to sex trafficking? If a family routinely sends its young boys to work in exploitative conditions in a quarry, and they send money home, are they victims of trafficking? If a young woman appears to consent to sex work but lacks papers that show that she is over eighteen, is she a trafficking victim, since consent is legally not possible for underage women? These are only a few of the reasons it is hard to count trafficking victims. Statisticians are being asked to count the uncountable.

Human trafficking is defined by exploitative labor and coercive recruitment, but neither of these is easy to specify. The term refers to both labor trafficking and sex trafficking, but whether adults can consent to sex work or whether it is always a form of trafficking is contested. A series of overlapping terms describes activities at this nexus of control and exploitation: modern-day slavery, bonded labor, forced labor, child labor, child sexual exploitation, prostitution, and forced marriage. Each of these terms points to a different conjunction of coercion and exploitation with a distinct theory of the source of the problem and the nature of the solution. Moreover, ethnographic research on trafficking shows that it takes widely varied forms and that the paths to victimhood are intricate and diverse (e.g., Agustin 2007; Brennan 2014; Cheng 2010; Kotiswaran 2011a; Molland 2012). Counting trafficking victims clearly requires making a highly diverse set of people and situations the same, at least in some ways, in order to render them countable. Any framework will simplify and distort this complexity, but each does so differently.

The major theoretical frameworks for conceptualizing trafficking focus on criminal justice, slavery, forced labor, and human rights. Each of these frameworks includes ways to count and control trafficking. The definitive conception of the problem will be determined by which mode of measuring trafficking prevails. Since the way a problem is defined points to the way it can be solved, the measurement system that prevails also determines what is done about it. These are the knowledge effects and governance effects of measuring trafficking.

This chapter examines the system of measuring human trafficking promoted by the US State Department. It shows how this system homogenizes and distorts a very complex array of interactions and relationships. The next chapter compares this framework with alternative models of trafficking based on conceptions of slavery, human rights, and forced labor and with recent ethnographic studies of trafficking. Finally, this chapter documents the global influence of the US State Department's indicators. A short case study of India examines how a powerful country identified as having a severe trafficking problem reacts to the charges. Its low ranking encourages domestic activism while rankling government officials. This chapter concludes that the State Department's system appears to be the currently dominant system of measurement, crystallizing the problem as being one of organized crime that requires a criminal justice response.

The US State Department's *Trafficking in Persons* (*TIP*) *Reports*, published annually by the US government, provide estimates of the number of trafficking victims, along with the numbers of prosecutions and convictions of traffickers, in most of the countries in the world. The reports rank countries according to their antitrafficking efforts. Although there are brief narratives about each country, it is the rankings that garner attention. Producing the rankings, however, is a deeply interpretive process with clear political dimensions. Even the authors describe it as a matter of art, requiring judgment. My genealogy of this indicator system examines its definitions of trafficking, its techniques for gathering data, its process of constructing the rankings, and its underlying theory.

My central argument is that the production of indicators about human trafficking homogenizes a highly diverse phenomenon and constructs a coherent theory to explain what trafficking is and how to fight it. For example, the

114

TIP Reports' theory about the nature of trafficking is that people who are trafficked are powerless and innocent victims and that it is up to states to warn potential victims and punish traffickers. They present such people as victims of traffickers rather than of larger structural conditions of inequality or closed borders (see Sharma 2005: 89). Modeled after drug trafficking, this theory assumes that humans, like drugs, are objects that are moved and exploited without their consent. As in the drug trafficking story, the trafficker is imagined as the head of a substantial organized crime network that understands the market and rakes in vast revenues. The solution, according to this theory, is for governments to enact laws, prosecute and punish traffickers, and absolve victims from criminal responsibility under the theory that traffickers will be deterred by the threat of punishment. This understanding of trafficking justifies the rescue, repatriation, and detention of victims to protect them and to hold them as witnesses pending the trials of traffickers while cracking down on traffickers. The system of measurement and ranking used in the reports is based on this underlying theory.

Unlike the UNSC's indicators of violence against women, this system is not a product of international collaboration but is a unilateral mechanism developed by one country. It evaluates and ranks countries according to US standards of adequate antitrafficking activity. Antitrafficking is a major US foreign-policy initiative, and the rankings are associated with rewards and punishments by the US government. Poor performers face sanctions, while good ones warrant praise. This is not an indicator in the making but an established system that has been in operation since 2001. It was initially criticized by academics and the Government Accountability Office (US Government Accountability Office 2006) for having thin data and politically influenced rankings. But over time, its data collection has improved, and it has acquired a more settled and legitimate status.

Defining Trafficking

Trafficking, as a publicly recognized problem, is not new. Concern about the sex trade dates back at least to the late nineteenth and early twentieth centuries, when it was named the "white slave trade," in contrast to the African slave trade, and was fueled by fears of white women from Europe and North America being lured into prostitution in the colonial regions of Asia, Africa, and South America (Chuang 2005–2006: 441, n. 8; 2010: 1667). This pattern was thought to be largely under the control of organized crime. The first international document on trafficking in women was the International Agreement for the Suppression of the White Slave Trade, adopted in 1904 and ratified by twelve states. It was followed by a series of treaties, culminating in the 1949 Convention for the Suppression of Traffic in Persons and of the Exploitation of the Prostitution of Others, ratified by forty-nine states. These endeavors focused on sex trafficking and did not provide a clear definition of trafficking in humans (Kangaspunta 2003: 82).

In the 1990s, a renewed concern about sex trafficking began, based on the perception that there was a substantial increase in trafficking. By the early twenty-first century, the prevailing view of trafficking was that it was rising rapidly as a result of globalization, privatization, rising global inequality, structural adjustment programs that cut back on government services, and the liberalization of the international market, along with the growth of organized crime networks and regional wars (Monzini 2005: 64). However, whether human trafficking has increased is much more difficult to determine than whether attention to trafficking has increased, which it clearly has.

Among the wide range of activities labeled as "trafficking," sex trafficking has long been the major focus of public concern. Sex trafficking is commonly represented by the image of a young girl, usually poor and brown, who has been kidnapped and passed from hand to hand until she ends up in a brothel in a large city or has been sold by impoverished parents to a criminal network. She disappears into a world of sex work where she services thirty men a night. As Carole Vance points out, these stories are produced by melodramatic films and media designed to generate outrage, but they fail to describe the complexity of trafficking or its structural conditions (2011; 2012: 201–2; see also Gulati 2011). Such stories have nourished an active rescue network of police and NGOs that invade brothels, seize women, and put them into rescue homes or deport them to their homes (Bernstein 2010; 2012). In the United States, victims of trafficking have great difficulty being recognized as victims rather than as criminals, unless they are rescued while chained to a bed in a brothel (or an equivalent situation; Haynes 2006–2007). Public interest in trafficking is fueled by concern for the plight of victims of sexual abuse and by the trafficking of drugs, arms, and organs. Labor trafficking is probably a larger problem than sex trafficking, but sex trafficking grabs more public attention.

There have been other ways of defining trafficking. In the 1990s, trafficking was seen as a human rights issue, not a security or organized crime one (Gallagher 2009: 792–93). Beginning in 1994, the US State Department's annual *Country Reports on Human Rights* included a section on trafficking. Unlike the *TIP Reports*, these country narratives did not contain recommendations, nor were they attached to ranks or sanctions. They simply described the state of human trafficking in each country and the range of state and civil society efforts to control it. These reports viewed trafficking as a problem of socially, politically, and economically marginalized groups caused by discrimination and societal abuse. However, as a human rights violation, trafficking was a marginal issue and received little attention.

In the late 1990s, human trafficking moved from the sphere of human rights to that of drugs and crime (Gallagher 2009: 793). The United Nations' major international trafficking treaty, called "the Palermo Protocol," took a criminal justice approach rather than a human rights approach despite considerable contestation (Chuang 2005–2006: 446–48). The Trafficking Victims Protection Act (TVPA), the major US antitrafficking law that created the *TIP Reports*, also adopted a criminal justice approach. As the 2013 *TIP Report* says, "Human trafficking is first and foremost a crime, so it is appropriate that law enforcement agencies lead most trafficking interventions" (US Department of State 2013d: 10). With the criminal justice approach, buttressed by anxieties about organized crime, terrorism, border control, and abused and vulnerable victims, the problem took off.

There is considerable debate about what trafficking means. In particular, there are deep disagreements about whether trafficking is the same as slavery, about how to differentiate between smuggled economic migrants and trafficking victims, and about whether all women who work in prostitution are trafficking victims. Various laws and organizations promote different definitions, and even within organizations, definitions change over time. Human trafficking generally refers to an individual's movement by force, fraud, or coercion for commercial sex, for performing a sex act under age eighteen, or for involuntary servitude, peonage, debt bondage, or slavery. The core features of trafficking are the recruitment or transport of persons by means of some form of force or fraud for an exploitative purpose (Chuang 2005–2006: 443). However, trafficking covers a very broad range of activities and is often quite varied in its forms of recruitment, the nature of the exploitation, and the extent to which a person has agreed to or accepted the labor — a decision typically made in the context of life circumstances and social and kinship expectations and obligations. It can only be understood within its social, political, and economic context. Since trafficking refers to a diverse set of practices shaped by local and national social structures, it is very hard to define it in a way that crosses national, local, and other social and cultural boundaries. As with the other case studies, joining quantification with detailed qualitative studies is essential for understanding trafficking in all its variation and complexity.

LEGAL DEFINITIONS OF TRAFFICKING

There are two important laws with international reach governing human trafficking, both of which date back to 2000. Each defines trafficking, although in somewhat different ways. In 2000, the US Congress passed the Trafficking Victims Protection Act (TVPA). It was originally envisioned as a way for the United States to help countries stem the flow of trafficked victims into the United States (Chuang 2010: 1661). This US law created the *TIP Reports* and a funding mechanism to support antitrafficking NGOs around the world. The TVPA emphasizes protection, prosecution, and prevention but emphasizes prosecution above all. It seeks to move trafficking from an exclusive concern with sex trafficking to a broader perspective that includes labor trafficking. The TVPA defines "severe forms of trafficking" as

(A) sex trafficking in which a commercial sex act is induced by force, fraud, or coercion, or in which the person induced to perform such an act has not attained 18 years of age; or
(B) the recruitment, harboring, transportation, provision, or obtaining of a person for labor or services, through the use of force, fraud, or coercion for the purpose of subjection to involuntary servitude, peonage, debt bondage, or slavery. (US Department of State 2013d: 8)

The 2013 *TIP Report* notes that a victim need not be physically transported from one location to another for the crime to fall within these definitions (US Department of State 2013d: 8). However, international trafficking remains an important concern.

A few months after the TVPA was passed, the Protocol to Prevent, Suppress and Punish Trafficking in Persons, Especially Women and Children, generally called "the Palermo Protocol," was created by the United Nations, with strong leadership from the United States among other countries (Chuang 2010: 1662). The UN protocol is an international law that has jurisdiction over all the countries that choose to ratify it. It is attached to a major international crime convention, the Convention against Transnational Organized Crime, but must be ratified separately from that convention. The Palermo Protocol was written under the auspices of the Commission on Crime Prevention and Criminal Justice and came into force in 2003. By 2015, 166 countries had ratified the treaty. In effect, the law creates a multilateral treaty regime, binding on all those states that ratify it.

The Palermo Protocol is the most widely used international definition of trafficking. It defines trafficking as recruitment intended for the purpose of exploitation. One of the goals of the Palermo Protocol was to distinguish trafficking from human smuggling (UN International Labour Organization 2005: 7). Article 3(a) of the Palermo Protocol defines trafficking in persons as

> the recruitment, transportation, transfer, harbouring or receipt of persons, by means of the threat or use of force or other forms of coercion, of abduction, of fraud, of deception, of the abuse of power or of a position of vulnerability or of the giving or receiving of payments or benefits to achieve the consent of a person having control over another person for the purposes of exploitation. Exploitation shall include, at a minimum, the exploitation of the prostitution of others or other forms of sexual exploitation, forced labour or services, slavery or practices similar to slavery, servitude or the removal of organs. (United Nations 2000, Art. 3[a])

The protocol further states that the recruitment, transportation, transfer, harboring, or receipt of a child for the purpose of exploitation is to be considered "trafficking in persons," even if this does not involve any of the means set forth above. As Anne Gallagher observes, here "trafficking comprises three . . . separate elements: (i) an action (recruitment, transportation, transfer, harboring, or receipt of persons); (ii) a means (threat or use of force or other forms of coercion, abduction, fraud, deception, abuse of power, or abuse of a position of vulnerability, or the giving or receiving of payments or benefits to achieve the consent of a person having control over another person); and (iii) a purpose (exploitation)" (Gallagher 2009: 811).

THE FIGHT OVER COMMERCIAL SEX WORK

The drafting of both the Palermo Protocol and the TVPA included fractious debates over the status of commercial sex — a deeply contentious issue within feminism (Chuang 2005–2006: 438–46; Gallagher 2009: 791). One faction views all forms of prostitution as inherently exploitative, while the other argues that adult women should be able to voluntarily consent to doing sex work and should not be regarded as victims. Although feminists agree that transnational prostitution is a reflection of sharp inequalities in class, gender, race, and nation, there is an intense debate between those who see prostitution itself as a form of violence against women and those who see providing sex as a form of work and want to improve its labor conditions. These groups take different approaches to trafficking (see Peach 2007). Many of those active in the antitrafficking movement are concerned about prostitution itself, not simply forced trafficking into prostitution. These activists include radical feminists and faith-based organizations that include evangelical Christians, many of whom are opposed to nonprocreative sex (Berman 2005–2006; Bernstein 2007; Chuang 2005–2006: 444; Soderlund 2005: 79–81). As Soderlund says, "These faith-based human rights organizations treat prostitution as an issue of conscience and morality rather than of income possibilities and labor, a stance that emphasizes protection over autonomy and empowerment" (Soderlund 2005: 81).

On the other side, liberal feminists argue that women should have the right to choose to engage in commercial sex work, although they should not be coerced into it. This group is joined by public health advocates concerned with combating the spread of HIV/AIDS, which is facilitated by making prostitution legal for consenting adults. Some advocates of sex-worker choice argue that the campaign against trafficking merges US interests in promoting its law enforcement tactics and its global power with increasing control over women's sexuality and rights (Soderlund 2005: 82). Thus whether trafficking refers to coerced and involuntary sex work or all forms of commercial sex is an unresolved issue, further complicating the effort to define trafficking.

This ideological division is reflected in the two international coalitions of NGOs working on sex trafficking: the Coalition Against Trafficking in Women (CATW), which condemns prostitution as a violation of women's bodies, persons, and rights, and the Global Alliance Against Traffic in Women (GAATW), which sees sex work as a form of work and advocates better working conditions and protections for those providing it (Coalition Against Trafficking in Women 2015; Global Alliance against Traffic in Women 2015). While feminists occupy both sides of this divide, the former tends to include conservative and religious groups, and the latter, secular feminists and public health advocates seeking to manage HIV/AIDS (Bernstein 2007). A third approach, advocated by the Network of Sex Work Projects, argues that prostitution is harmful because of moral condemnation and criminalization of the activity, advocating decriminalization and a human rights framework that includes migrant and labor rights (Cheng 2010: 200).

The fight over commercial sex dominated the drafting of these antitrafficking laws. Janie Chuang, who participated in the process of drafting the Palermo Protocol and with whom I have discussed it, says it took over the drafting process (2010: 1662). In the fierce debates over prostitution, the human rights perspective, concerned with the circumstances of the trafficking victim and the structural conditions that produce trafficking, fell by the wayside (Chuang 2010: 1703).

The US debate over the TVPA followed similar lines (Berman 2005–2006: 283). A series of horror stories about the treatment of victims and a film on brothels and brothel raids in India called *The Selling of Innocents*, combined with huge estimates of the number of victims, evoked serious concern in Congress. Supporters of the antitrafficking bill included liberal feminists such as Hillary Clinton, Christian conservatives such as Chuck Colson and Gary Haugen of the International Justice Mission, political liberals such as Paul Wellstone (D-Minnesota), and conservative politicians such as Christopher Smith (R-New Jersey). As Berman points out, Smith responded to the coalition of conservative religious groups and radical feminists targeting the sexual exploitation of women and girls while Wellstone expanded the bill to include all forms of forced labor relating to human trafficking (Berman 2005–2006: 283). The criminal justice approach, already accepted for domestic violence and sexual assault, was incorporated into the bill, which was attached to the reauthorization of the Violence against Women Act (VAWA). Thus Congress focused on both sex and labor trafficking and saw human trafficking as a criminal justice problem. Much later, in 2007, a *Washington Post* article noted that the size and scope of the sensationalistic stories of horrific abuse depicted in these Congressional discussions were contradicted by the small numbers of victims actually identified and prosecutions carried out, despite substantial investment in the identification of victims of trafficking in the United States (Markon 2007).

These debates over prostitution, along with fights over the relative focus on sex or labor trafficking, produced some of the ambiguity in these laws. For example, the TVPA defines severe trafficking in two clauses, with sex trafficking identified separately in Clause A, though it is conceptually incorporated in Clause B. By naming it as a separate offense, the law brings greater visibility to the issue of sex trafficking.

A major point of contention in both laws is whether it is possible to consent to exploitative work, particularly sex work. According to the Palermo Protocol, the consent of the victim of trafficking is irrelevant in cases where the forms of coercion listed in Article 3 have been employed or when the victim is under the age of eighteen. As Kay Warren notes in her analysis of the protocol, it continually stresses the vulnerability of the victims of trafficking, portrayed repeatedly as "women and girls," and denies the possibility of their consent or agency (2007: 12). Indeed, inserting the phrase "abuse of a condition of vulnerability" into the list of factors that define a victim of trafficking was a major triumph for some feminist activists. Adding the abuse of a position of vulnerability to the factors that constitute trafficking in the UN protocol expands the number of sex workers who could be considered to be trafficked, since Section B of the definition says that the consent of a victim is irrelevant in cases where any of the means set forth in Subparagraph A have been used. Conversely, it shrinks the number of individuals who can be seen to have consented to sex work, since even if they have chosen to do sex work because it was their best option, they may have done so under conditions of poverty, discrimination, or gender-based violence that constitute a position of vulnerability (see Gallagher 2011).

Halley et al. argue that the TVPA, developed with a more liberal human rights perspective under the Clinton administration, allows greater space for consent to forms of labor such as sex work than the Palermo Protocol, which is more influenced by abolitionists who are opposed to all commercial sex work (2006). On the other hand, Chuang argues that the TVPA takes a stronger stand against prostitution than the Palermo Protocol, which left the ultimate decision about the legality of prostitution to the states themselves (Chuang 2005–2006: 469). This flexibility probably reflects the more international nature of the Palermo process and the need to provide flexibility about the legality of prostitution in order to win countries' participation and support.

The ambiguity of the UN definition's reference to "abuse of a position of vulnerability" has proved difficult to work with. As a result, the UNODC has initiated a series of expert group meetings and reports to delineate more clearly the meaning of the phrase and to examine how it is being used in a series of particular countries (Gallagher 2012). Because of the addition of the reference to "the abuse of power or of a position of vulnerability or of giving or receiving of payments or benefits to achieve the consent of a person having control over another person," it incorporates the idea that a person's personal relationships and situation can have coercive influences (Halley et al. 2006: 359). Economic migrants are, in general, excluded from the definition of trafficking victims unless they moved under these conditions, but this is of course a very broad and ambiguous category. The US State Department's indicator system plunged into these tumultuous definitional waters.

Framework of the *Trafficking in Persons Reports*

The 2000 TVPA authorized the US State Department to publish an annual report on the status of efforts to control trafficking by countries around the world. As of 2013, the report classified 188 countries according to a three-tiered scale based on how well they were working to control trafficking. The *TIP Reports* are published by the Office to Monitor and Combat Trafficking (called the G/TIP office) of the US State Department, comfortably housed in a vast and impressive State Department building in Washington, DC, as I discovered when I visited it. In addition to the report, the G/TIP office funds many anti-trafficking NGOs. Weitzer reported in 2007 that in the previous five years, the US government had awarded more than $300 million to international and domestic NGOs involved in antitrafficking and antiprostitution work (2007: 460). Many of these were prominent antiprostitution organizations that sought to rescue victims, usually from brothels (Weitzer 2007: 460).

Since the first report was published in 2001, the *TIP Reports* have become a tool for pressuring countries to fight trafficking. They use shaming and encour-agement, as well as the application of sanctions. Some commentators, even those critical of their unilateral approach, credit these reports with a signifi-cant increase in action by governments to control trafficking (Gallagher 2011). The TVPA has been reauthorized and revised regularly — most recently in 2013 as an amendment to the Violence against Women Act.

The *TIP Reports* judge countries according to a clearly articulated set of standards established by the United States. They promote prosecution, pre-vention, protection, and more recently, participation. These standards are based on the theory that trafficking is the product of criminal networks that recruit and transport innocent, naïve victims. The reports present the prose-cution and conviction of traffickers as the primary solution. The reports also advocate prevention by warning potential victims and protection by not arrest-ing trafficking victims when they engage in illegal behaviors such as crossing borders or engaging in prostitution. States are held responsible for carrying out prosecutions and sentencing offenders to significant terms in prison. The US government sees the state as responsible for protecting persons in exploitative forms of labor who are unable to protect themselves and puts pressure on other states to follow this path.

Prosecution, protection, and prevention are to be weighted and assessed equally. *Prosecution* is measured by the number of antitrafficking laws passed and the number of arrests and convictions of traffickers, *protection* of victims through collaboration between law enforcement and service providers, and *prevention* of trafficking through public awareness campaigns and a variety of policies such as enforcing labor laws, eliminating restrictive visa practices, and increasing criminal and civil penalties for companies that rely on forced labor. Although the reports emphasize the importance of victim protection and assistance, their core concern is the number of prosecutions, convictions, and sentences; the number of new or amended antitrafficking laws; and the overall quality and impact of countertrafficking law enforcement efforts (US Department of State 2010: 6). Tables within the reports provide data on prosecutions and convictions, not the number of visas issued to trafficked people, the number of people who have found other livelihoods, or the number of people who received legal permission to travel and work so that they would not have to move illegally. Since 2004, following a 2003 amendment, the *TIP Reports* have provided the annual numbers of prosecutions, convictions, and victims identified and new or amended legislation. In recent reports, these data are presented globally by six regions and across six years (US Department of State 2013d: 46, 57–620). Moreover, each country narrative covers all three areas, but prosecution comes first. Twice as much funding was provided for groups doing law enforcement as those protecting rights or diminishing the demand for commercial sex (Huckerby 2007: 236). Thus statistical measures, narrative accounts, and funding all reflect the primary concern with prosecution.

The underlying theory of the *TIP Reports* is that trafficked persons are ignorant of the risks they are taking and that they act illegally only under coercion. The forms of economic, gender, or structural inequality that foster trafficking or the restrictive immigration policies that encourage migrant smuggling and illegal immigration are not considered in the *TIP Reports*. The framework blames organized crime rather than economic disparities, violence in families, established patterns of servile labor, a lack of legal modes of movement, or a desire to travel.

The reports present their policy in terms of American values. They describe trafficking victims in the language of slavery, drawing parallels between the US emancipation of slaves and current efforts to free victims of trafficking. The 2010 report includes a quote from Frederic Douglass (US Department of State 2010: 5) and juxtaposes a bill of sale for a slave in Virginia in 1819 with an official document releasing a man from bonded labor in India in 2007 (US Department of State 2010: 33). The 2013 *TIP Report* calls all forms of trafficking in persons "modern slavery" and explicitly connects its work to the historic American fight against slavery and the search for freedom (US Department of State 2013d: 7). In July 2013, the ambassador at large of the Office to Monitor and Combat Trafficking, Luis CdeBaca, noted that the linkage between human trafficking and the fight against modern slavery had made it through the transitions between the Clinton, Bush, and Obama administrations, saying, "I think this shows it is a bipartisan fight, it's quintessentially an American fight" (US Department of State 2013d).

While the leaders of the G/TIP office during the Bush administration were committed to the evangelical Christian perspective, CdeBaca, who took over as director of the office in 2008, had a background as a prosecutor. When I interviewed Ambassador CdeBaca in 2010, he emphasized combating slavery, increasing prosecutions, and improving victim protection as the key work of the office. Movement was no longer a criterion of trafficking. Under his leadership, the G/TIP office has increasingly focused on forms of forced labor. In response to a Congressional mandate in 2008, child soldiers were added. In 2013, Luis CdeBaca said that the basic point of trafficking is that it is a crime and that governments are responsible (US Department of State 2013d: 2).

The Challenge of Counting Trafficking Victims

The antitrafficking movement continually seeks to count the number of victims in order to build the case that this is a serious problem. Yet victims are hard to find and count: trafficking is illegal and hidden, the victims are often afraid to speak up, and their situations and experiences are very diverse. Estimates are based on differing theoretical frameworks and describe different categories of people. Some refer to internationally moved people, some to people trafficked into commercial sex work, some to slaves, child soldiers, child brides, or forced laborers. Over the last few years, a wide range of numbers has been offered by various organizations, each with its own methodology and definition of trafficking (Feingold 2010: 54). In this swamp of competing ideas and categories, the organization that establishes the definitive measurement system will be the one whose definition prevails.

There is a wild divergence in numbers. In 2005, for example, estimates ranged from 27 million slaves (Bales 2005) to 12.3 million forced laborers, of whom 20 percent were trafficked (UN International Labour Organization 2005: 7, 10), to 600,000–800,000 men, women, and children victims trafficked across international borders annually, of which 14,500–17,500 were trafficked into the United States (US Department of State 2005: 6). However, the number of victims actually identified is far smaller than these estimates. For example, according to the *TIP Reports*, in 2008, the first year for which this information was provided, there were only 30,961 identified victims, and by 2012, there were 46,570 (US Department of State 2013d: 46). It is not clear how many of these were commercial sex workers, although that is the prototype of the trafficking victim. Of the 600,000–800,000 victims estimated by the 2005 *TIP Report*, approximately 80 percent were women and girls, and up to 50 percent were minors. Of these, there were "hundreds of thousands used in prostitution" (US Department of State 2005: 6).

Despite the variation in numbers of trafficking victims, a few estimates circulate widely, gaining credibility through their use and repetition (Tyldum and

Brunovskis 2005). Some are repeated over and over in various documents until they acquire an aura of truth and are commonly cited simply as, for example, "US government" data. In this situation, as in many other ambiguous situations, the act of measurement creates the object of measurement. We may not know what intelligence is, but we do know that there is something that IQ tests measure that we call intelligence.

Although the *TIP Reports* are among the most widely cited sources on trafficking victims, their estimates of the size of the problem vary greatly, and the documentation for them is quite minimal, leading to critiques of the data during the reports' early years (Gallagher 2001; US Government Accountability Office 2006). The first *TIP Report*, in 2001, cites "reliable estimates" that the global traffic in persons is seven hundred thousand each year. The 2002 report opens by stating, "Over the past year, at least 700,000, and possibly as many as four million men women and children worldwide were bought, sold, transported and held against their will in slave-like conditions" (US Department of State 2002: 1). The 2003 *TIP Report* estimates that between eight and nine hundred thousand people are trafficked across borders each year (US Department of State 2003: 4). The 2004 and 2005 reports both give estimates of six to eight hundred thousand men, women, and children having been trafficked across international borders during those years (US Department of State 2005: 6). The 2004 report does not credit an organization for this estimate; however, both the 2005 and 2006 reports cite "US Government data" without further elaboration. These numbers are notable because of their fluctuation; global estimates range from six hundred thousand to as many as four million people per year. The absence of citations linking these numbers to a report, methodology, author, or sponsoring department further mystifies the estimates and the differences among them.

Nevertheless, US government estimates circulate widely and gain credibility as they are repeated. Vera Institute researchers Weiner and Hala found that 40 percent of the prevalence estimates they encountered in a literature review were attributed to the *TIP Reports* (2008: 9). Weiner and Hala concluded that as these estimates circulate, they appear to gain credibility despite the absence of an explicit methodology.

Since 2005, when the International Labour Organization (ILO) produced a global estimate of forced labor, the *TIP Reports* have used ILO global estimates of trafficking. During that year, the ILO estimated that there were 12.3 million forced laborers, of which 2.45 million, or 20 percent, were trafficked (UN International Labour Organization 2005: 10, 14). Of the forced laborers, 1.39 million, or 11 percent, were in commercial sexual exploitation, 98 percent of whom were women and girls (2005: 12, 15). Of the trafficked population, 1.05 million, or 43 percent, were trafficked for commercial sexual exploitation (2005: 14). The ILO, according to the Forced Labor Convention of 1930 (no. 29), defines forced labor as "all work or service which is exacted from any person under the menace of any penalty and for which the said person has not offered himself voluntarily" (Article 2[1]; UN International Labour Organization 2005: 5). The report acknowledges that these data are the ILO's best estimates, but only estimates. The ILO uses the UN's Palermo Protocol definition to develop four sets of operational indicators to measure trafficking for labor and sexual exploitation (2009). In general, it defines the concept of trafficking in terms of labor: "In its many projects and advocacy activities, the ILO addresses trafficking from a labour market perspective. It thereby seeks to eliminate the root causes, such as poverty, lack of employment and inefficient labour migration systems. ILO led responses involve labour market institutions, such as public employment services, labour inspectors and labour ministries" (UN International Labour Organization 2008: 2). The 2010 *TIP Report* used these ILO figures, estimating the number of adults and children in forced labor, bonded labor, and forced prostitution globally at 12.3 million. In contrast, it says that the total number of identified victims in 2009 was 49,105, and the number of successful trafficking prosecutions was 4,166 (US Department of State 2013d: 46).

The 2013 *Tip Report* takes a different approach, turning to estimates from antislavery activists and scholars. These data create an even starker gap between estimated and identified victims, claiming that 46,570 victims were identified in 2012 (US Department of State 2013d: 46) but that social scientists reported as many as 27 million men, women, and children who were victims of trafficking (US Department of State 2013d: 7). The number 27 million is imported from Kevin Bales's work on "modern-day slavery." He first proposed it in 1999 in his book *Disposable People* (originally published in 1999 and reissued in revised editions in 2004 and 2012) as a rough estimate of the number of modern-day slaves. This category includes people who move across borders into exploitative labor and child marriages, as well as people in debt bondage, commercial sex work, and other forms of labor where they are not free to leave and are under the total control of another person (2004; 2005). Kevin Bales, an academic sociologist who heads the Free the Slaves organization, says he realized that 27 million was a very rough guess. Despite this conjecture, the estimate has now been adopted and repeated widely (Bales 2005). According to Elizabeth Bernstein, the number 27 million is frequently cited by a variety of evangelical Christian and secular feminist activists, NGOs, and state agents (2007). Bales says that he expected a critical reception to the figure but found that it was "seized upon with alacrity and [he] found [himself] an 'expert.'" The number helped shift public debate from definitions to responses, a reaction he found both heartening and worrying: "It was heartening because the response was to use the estimate in many informative ways, worrying because of an often uncritical acceptance of the estimate" (Bales 2003: 344).

These examples underscore the magic of numbers: their ability to create certainty in spaces of great ambiguity. These numbers are frequently cited, often with minimal attention to their original source or data collection methods. Numbers gain credibility through frequent repetition, as in the case of the 27 million figure, often distancing them from their original sources. As Andreas and Greenhill point out, the politics of counting as a way of generating truth occur in a wide variety of places, from drug trafficking to body counts after a war (2010).

The *TIP Reports* do not explain the wide swings in numbers beyond pointing out that counting victims is very difficult. As Weitzer notes, large numbers help to generate a sense of crisis — what he calls a "moral panic" — and spur media attention and support (2007: 455). Such attention also generates funding and donors. Yet neither in the movement against modern-day slavery nor in the *TIP Reports* is it at all transparent who is being counted (Bernstein 2007). Nor do the *TIP Reports* explain the huge discrepancy between the estimated and identified number of victims, except to say that trafficking is illegal behavior and is thus hard to uncover. Indeed, the theme of the 2013 report is how to identify victims, under the assumption that there is indeed a large number of victims who are not being detected (US Department of State 2013d: 7–23). But perhaps the kinds of victims we imagine are less numerous than are people in other kinds of bad and exploitative labor situations who do not fit this model of trafficking.

Counting things or people requires constructing a category based on a single principle that crosses national, regional, and cultural lines and is clear regardless of context. This means that there must be an essential common denominator that describes the situation of all persons labeled as trafficked. For both the United Nations and the United States, the fundamental element is coercion (Monzini 2005: 50, n. 11, pp. 56–57; see Warren 2007). Yet the steps by which individuals become enmeshed in bad labor situations are highly varied and contextually specific, involving various degrees of coercion. While trafficking is typically imagined as the work of large organized crime networks, it is often carried out by neighbors, relatives, or people known to the victims and may not involve international travel. A key criterion is that a trafficking victim has not consented to his or her work situation, but consent is very difficult to determine. The move into exploitative labor typically takes place within a social context of vulnerability in which a person is faced with a range of undesirable options whose costs and benefits are socially and culturally specified. Moving into sexual labor may seem better than starvation or living with a sexually abusive parent. A person who has had a series of abusive partners may decide it is better to be paid for sex work than to be sexually exploited for free. A woman may agree to travel to a city for sex work because she is seeking to escape a violent marriage or because she has been invited by a friend to join her in an adventure that ends up as work in a brothel. Most trafficking laws establish an age below which a person is considered too young to consent, but even determining a person's age, in the absence of documentation such as birth registration or other forms of identification, is difficult. The quantification of trafficking fits uneasily into these complexities of everyday practice.

Sverre Molland demonstrated this mismatch between conception and reality in his research on trafficking and antitrafficking movements across the Thailand-Laos border (2012). He showed antitrafficking lawyers and activists in the region case studies of the women whose recruitment stories he had heard and asked them if these women had been trafficked. Intriguingly, the antitrafficking lawyers found it difficult to decide, often did not agree with each other, and even changed their minds over time (2012: 204–11). He argues, based on his ethnographic field research on women in the sex trade in this region, that the bipolar logic of "trafficker" and "victim" fails to describe the complex ways a person enters into and leaves sex work (2012: 108). Some might arrive to do factory work and find that sex work pays better. Others might come to do sex work to support their families back home. Others might be reluctant at first to do sex work and instead work serving drinks in a bar. They might then decide that the money is worth doing sex work as well. There is no simple distinction between being forced and choosing to do this work. Similarly, Denise Brennan's detailed portrayal of the lives of trafficking victims in the United States reveals considerable diversity in the way people become trafficked and manage to escape (2014).

The G/TIP office is also changing its definition of trafficking. Although in their first decade, the reports focused extensively on cross-border movements, the 2010 report says that a person need not be physically transported to be a trafficking victim but can be considered trafficked if there is exploitation of labor (US Department of State 2010: 8). The office is now focusing on exploitative labor instead of movement across borders. In my interviews with the G/TIP office, Ambassador CdeBaca was clear that movement is not an essential criterion of trafficking. Thus, as the struggle to count proceeds, what gets counted is also shifting.

Within this highly varied and complex world of trafficking and forced labor, the *TIP Reports* seek to build a coherent, global framework that defines the phenomenon and enables comparisons among countries of their efforts to combat these practices. The powerful stories of abuse and suffering generated by antitrafficking activists have drawn attention to the issue, but numbers are necessary to assess the size of the problem. Under these conditions, it is not surprising that the estimated number of trafficking victims is far larger than that of actually identified victims.

The case of trafficking illustrates the challenges of quantification and governance. In order to draw attention to a social problem, it is essential to show that the problem is significant: that it involves a substantial number of people or that it costs society a great deal of money. Building a social movement frequently requires quantification to establish the size of the problem. Yet when a problem is newly discovered, poorly understood, and not well defined, gathering these data is extremely difficult. The phenomenon needs to be defined clearly, principles of equivalence created, categorizations established, and data collection systems put into place. Trafficking has proved particularly elusive.

TIERS AND RANKING

The *TIP Reports* tackle this tangled issue as a central actor in knowledge production. They estimate the number of victims globally and combine numbers, narratives, and analyses to assess which countries are working effectively to eliminate trafficking and which are not. The reports rank countries into tiers based on their compliance with the standards articulated in the report. In order to rank countries, it is necessary to find some criteria for comparison. The *TIP Reports* count the numbers of prosecutions, convictions, and sentences, as well as the number of antitrafficking laws passed in each country. They assess government efforts to combat trafficking. In order for the reports and their rankings to appear authoritative and objective, they must rely on numerical data, but finding these data and determining what the scant figures actually represent is very uncertain.

The tiered ranking system is a composite indicator based on counts of antitrafficking laws passed, criminal justice actions against traffickers, and country narratives. The US government determined what it considered to be good practices for controlling trafficking and established these as the standards against which other countries were to be judged. Early *TIP Reports* made little reference to international standards, although that has changed more recently.

The TVPA sets minimum standards for the elimination of trafficking that it sees as the responsibility of governments. The minimum standards specify obligations of governments to prohibit severe forms of trafficking; to punish acts of trafficking; to prescribe punishment commensurate with that which is given for grave crimes, punishment that is sufficiently stringent to deter and that adequately reflects the heinous nature of the offense; and to make "serious and sustained efforts to eliminate severe forms of trafficking in persons" (US Department of State 2013d: 410–11). Clearly, these standards rely on vague and unspecified terms such as "severe" and "grave." The act then lists eleven factors considered to be indicia of serious and sustained efforts by governments. The first one specifies investigation, prosecution, conviction, and sentences for principle actors in serious cases of trafficking, with a failure to provide information creating the presumption that such efforts have not been made. The second one requires the government to protect victims and ensure that they are not inappropriately incarcerated, fined, or otherwise penalized, which includes training police on approaches that focus on the needs of the victims. Other indicia are public education, cooperation with other governments, extradition of traffickers, monitoring of immigration and emigration for evidence of trafficking, prosecution of complicit public officials, progress over the previous year, and efforts to reduce demand for commercial sex and international sex tourism (US Department of State 2013d: 410–11). Thus the law sets out general principles for state action and develops a series of more specific indices, most of which center on prosecution. Gallagher and Holmes point out the enormous difficulties of prosecuting traffickers, however, noting the need for institutional support, generous donors, and interagency and international collaboration (2008). Despite these clear challenges to the criminalization approach, it remains the dominant way of tackling the problem in the *TIP Reports*.

The *TIP Reports* rank countries into three tiers based on their compliance with the minimum standards established in the TVPA. Tier 1 countries are the most compliant, Tier 3 the least. A fourth tier, the Tier 2 Watch List, was added in 2004. Countries that fall into Tier 3 face the possibility of sanctions by the United States, while a 2008 amendment consigns those ranked in the Tier 2 Watch List for two consecutive years to Tier 3 for the next year unless there is a presidential waiver (US Department of State 2010: 25). Three countries were downgraded in this way in 2013: Russia, China, and Uzbekistan. Sanctions include withdrawal of non-humanitarian aid and non-trade-related foreign assistance, exclusion of government employees from funding for cultural and educational exchange programs, and US opposition to assistance from international financial institutions such as the IMF and the World Bank (US Department of State 2013d: 47). However, sanctions may be waived by the US president if they are not in the national interest, including its security interests, or if they would harm vulnerable populations such as women and children. As of 2005, seven countries had been sanctioned: Burma, Cuba, North Korea, Equatorial Guinea, Sudan, Venezuela, and Cambodia (Chuang 2005–2006: 484). As Chuang points out, none of these countries had significant economic or strategic relations with the United States (Chuang 2005–2006: 484–85).

The *TIP Reports* present their ranks in color-coded regional maps that indicate the relative merit of a country at a glance in print and online. A striking feature of indicators as a cultural practice is that many of them present global country rankings in the same way: on a world map with countries color-coded by rank, often with green representing the best countries and red the worst. In addition, many websites with maps add a feature in which clicking on a country reveals further details of its rank and number. In addition to the maps, the *TIP Reports* offer personal stories and pictures, mostly of faceless victims, alongside the quantitative data. The numbers require context and individual stories to be persuasive, but the context is often that of a generic, poor country or a nameless, universalized victim rather than a specific political, economic, and cultural situation. In addition, the ranks and counts are supplemented by brief narratives about each country's antitrafficking efforts.

Until 2010, the United States did not rank itself, but in response to global complaints, it has since done so. Until 2010, rankings were presented in layers based on the tiers to which they belonged, but since then, they have been listed alphabetically by country, with the tier ranking following the name of the country. Perhaps this was an effort to soften the visual blow the tiers made when countries were arrayed in ranks. However, at the same time, rankings were made visible through vivid regional maps colored according to the tier of each country. There were clearly some who felt that the categories were not specific enough, since a bill introduced to the Senate in July 2011 (S. 1362) sought to simplify the *TIP Reports* by reducing the number of country categories and by ranking countries within each tier (US Congress 2011). The bill asked for a list of countries in full compliance to be ranked on a single scale and for those that were not also to be ranked on a single scale in terms of their relative adherence to the TVPA standards. The bill died in the Senate in 2011.

Tier rankings depend on the extent to which governments comply with the TVPA's minimum standards for the elimination of trafficking or are seen as making significant efforts to come into compliance with them. Tier placement is based more on government efforts than the size of the problem (US Department of State 2010 Report: 20). According to the reports, the efforts they assess include passing antitrafficking laws; implementing these laws through prosecution; providing victims with protection and services and not harming their rights, dignity, or well-being; developing victim identification systems; imposing criminal penalties on traffickers; curbing practices that contribute to forced labor migration; and developing partnerships with NGOs to provide victims with services such as health care and counseling (US Department of State 2010: 20–21). Countries that are making efforts but have a large or increasing number of victims, have not provided evidence of increasing efforts, or have not fulfilled commitments made the previous year are classified as being in the Tier 2 Watch List. Numbers of prosecutions are important. For example, India was in the Tier 2 Watch List from 2004 to 2010 but was raised to Tier 2 in 2011. According to the report, its Watch List status was primarily based on a lack of government effort concerning labor trafficking, especially with regard to bonded labor, rather than sex trafficking (US Department of State 2010: 171–72). There were very few convictions for bonded labor in India. Sex trafficking resulted in more convictions, although largely in Mumbai and Andhra Pradesh (US Department of State 2010: 173). Overall, it noted several positive government programs, such as the Anti-Human Trafficking Units (AHTUs) of the police, and progressive laws but cited a lack of implementation of these laws and policies.

NONGOVERNMENTAL ORGANIZATION FUNDING

The tier rankings are important in determining how the G/TIP office allocates its substantial funds for antitrafficking work, reaching $19 million in 2013. In both the 2013 and 2014 solicitations for proposals from NGOs, universities, and public international organizations, such as International Organization for Migration (IOM) and UNODC, the office specified a small number of countries (fifteen) where funding would be provided based on their low-tier rankings. The solicitation also specified general goals and activities based on the recommendations of the previous *TIP Report*. Thus the information, recommendations, and rankings in a report shape the allocation of funding for the following year and thereby promote the solutions favored by the G/TIP office (US Department of State 2013b).

The extensive funding for antitrafficking programs is a significant part of the *TIP Reports'* influence. In 2004, they supported thirty-eight programs in Latin America and twenty-two in the United States, with grants totaling almost $17 million. In 2005, the G/TIP office funded thirty-three programs in the region, with grants of $16.5 million. A significant part of this funding has gone to law enforcement, particularly training programs. These provide readily quantifiable activities for responding to US demands, particularly when offered by nongovernmental organizations rather than the government (Quinn 2008: 139–40).

This approach to controlling human trafficking—assessing country performance, ranking countries on the basis of their criminal justice activities, and imposing sanctions for noncooperation—follows a model created for dealing with drug trafficking during the 1970s and 1980s. In the mid-1980s, Congress required the president to report annually on US international drug control policy, identifying and providing information on countries that were sources of narcotics and controlled substances affecting the United States, and to use this information as the basis for cutting US assistance and voting against financial assistance in multilateral institutions such as the World Bank and regional development banks (Friman 2010: 77). Trade sanctions were also imposed for noncompliance. Beginning in 1987, countries that were significant sources of illicit drugs were placed on a special list and ranked according to their level of cooperation with the United States, with national interest waivers given to countries where continued financial assistance was "vital to the national interests of the United States" (Friman 2010: 85–86). Friman notes, "In effect, by the late 1980s, the United States had introduced a rating and ranking system to assess foreign compliance in counternarcotics efforts" (2010: 78). Countries are ranked into three broad categories: cooperating fully; failing, but where continued assistance is vital to US national interests; and failing demonstrably in the previous twelve months to make substantial efforts to adhere to obligations under international counternarcotics agreements (Friman 2010: 85).

The TVPA took a similar approach, classifying countries on the basis of their compliance with the US government's minimum standards. At first, only those countries with a significant number of victims were classified, but since 2008, the scope has expanded to include most countries. The sanctions regime is also modeled on the US International Religious Freedom Act (USC 6445[a] of 1998; Chuang 2005–2006: 452, n. 62). A template developed to deal with drug trafficking has been adopted to deal with these other issues as well.

Clearly, this model draws a parallel with drug trafficking, with its extensive networks and vast revenues (Feingold 2010: 47), but the model does not map well onto human trafficking. It denies agency to those who are trafficked, who become theorized as passive objects rather than actors trying to make the best of a difficult situation. Similarly, there is confusion between migrant smuggling and other forms of economic migration and human trafficking, which are sometimes hard to distinguish in practice (Gallagher 2009; Hathaway 2008–

2009). Countries themselves sometimes fail to distinguish between these patterns legally and may well not separate them in their measurement systems (Gallagher 2001: 1140; Haynes 2009; Kangaspunta 2003: 85).

GATHERING DATA AND RANKING COUNTRIES

How are these vague standards converted into rankings? In my interviews with State Department officials in the G/TIP office, they said that embassy personnel supply the data but that decisions are made within the State Department in Washington, DC. The US State Department gathers information on trafficking efforts through the political officers in its embassies and local antitrafficking NGOs — particularly those supported by G/TIP grants. Embassy representatives seek information from governments as well as advocates. Political officers deal with many issues, not just trafficking, and may have relatively little time to collect the required information, leading them to collect readily quantifiable information such as the number of laws passed, the number of training sessions for officials, and the number of prosecutions. Governments striving to satisfy US requirements will, consequently, tend to privilege these readily countable activities (Guinn 2008: 139). Countries that refuse to cooperate in providing information are chastised in the narratives and are potentially downgraded in the rankings, since failure to provide information is interpreted as failure to act.

According to the head of the report division of the G/TIP office, whom I interviewed in 2009 and 2010, a fifty-two-page questionnaire is directed to the political officers of all the embassies in late December, asking them for information. They are required to respond to the questionnaire by February. These embassy officials are asked to write many reports, so the quality varies. The questionnaire asks for information on the country's legal structure as well as its number of victims, prosecutions, convictions, and sentences. Prosecutions are important, but it tries to emphasize prevention as well. The office also e-mails their "NGO partners," primarily present and former grantees of the G/TIP office, asking for information. Data gathering may also include town hall meetings. The G/TIP office also publishes an annual public notice online in the Federal Register soliciting answers to an extensive questionnaire on trafficking and government responses to it. This questionnaire says that governments are requested to provide data on investigations, prosecutions, convictions, and sentences and that if a government is judged capable of doing so but fails to provide these numbers, it will be presumed not to have "vigorously investigated, prosecuted, convicted or sentenced such acts" (US Department of State 2013a: 76185).

Embassies also rely on local NGOs for information. In India, some of the embassy staff were Indian nationals who had good contacts with NGOs in the antitrafficking field. My interviews with antitrafficking NGOs in India indicated that sex-worker NGOs were not consulted by US State Department officials gathering information for the *TIP Reports* but that some antitrafficking NGOs were — particularly those funded by the G/TIP office. During the era of George Bush's presidency, only organizations that took an antiprostitution pledge were eligible for G/TIP funding.

The process of data collection, while originally criticized by scholars as well as the General Accountability Office (Gallagher 2001; US Government Accountability Office 2006), has improved over the years (Gallagher 2011). The 2013 *TIP Report* lists seventy-one staff members engaged in producing the report and managing its grant activities, a list that probably includes interns (US Department of State 2013d: 416). In a 2010 interview with the report writing team, I was told that nine analysts wrote the country reports based on the questionnaires and some site visits. In 2012, thirteen staff members were responsible for assessing 180 countries (Gallagher and Chuang 2012: 333). Each analyst covers between eighteen and twenty countries. The *TIP Reports'* narratives are written in Washington, DC, based on the information provided by embassies, NGOs, and international organizations, as well as some short field trips. For example, one staff member spent ten days in India in 2010, and staff trips have increased since then. The G/TIP office runs training sessions for embassy personnel on how to provide data for the report. Yet because the analysis and writing are done in Washington, DC, the report lacks the in-depth knowledge of the State Department's *Human Rights Reports* on trafficking, which are written by local embassy personnel. The system of using a single office based in Washington, DC, to make assessments enables better comparison and commensuration but reduces contextual knowledge. This trade-off is inevitable in measurement and ranking systems.

After the information arrives in Washington, DC, the office spends March writing the report. Then the political struggles begin about what to say and how to interpret the data. There is tension because the embassies only report information, and the G/TIP office writes the reports and establishes the ranks. Embassies are unhappy about this loss of control, but the team's head pointed out to me that it is the State Department that is responsible for making policy. Embassies get close to their countries and tend to take on their interests. They often want their countries to look as good as possible, he said. For example, in 2014, a trafficking activist in Denmark told me that the US embassy encouraged her country to pass a particular law to improve its TIP position. Conflicts may erupt at the regional level or between national and regional perspectives, possibly ending up in a dispute-resolution process. Conflicts go up the hierarchy, even fairly high. The head of the report-writing office told me that the fights often occur between the G/TIP office and the officials running regional offices in the State Department. According to Gallagher and Chuang, rankings and narratives have to be approved by relevant political officers in the State Department, leading to what the Government Accountability Office report referred to as some "horse-trading" in tier rankings (Gallagher and Chuang 2012: 334; US Government Accountability Office 2006: 33).

In conversations with US embassy personnel in India, my research assistant Vibhuti Ramachandran found that some embassy officers establish long-lasting relationships with NGOs, while others know little about the local trafficking situation. Since political officers are responsible for gathering information on a wide range of issues, they are not necessarily conversant with this one. In her analysis of the methods of data gathering in 2005 based on her interviews in Southeast Asia and Central and Eastern Europe, Janie Chuang notes that some NGOs are reluctant to provide data on poor government performance lest it jeopardize their ability to work in the country, and some disengage from the process because they do not share the abolitionist perspective (Chuang 2005–2006: 475). She also notes a lack of coordination, or even agreement, in the data presented in the *TIP Reports* and in the trafficking section of the annual *US Department of State Country Reports on Human Rights Practices*.

The *TIP Reports* offer very little indication about how the data are assessed and countries are ranked. In one interview with the head of the report-writing office, I asked if all three criteria — prosecution, protection, and prevention — were counted and weighted equally, but he said that would be difficult to do since data were very uneven among those three categories. He told me that Congress always asks him that same question. The staff discussed the pressure they experience from Congress and from elsewhere in the State Department to provide more metrics. In response, they have tried developing a checklist with thirteen points in order to make ranking more systematic. But the head of the report-writing team said that in the end, he wants to preserve the process of ranking as an art and a matter of judgment. He sees the need for flexibility. A more discretionary system allows taking into account the differing capacities of the countries. In effect, he is resisting the creation of an evaluation system where the numbers determine the ranking. Thus this office grapples with the fundamental paradox of governance by indicators: to be objective, it is important that numbers directly determine outcomes, yet the flexibility to assess various factors together can provide more nuanced and fairer, but potentially less objective, outcomes.

Chuang notes that the tier rankings are inconsistent and sometimes do not mesh with the standards of the TVPA (2010). Inevitably, ranking involves considerable interpretation and judgment. There are clearly politics involved in some cases. Several of the Tier 3 countries are those already viewed as problematic by the United States. For example, Cuba, North Korea, and Iran were all in Tier 3 from 2003 to 2013 with the one exception that Iran was in Tier 2 for two of those ten years. However, Tier 3 also includes US allies such as Saudi Arabia.

Although each country is described in a narrative of two to four pages, the report and the rankings still rely very extensively on statistical information, particularly about criminal justice activities (number of convictions, number of shelters, number of training programs) rather than more qualitative information on, for example, the nature and impact of support for victims (Gallagher 2011: 15, 20). There is little discussion of the limitations of the data or the difficulty of counting trafficking victims and activity. The 2013 report does include a section on how to identify victims but focuses on the need for training, particularly of law enforcement personnel, rather than on any specific guidelines for identification (US Department of State 2013d: 7–27). The reports focus on what is measurable, such as laws passed, convictions, sentences, number of trainings, number of shelters, number of special police units, and so forth, rather than the unmeasurable quality of life of victims or of poor communities from which people are trafficked. As the 2013 report says, "While holding regular inter-ministerial meetings are an important step, governments must also achieve measurable results, including in numbers of victims helped and traffickers brought to justice" (US Department of State 2013d: 15).

Yet it is clear that it is difficult to distinguish trafficking victims from labor migrants and people who more or less voluntarily move to seek sex work or other forms of exploitative work and that the number of victims claimed is highly dubious (Agustin 2007; Feingold 2010: 51–53; Warren 2010). Even the terminology can be misleading. For example, the 2005 *TIP Report* says, "The vast majority of women in prostitution do not want to be there. Few seek it out or choose it, and most are desperate to leave it. A 2003 study in the scientific *Journal of Trauma Practice* found that 89% of women in prostitution want to escape prostitution" (US Department of State 2005: 19). Although there was no citation for this article in the *TIP Report*, when I tracked it down, I found that it was a major study of prostitutes in nine countries in which they were asked on a questionnaire if they would like to leave prostitution (Farley et al. 2003). Yet when this information was described in the text of the article, the authors referred to the percentage of women who wanted to "escape" prostitution. The author, an abolitionist, shifted the language from "leave" in the questionnaire to "escape" in her analysis. It is the latter word the *TIP Report* picks up. "Escape" implies a need for rescue that the phrase "leave" does not. As well as arguing that women want to "escape," the *TIP Report* uses this study to claim that 60–75 percent of women in prostitution were raped and that 68 percent suffered posttraumatic stress disorder (US Department of State 2005: 19). Thus the statistics and their presentation promoted the antiprostitution orientation of this period.

Despite the ambiguity of the concept of trafficking, the flaws in the data, and the interpretive work required to evaluate a country's performance and produce rankings, this information is translated into apparently objective tier rankings, producing a "truth" of the status of trafficking in each country. Arguing that the quality of government is relevant to these rankings, the 2010 report shows a correlation between low tier rankings and poor performance on Freedom House's indicators of freedom and Transparency International's Corruption Perception Index, thus using one composite index to verify the underlying theory of another (US Department of State 2010: 28–29).

Conclusions

This study shows how measurement systems, once established, can provide an apparently objective way of understanding the world. The *TIP Reports* examine numbers of victims, numbers of prosecutions, and numbers of convictions as a way to gain certainty about a problem for which the actual size and nature of population flows is extremely hard to determine and the very category of trafficking so diverse as to render counting it impossible. The concept of human trafficking is defined by what is counted as trafficking. Because the United States has taken a major stand on trafficking, using rewards and sanctions, it has been able to determine the prevailing conceptualization of it. The reports' use of numbers and scores adds to their credibility. Other measurement systems proposed by the ILO, the UNODC, and the International Organization for Migration (IOM) also count trafficking victims, but at this point, none exercises the global authority of the *TIP Reports*. At least for now, trafficking is what the *TIP Reports* measure.

This case study also demonstrates the power of country rankings to mobilize action. The *TIP Reports* constitute a classic example of the use of ranking to shame states or people into changing their behaviors to conform to the standards established by the ranker. The TIP system responsibilizes states to conform to the standards established by the United States, and many have responded by passing laws and changing policies, even if they have done so grumpily. While the impact of the *TIP Reports* seems greater on smaller, more donor-dependent countries, even a large and powerful country like India is somewhat affected, although mostly in the way this effort draws attention to the problem and reshapes the relations among domestic activists, as discussed in the next chapter.

This indicator demonstrates the power of new governance techniques based on evidence. Rather than implementing change itself, the measurement system creates knowledge: it sets standards, collects information, and assesses compliance. Its new systems of measurement build on existing templates — in this case, from drug trafficking. It also exercises power as it offers rewards and sanctions for compliance. Neither of the other indicators discussed in this book have the economic and political power behind their measurement systems that the *TIP Reports* have.

Finally, this example again shows the power of composite indicators that lump many variables together into a single rank or score. Prosecution, protection, prevention, and participation are rolled into a single tier ranking that provides simple and easily grasped knowledge. However, while such indicators clearly draw attention, it is less clear to what extent the changes they bring improve the lot of trafficking victims, diminish trafficking, or prevent future victimization.

One of the puzzles of indicators is the extent to which they are used and even considered reliable despite widespread recognition of their superficiality, simplification, and neglect of context and history. This critique is particularly applicable to the field of trafficking, in which estimates of victims are widely divergent and the social practices of trafficking so varied. Yet numbers offer the illusion of knowledge, even if it is a false specificity. This is a seductive form of knowledge. It promises certainty and clarity and provides readily comparable information that facilitates decision making. I think this apparent clarity accounts for the growing popularity of composite indicators. Indicators and other numerical forms of knowledge subdue the thorny difficulties of making decisions about incommensurable social practices, issues, and problems. With such an uncountable problem as human trafficking, the *TIP Reports* offer knowledge and certainty. Such clarity is hard to resist in a complex world. The indicators provide a way to know a world that is unknowable and to govern a world that is ungovernable.

Knowledge Effects and Governance Effects of the *Trafficking in Persons Reports*

What kind of knowledge do the *TIP Reports* provide about trafficking, and what do they miss? The effort to measure the number of victims, the passage of new antitrafficking laws, and the prosecution of traffickers in the *TIP Reports* system serves to solidify and fix the narrative and definition of trafficking it espouses. It merges a highly diverse series of practices and situations into a single problem with a relatively uniform solution. As it does so, it renders the complex processes that constitute trafficking simpler and more homogeneous and thus crystallizes the underlying theory of trafficking as being a criminal activity. Through this homogenizing strategy, it has made a major contribution to increasing the visibility of the problem and pressuring states to take action by passing laws and enhancing policing.

However, careful ethnographic studies offer a different perspective on trafficking. Quantitative forms of knowledge tend to explain trafficking through dyadic relations between traffickers and victims, without paying attention to the larger set of conditions that produce the suffering that compels victims to become vulnerable to exploitative labor situations. In contrast, ethnographic studies show that trafficked people do make choices, but within the constraints of economic, political, and social structures that persuade or drive them to move, even into exploitative labor conditions. Structural violence, inequality, political conflict, and poverty, along with state practices that inhibit legal movement across borders and fail to provide adequate protection for workers, foster trafficking. Without a clear analysis of the phenomenon being counted, it is clearly difficult to develop a reliable system of measurement or an adequate response. This chapter contrasts the knowledge provided by ethnographic studies with that provided by quantitative data, examines alternative frameworks for understanding and counting trafficking based on conceptions of slavery and human rights, and assesses the impact of the *TIP Reports'* framework on knowledge and governance.

Ethnographic Perspectives on Trafficking

In the standard narrative, victims of sex trafficking often live in semi-imprisonment, isolated from the rest of society and constantly subjected to physical and mental violence. They may work ten to fifteen hours a day for days at a time yet get little money. They often agree to unprotected sex or do dangerous or humiliating acts in order to increase their income or because they have no choice. They are charged large fees for their living expenses, propelling them into a situation of permanent debt. In many cases, the trip to their place of work is also charged to them, further increasing their levels of debt. They are intensively supervised and have great difficulty escaping. Typically, they are under the control of criminal gangs that use violence, debt, and threats to reveal their activities to their families to keep them under control. Traffickers may take the women's passports and other documents so that they are unable to travel and so that they fear the police (Monzini 2005: 41–48). Given this scenario, the solution is rescue.

While there are undoubtedly situations where this scenario takes place, it does not describe all prostitutes. It seems to describe those in the most marginal positions in the business. Brennan describes similar forms of control of labor trafficking victims in the United States (2014). There are undoubtedly cases of highly coercive labor situations, but when and how often this takes place is not only contested but uncounted. Sex workers range from those who are independent, choose their hours and working conditions, and keep all their earnings to those who have no control over their work or their income (see Cheng 2008; 2010; Kotiswaran 2008). Women who are coercively moved, or trafficked, tend to fall into the least independent positions. Once a woman has started working in commercial sex, she may have the opportunity to improve her situation. As Prabha Kotiswaran shows in Kolkata, India, some brothels cater to trafficked women, while others rely more on local women (2008; 2011). Women can move from the former to the latter over time and gradually become property owners and rent to other sex workers. Some will eventually become brothel owners and may even run trafficking networks themselves. In practice, there are significant variations among workers in the sex trade, with coercion being more common in some areas than others.

Ethnographic research on sex trafficking in India, Laos, Thailand, South Korea, the United States, and Latin America suggests that women end up in sex work through many paths (see Agustin 2007; Brennan 2014; Cheng 2010; Kotiswaran 2008; 2011; Molland 2012; Montgomery 2001). In practice, there is not a sharp distinction between entering into sex work and entering into other forms of exploitative labor. A migrant may intend to take on one kind of work and find herself in another or go back and forth between both sex work and other forms of work depending on her circumstances (Agustin 2007). Some trafficking is the result of organized crime networks, while other cases are the product of informal networks of neighbors, relatives, or friends. Sometimes victims know what they are getting into; other times, they do not but gradually accept their situation and choose to stay, as Sealing Cheng shows in her detailed ethnographic study of sex workers in South Korea (2010) and as Sverre Molland shows in his study of those on the Thailand-Laos border (2012). Denise Brennan documents similar variability in the circumstances of trafficking victims in her ethnographic study of trafficking in the United States (2014).

In Molland's ethnography of sex trafficking in the Mekong River region, he finds that movement into the sex trade depends primarily on social relationships, not physical coercion (2012). He shows that while some women are brought to beer shops and brothels who have been deceived about the nature of the work, many are recruited by friends or family members and chose sex work over lower-paying service jobs in noodle shops or garment factories. In general, traffickers may be part of organized crime networks, or they may be relatives or even family members from poor villages. Molland notes that many traffickers are not even sophisticated about the market for sex workers (Molland 2012: 140). It is not unusual for sex workers themselves to become involved in trafficking as they get older (Kotiswaran 2008; Molland 2012; Warren 2012).

In many parts of the world, women who go into prostitution are seeking a better life, enticed by ideas of modernity and consumer goods. Many move into the sex trade to escape difficult situations such as abusive husbands, oppressive relatives, or simply grinding poverty. They may well recognize that they are taking risks but are desperate to improve their situation (Brennan 2014). Some go for adventure and the money they can earn. For example, my research assistant Vibhuti Ramachandran and I interviewed a woman in Kolkata, India, who left high school just before graduation, went with her boyfriend to Pakistan and the Gulf states to do sex work, then traveled back home. Here she persuaded a friend to go with her on another trip. Is this trafficking? In many rural villages, those who introduce women to the sex trade may be relatives, neighbors, or friends, as occurred in this case. Similarly, Cheng's study of Filipina entertainers in South Korea shows a complex series of paths by which women move into sexual labor, sometimes through friends or through their desire for money for consumer goods or to support their children (2010).

Ethnographic research also sheds light on the strategy of rescue. Rescue is often promoted as a solution for trafficked persons, particularly for women engaged in sex work, yet this mode of intervention fails to recognize the complexity of the trafficking situation that these ethnographies reveal. While the homogenizing approach of the *TIP Reports* makes rescue appear to be a reasonable solution, it does not take into account the many ways people become trafficked or the structural conditions that have produced their vulnerability to exploitation. Nevertheless, many of the prominent US antitrafficking groups, inspired by radical feminism and Christian evangelism, use the language of freedom to stage rescues from brothels and to restore women to their families, with whom they can be rehabilitated as workers (Bernstein 2007). For example, the International Justice Mission (IJM), one of the most prominent Christian antitrafficking organizations, offers both legal aid and rescues to both labor and sex trafficking victims. At this organization's annual Global Prayer Gathering, which I attended in 2014, this work was presented to supporters as dispelling the darkness from and bringing light to the lives of the victims. The IJM recognizes the importance of legal assistance as well as rescues, but rescues are a centerpiece of its work. After rescues, traffickers can be arrested and prosecuted.

Yet rescue homes may hold women in prisonlike conditions to protect them, prevent their return to sex work, rehabilitate or train them, and be sure that they testify against their traffickers. It is almost exclusively women and girls who are detained in shelters. Some are open and allow women to leave, while others are closed and hold women in semicaptivity (Gallagher and Pearson 2010: 78). Trafficking victims are sometimes held in closed shelters pending their return home, rehabilitation, and/or testimony against traffickers in order to protect them (see Cheng 2010: 196–97; Gallagher and Pearson 2010; Soderlund 2005: 66). Foreigners may be left in shelters pending repatriation. Rescue satisfies a savior mentality and the idea of home as the ideal place for a woman to be. Raids help keep shelters full, which looks good to the G/TIP office and brings in donor funding. By 2010, the US government had contributed more than $4 million to the IJM and its work with labor and sex trafficking victims focusing on rescues and legal aid to help victims prosecute traffickers (Chuang 2010: 1715).

Yet raids are difficult: women do not always wish to be rescued, and they often leave open shelters or escape from closed ones. We have little information about the rehabilitation dimensions of rescue work, as rescued women typically disappear. For example, Kay Warren reports that few Columbian women repatriated from Japan stay in shelters, while social service workers seeking to repatriate Columbian workers find that relatively few return to Columbia after working overseas in Japan or elsewhere (2010: 119–22; 2012). Nor has there been any mobilization of formerly trafficked women into a social movement in Columbia (Warren 2012: 111; see also 2007). Denise Brennan's research in the United States, however, finds that trafficking survivors are often very poor and struggle to get by, which does not allow them the time to organize (2014). Scattered evidence suggests that rescued sex workers often return to sex work. In Soderlund's study of rescues, for example, she reports that in Phnom Penh, Cambodia, one shelter manager said that 40 percent of women escape and return to sex work and that in Chiang Mai, Thailand, half of rescued women escaped from a shelter within one month (2005: 66). Anne Gallagher reports that in an open shelter in Cambodia, up to 70 percent of rescued women and girls choose to leave within two weeks (2010: 106, n. 156).

Even if women are repatriated to another country, many return, usually because of the same pressures that persuaded them to move in the first place. This tendency to return does not mean that these women would not prefer a different kind of work but that sex work may be the best available option, in contrast to low-paid factory or service work (see Molland 2012). Cheng's depiction of women's return home to the Philippines from South Korea shows clearly how the pressures of earning money to support children and family along with the desire for the consumer goods that mark modernity drive women back to migration for entertainment and sex work after coming home (Cheng 2010: 166–91). As these examples suggest, it can be difficult to distinguish between voluntary and coerced entrance into commercial sex, since people move into this work under varying degrees of coercion.

Finally, rescues confront the problem of distinguishing between trafficked victims and consenting prostitutes. Brothel raids in India only rescue women who did not consent, but this is hard to know, particularly in the tumult of a raid. One solution is to focus on "rescuing" children, who are legally unable to consent, but it is also hard to know the age of young people in many parts of the world where individuals lack reliable documentation of their age or are able to forge them. In my research with Vibhuti Ramachandran in India, we discussed with NGO activists the difficulties of determining the ages of rescued women. Few women have reliable birth certificates or identity documents. In Kolkata, the state and NGOs relied on bone ossification tests to determine a girl's age, using a doctor's signature to certify the truth of the test. However, this test cannot precisely pinpoint age and is accurate within only about a two-year time span. Thus it is impossible to precisely determine which women in a brothel are adults and could consent and which are children (under eighteen) and, by definition, cannot.

Alternative Frameworks for Trafficking

MODERN-DAY SLAVERY

In recent years, coerced and exploitative labor has been increasingly referred to as modern-day slavery. The *TIP Reports* conflate the two terms, treating them as the same. The first *TIP Report* in 2001 claimed that slavery is another name for trafficking (US Department of State 2001). The 2002 National Security Presidential Directive 22 pronounced the US government's opposition to prostitution and related activities and called trafficking in persons "a modern-day form of slavery" (Chuang 2010: 1680). Introducing the 2013 *TIP Report* eleven years later, President Obama urged nations to be concerned about "the injustice, the outrage, of human trafficking, which must be called by its true name — modern slavery" (September 25, 2012; US Department of State 2013d: 7).

The turn to the concept of slavery has produced yet another definition of trafficking and an ongoing debate about whether slaves and trafficking victims are the same. Kevin Bales has taken a leading role in merging trafficking and slavery. In counting slaves, Bales notes that "finding measurable variables is difficult with a phenomenon like slavery, which has an essential core but varies dramatically from place to place (and from time to time)" (2005: 91). He defines the essential core as three factors: the use of violence to control a person, the resulting loss of free will, and economic exploitation such that normally the person receives no compensation for his or her work (2005: 91). However, Anne Gallagher argues that this broad definition does not conform to the definition of slavery in international law (2009). In the 1926 Convention against Slavery, it is defined as the exercise of "any or all of the powers attached to the right of ownership" (Chuang 2005–2006: 1709). In contrast, Bales says, "At its most basic level, slavery is a social and economic relationship played out in systematic ways." He continues, "Slavery is a relationship between individuals (as is marriage, for example), but it exists primarily within communities and is governed by those communities (also like marriage)" (2005: 90–91). He emphasizes the power differential between slave and slaveholder and the importance of understanding slavery in its full social context. The expansion of the international law concept of slavery to a range of other forms of exploited labor undermines international law in Chuang's view (2010). She refers to this shift from trafficking to slavery as "exploitation creep" (Chuang 2014). Despite the ambiguity of the concept of slavery, in 2013, an antislavery NGO, the Walk Free Foundation, launched its Global Index on Modern Slavery, updated in 2014 with more numbers and country classifications (Walk Free Foundation 2013).

The *TIP Reports* have always used the phrase "modern-day slavery" to describe trafficking (US Department of State 2001: 2), but measuring slavery is different from the approach the *TIP Reports* take to measuring trafficking. The *TIP Reports* provide data on the number of victims but focus on measuring state efforts to combat trafficking. It is clearly easier to count the number of laws passed, training processes held, and special police stations created than it is to count the number of people living and working in exploited, illegal situations. Moreover, there is disagreement about what constitutes slavery. Orlando Patterson, an eminent scholar of slavery, disagrees with the definition used by Kevin Bales (see Bales 2005; 2012; Feingold 2010: 48–50; Patterson 2012). When the institution of slavery is legal and enforced by a state, for example, it is quite different from illegal slavery, which must remain hidden. The absence of a clear definition makes it hard to collect data in a systematic way (Bales 2005: 88).

The move to a focus on slavery rather than trafficking changes the measurement problem. Instead of counting individuals who are in exploitative labor because of a particular process of coercion or deceit, it focuses on counting individuals who are of the status of not being free to leave. While neither is easy to count, it is conceptually easier to count people of a status than people who have moved into a status through a particular process. Thus the demands of measurement may push activists toward adopting the slavery framework. It is also a more politically charged term with particular resonance in the United States and is thus valuable for gathering supporters and donors.

HUMAN RIGHTS

The United Nations has worked to develop a human rights approach to trafficking in recent years. In 2002, the OHCHR adopted a set of Recommended Principles and Guidelines on Human Rights and Human Trafficking (UN Office of the High Commissioner for Human Rights 2002). In August 2011, the UN special rapporteur on trafficking in persons, especially women and children, presented a report to the General Assembly that provided draft principles on the right to an effective remedy for trafficked persons (UN General Assembly 2011). In June 2012, the UN special rapporteur advocated a human-rights-based approach to the prosecution of trafficking in her annual report (UN Human

Rights Council 2012a). In July 2012, the Human Rights Council passed a resolution advocating access to effective remedies for trafficked persons and their right to an effective remedy for human rights violations (UN Human Rights Council 2012b).

The *TIP Reports* also refer to the human rights of victims, but because of the pressure to prosecute traffickers, victims' human rights are sometimes compromised. Prosecution often requires testimony from reluctant or frightened victims. Rescued victims may be held in protective shelters until they can testify, which can mean long periods of time in quasi-prison conditions. Many rescued victims fear testifying against their traffickers and seek to escape these shelters. Some women wish to testify, while others are held against their will pending trials and other court procedures. In a conversation Ramachandan and I had with representatives of a Christian group in India, for example, we were assured that rescued women were eager to testify against their traffickers and that the organization offered them training and support for testifying. On the other hand, some shelter homes are restrictive, and victims try to escape. The 2013 *TIP Report*'s country report for India describes abusive and carceral conditions for rescued women in shelter homes (US Department of State 2013d: 197). Ratna Kapur notes that in India, rescued women can be held in remand homes for long periods because of delays in medical examinations and court proceedings (Kapur 2007: 123).

Moreover, many countries allow victims to stay only if they participate in prosecuting their traffickers (Global Alliance against Traffic in Women 2007). In the United States, for example, trafficked persons are only eligible for immigration relief if they assist law enforcement or comply with "reasonable requests" to assist in the investigation and prosecution of their traffickers (Haynes 2006–2007; Huckerby 2007: 243). Similarly, Australia offers assistance and the right to remain only to those potentially useful in providing evidence to prosecute traffickers (Pearson 2007: 29). Sweden, a leader in criminalizing customers of sex workers, extends limited residence rights to trafficking victims willing to testify against their traffickers (Shamir in Halley et al. 2006: 396). The Netherlands offers an initial, short visa to a trafficked victim so she can decide if she will testify against her trafficker and a longer one to those who agree to testify that lasts until the end of the trial (Shamir in Halley et al. 2006: 399; see also Nelken 2011).

Indeed, feminist critics of the new regime of antitrafficking activism argue that it has increased the control that states exercise over women and their expressions of sexuality in the name of protecting women. Women moving across borders are more likely to be suspected of being trafficked than men

148

and, in order to protect them, are subjected to increased surveillance and even deportation (see Sharma 2005). The failure to develop a more nuanced understanding of trafficking and the overreliance on a single model for intervention can deeply disadvantage young women on the move by subjecting them to increased surveillance and control (see Agustin 2007). Sociologist Jennifer Musto argues that advocacy efforts to protect trafficked persons have been appropriated by the criminal justice system, merging the efforts of NGOs and law enforcement to create a regime of "carceral protection" that joins criminal justice and social service interventions (2011). The pressure the *TIP Reports* place on countries to convict traffickers increases the importance of holding victims as witnesses and subjects them to greater state control. Thus the indicator, with its emphasis on prosecution as the basis for ranking, has produced effects that are at odds with its own goals of protecting victims.

The Impact of the *Trafficking in Persons Reports*

To what extent are the *TIP Reports* effective in combating trafficking? Despite concerns that the reports have thin data, an overemphasis on prosecution, a unilateral approach to the problem, and a tendency to construe trafficking as a moral panic (Chuang 2005–2006; Gallagher 2001; 2006a; 2006b; US Government Accountability Office 2006; Weitzer 2007), US pressure has encouraged countries to take stronger action against trafficking and has empowered activists within countries to mobilize. Even some of the reports' critics, such as Anne Gallagher, acknowledge that they have raised the visibility of the problem and led to some positive changes (2011). Gallagher and Holmes point out that despite their unilateralism and weak data, the *TIP Reports* have had considerable influence on national antitrafficking responses (2008: 319). States have passed new laws, amended existing laws, and developed some new policies, although some have also resisted and resented US pressure. The sanctions regime has clearly raised the visibility of the issue and induced some governments to develop new legislation and initiatives, even though these are sometimes based more on TIP requirements than on what makes sense for individual countries (see also Chuang 2005–2006: 489–90). As has occurred with other indicators, the reports have contributed to the development of an international consensus that something called "human trafficking" exists and is a problem, as well as some agreement about how to address it (Gallagher and Holmes 2008: 320). In their recent study of trafficking, Kelley and Simmons have found that inclusion in the *TIP Reports* and shaming by being placed on the Tier 2 Watch List or in Tier 3 are correlated with the criminalization of trafficking (Kelley and Simmons 2015).

As a major donor with considerable influence on stakeholders and their ideas of how to define success, the United States has had a significant impact on the way activists and organizations define trafficking (Gallagher and Surtees 2012: 17). By 2005, the United States had spent $295 million combating trafficking in 120 countries, making it the largest source of antitrafficking funds globally (Chuang 2005–2006: 470: n. 162). The *TIP Reports*, with their threat of sanctions, are "highly influential" in this field (Gallagher and Pearson 2010: 76, n. 11). Trafficking in persons has been a major foreign-policy issue for the United States, particularly for the George W. Bush administration (2000–2008), which spent $100 million per year on domestic and international trafficking — perhaps more than any other country (Soderlund 2005: 67). With a system of carrots and sticks, the United States offers rewards in the forms of grants to antitrafficking NGOs and sanctions on countries that fail to work on improving their trafficking records. The United States acts, in effect, as a "global sheriff" (Chuang 2005–2006). According to Janie Chuang and Anne Gallagher, two leading academic experts on global trafficking, "By placing itself squarely at the centre of knowledge production and global governance, the United States government has been able to play a pivotal role in global anti-trafficking efforts with its primary instrument, the TIP Reports, exercising a profound influence over the way in which states and others understand and respond to trafficking" (Gallagher and Chuang 2012: 342). Some experts say that these reports constitute the most far reaching and comprehensive global review of human trafficking undertaken by a government (Laczko and Gramegna 2003: 179). To a significant extent, trafficking is what the *TIP Reports* measure.

The *TIP Reports* have had a substantial global influence. Chuang notes that they have led to an "unprecedented number" of states adopting antitrafficking legislation and developing domestic infrastructure to meet US minimum standards in order to avoid US sanctions (Chuang 2005–2006: 464). She argues that states have passed laws and changed policies in order to avoid sanctions (2005–2006). The *TIP Reports* have had a major impact on protecting and supporting victims, on questioning the fairness of holding victims in shelters, and on drawing attention to the problem of forced labor more generally (Gallagher and Chuang 2012: 339–40). Through this mechanism of information gathering, evaluation, and ranking, the United States has exercised "disproportionate influence" (Gallagher and Chuang 2012: 335). Gallagher and Chuang comment that it appears, from their contacts with countries and activists, that the rankings, more than the country reports, have had an influence — a judgment confirmed by my own ethnographic observations of antitrafficking activists (Gallagher and Chuang 2012: 331). While there are other international initiatives, the United States stands out for its sizeable investment in this issue.

The *TIP Reports* appear to have influenced both legislation and policy in many countries. In Latin America, many governments have adopted anti-trafficking laws modeled on the TVPA, rather than laws designed for local concerns, in response to the *TIP Reports'* demands to comply with its standards (Quinn 2008: 128). Countries concerned about their reputations — particularly if tourism is a major industry, as in Costa Rica or Jamaica — worry about poor rankings. Such worries may inspire them to avoid producing accurate data in order to escape a low-tier ranking (Quinn 2008: 128). Japan developed an action plan and started to enforce some of its laws further (Warren 2010: 119–20), while both Laos and Thailand increased their policing efforts and international agreements in response to US pressure by means of the *TIP Reports* (Molland 2012: 13–14, 197). In 2006, Japan cut entertainer visas for Filipinas as part of its antitrafficking efforts in response to US pressure (Cheng 2010: 220). Australia changed its criminal law in part because of the *TIP Reports* (Pearson 2007: 32).

Israel responded to the pressures of the TVPA, US law, and US feminists by passing an amendment to its 2000 Penal Code that criminalized sex trafficking (Halley et al. 2006: 362). In 2001, Israel was placed in Tier 3, but in light of the economic consequences of this tier placement, the Israeli government began to take the problem more seriously. Once a parliamentary committee was convened on trafficking of women, Israel was rewarded with an upgrade to Tier 2 (Halley et al. 2006: 363–64). Hila Shamir argues that the Tier 3 placement enabled politically powerful feminists in Israel to become visible (Halley et al. 2006: 364; Shamir 2012).

When South Korea was ranked in Tier 3 in 2001, along with Burma, Sudan, and Albania, it was embarrassing to the country, which saw itself as promoting human rights and gender equality. Cheng argues that this encouraged the country to take up the problem of trafficking, defined by its government as one of prostitution, and to pass new laws against it in 2004. The 2002 *TIP Report* moved South Korea to Tier 1 and declared it a country of International Best Practices in 2005 (2010: 201–2, 207–8), even though a closer look at South Korea's laws and policies suggests that it did not actually fulfill the minimum standards of the TVPA during that time period (Weiss 2012: 325–29). US foreign policy's emphasis on trafficking has succeeded in establishing it as a major issue for reform and in promoting a criminal justice response.

A Case Study of India

A closer look at the impact of the *TIP Reports* in India highlights the way they exert pressure on powerful states with significant numbers of trafficked people.

In order to examine India's reaction to the *TIP Reports* in greater detail, Ramachandran spent two summers, in 2009 and 2010, doing ethnographic research in India with antitrafficking NGOs, women's organizations, police, and government officials to assess responses to the reports. I joined her for some of this ethnographic research in 2010. Ramachandran's work provides much of the ethnographic material in this section.

Overall, the reports empower some nonstate groups over others, foster certain programs and approaches to trafficking while marginalizing others, and elicit attention as well as resentment from state actors. They strengthen antitrafficking groups, separate them from sex-worker organizations, encourage police intervention, and generate some resistance and hostility from government officials who do not think the United States should be telling India what to do. It appears that Indian government officials experience the *TIP Reports* as finger pointing or as threats. Some government officials say they are adamant about following what the Indian government wants, not what the US government wants. The *TIP Reports* are sometimes described by NGO activists as imperialist, mostly talk, patronizing, and lacking in respect for them. Some antitrafficking activists appreciate the pressure on governments the reports generate but also express some skepticism about their effects. According to one, the reports put pressure on India to act, but the result is often tokenism. Another leader of an antitrafficking organization complained that filling out the questionnaires was time consuming and of little use, since they narrow down all the information into one indicator, which does not describe a country as large and diverse as India. This person said that the *TIP Reports* have little standing with the Indian government, in part because they focus on convictions rather than prevention, while domestic reports and organizations, such as a major report by India's National Human Rights Commission or the views of its Central Social Welfare Board, do have influence.

Many of those interviewed who were working in the antitrafficking area preferred the UN approach, which is more collaborative. The UNODC has played an important role in supporting criminal justice interventions for trafficking such as the Anti-Human Trafficking Units (AHTUs) of the Indian police. On the other hand, a police officer who played a prominent role in the antitrafficking movement said that although the Indian government does not accept the *TIP Reports*, it indirectly is an indicator for them.

India has taken steps to control trafficking based on domestic mobilization as well as international pressure from the United Nations and the United States. India was listed on the Tier 2 Watch List in 2004 for its failure to work on labor trafficking and only moved to Tier 2 in 2011 — a position it continued to hold in 2012 and 2013. When Ramachandran met with US embassy officials in India and Indian NGOs in 2009, the embassy staff emphasized that it wanted to help India move up to Tier 2 and that Washington was mostly concerned with prosecution rates. They talked about having to explain to Washington that the Indian judicial system moves slowly. India subsequently ratified both the convention against organized crime and the Palermo Protocol in 2011 (UN Office of Drugs and Crime 2013: 3).

The narrative report for India in the 2013 *TIP Report* focused in particular on labor trafficking, although it also argued that sex trafficking was widespread. On the positive side, it noted the passage of the Criminal Law Amendments Act of 2013, which amended Section 370 of the Indian Penal Code so that "all forms of labor trafficking and most forms of sex trafficking" became prohibited and penalized with sufficiently stringent penalties (US Department of State 2013d: 196). It also commended the further development of AHTUs for law enforcement and rehabilitation. However, the report noted that the amended Section 370 did not define the prostitution of a child under age eighteen in the absence of coercive means as trafficking, contradicting the standard of the Palermo Protocol. It also complained about a lack of effective enforcement of antitrafficking laws, especially for labor trafficking, and a failure to address official complicity in trafficking.

Although India's Immoral Traffic Prevention Act (ITPA) prohibited sex trafficking, the report noted that it also criminalized prostitution and was often used to prosecute prostitutes, at least some of whom are sex trafficking victims. It complained about the government's failure to provide statistics on antitrafficking efforts and noted that official crime data from the National Crimes Record Bureau did not disaggregate data on trafficking, nor did it specify the number of investigations, prosecutions, and convictions for trafficking. The TIP narrative relied instead on information from publicly available criminal records and NGO reports. It labeled government efforts as piecemeal and uncoordinated, and said that the prioritization of trafficking decreased over the previous year (US Department of State 2013d: 195–96).

The 2013 *TIP Report*'s recommendations included ceasing to penalize victims of human trafficking, increasing prosecutions and convictions for all forms of trafficking including bonded labor, and providing greater support for AHTUs, fast-track courts for traffickers, shelter homes, and rehabilitation of victims (2013d: 196). Thus the focus of this report, congruent with the underlying theory of the TIP project, was on law enforcement activities as well as decriminalizing victims and providing preventive information to potential victims. While there was reference to the human rights of victims, this was not the central focus of the report, nor was there any analysis of structural conditions that might produce trafficking. Despite the attention to labor trafficking, the country narrative did not recommend changes in labor laws or other forms of labor regulation except to note a lack of effective enforcement of the Bonded Labor System Abolition Act (US Department of State 2013d: 196).

It is unclear what impact the US effort has had in India. In comparison to some smaller countries in the region that passed new antitrafficking laws or developed new policies, India's response was less direct. As Kotiswaran argues, it is important not to overemphasize the impact of the international in India. Rather than seeing its role as determinative, it is more accurate to see it as a resource within national political struggles (Halley et al. 2006: 376; Kotiswaran 2011a). Kotiswaran thinks it is likely that the TIP project deepened the divide between sex-worker organizations and antitrafficking groups, since US intervention supported antitrafficking groups but not sex-worker organizations.

One of the ways in which the *TIP Reports* affect India's approach to trafficking is through the organizations the United States funds. Indian antitrafficking work gets some funding from USAID, either directly or through UNIFEM (now called UN Women) and UNODC, in addition to direct funding from the G/TIP office. NGOs favoring the legalization of sex work do not receive US funding, while those promoting an abolitionist position, including US church-based organizations, are more often funded.

Several people Ramachandran and I interviewed in India, particularly government officials, revealed resistance and even resentment about US judgment of India's performance in antitrafficking work. However, some also speculate that US pressure contributed to domestic policy initiatives such as efforts to criminalize customers and to develop antitrafficking police stations. It is clear that the United States exerts influence in India by funding prominent antitrafficking NGOs through the G/TIP office. These groups contribute to a government policy of rescue and prosecution, in which NGOs and law enforcement personnel work closely together to rescue and rehabilitate women who are coerced or duped into prostitution. This collaboration also includes the UNODC, which orchestrated the formation of AHTUs, in partnership with certain state governments and NGOs, with some funding from USAID. These groups form part of the Central Advisory Committee to Combat Trafficking for Commercial Sexual Exploitation, instituted by India's Ministry of Women and Child Development (MWCD). In all these legislative and policy-making initiatives, it is antitrafficking organizations rather than sex workers' unions whose work and perspectives are taken into account. Our interviews with NGOs in 2010 suggested that those with an abolitionist approach were more likely to be contacted by the US embassy's personnel for information for the report than those with a sex-worker orientation.

US pressure may also have contributed to a proposed 2006 amendment to the ITPA. Some scholars and activists suspect that this proposed amendment was designed to raise India out of its position in the Tier 2 Watch List, but there is no clear evidence (Halley et al. 2006: 375–76; Kapur 2007). Kotiswaran says that it is commonly believed that the government pursued this amendment with urgency in relation to its TIP rankings and that whether or not one believes this, the belief has had an effect on the academics, activists, and NGOs in this field (2011b). The proposed ITPA amendment followed a strategy of partial decriminalization rather than either legalization or full criminalization. Criminalization is the strategy generally adopted by countries responding to US pressure (Kotiswaran 2011a: 190). In contrast, the proposed amendment criminalized customers of sex trafficking victims, broadly defined, while seeking to decriminalize the sex workers (Kotiswaran 2011a: 190–91). Supported by many antitrafficking groups, the proposed amendment advocated more stringent punishments for traffickers and brothel owners as well as the criminalization of clients. The Ministry of Women and Child Development, which introduced the proposed ITPA amendment bill, regularly invited antitrafficking NGOs to contribute to the proposal for the new bill and to the National Plan of Action to Combat Trafficking. Thus the proposed bill took a crime prevention approach to trafficking, decriminalizing prostitutes and reframing them as victims but not recognizing them as workers with rights. Some sex-worker and public health groups opposed the amendment. It subsequently lapsed in Parliament and, as of 2014, had not moved forward.

There are some indications that the Indian government resists US pressure. Ratna Kapur argues that the *TIP Reports* have been an important source of external pressure on India to change its laws and policies about trafficking but that the tier placements are "regarded with considerable suspicion by some state and non-state actors, as they are frequently based on criteria that has little to do with trafficking" (2007: 128). The Indian government's failure to provide law enforcement data for the 2013 *TIP Report* also suggests resistance to scrutiny. A discussion about the *TIP Reports* during a question-and-answer session of the Indian Parliament in 2009 indicated more explicit resistance. In response to a question posed to the home minister about the report the minister, Shri P. Chidambaram replied,

> Sir, I cannot stop an American Government's agency submitting a report to the American Congress. We do not take cognisance of that report. And,

I do not see any reason why we should feel that we have been defamed. In the Tier II Watch List, along with India, there are 52 other countries. They have included China, Russia, Argentina, Egypt, Pakistan, Sri Lanka and Bangladesh. So, I do not think we need to attach too much importance. Nevertheless, the problem is a problem in India; human trafficking is indeed a problem in India. We should address it in our own self-interest and we are addressing it. I have set out the various measures that we are taking to address the problem of human trafficking. We should do it as an enlightened nation, not because somebody else points it out to us. (India 2009: 48–49, answer to question no. 65)

Another questioner began,

Sir, the assertion of the Government that they do not take cognisance of a report made in the U.S. is very pleasant to hear when normally, we see that the Government is very sensitive to the U.S. judgement about us and goes out apologising to them for things that did not . . .

MR. CHAIRMAN: Question, please.
SHRI BALAVANT ALIAS BAL APTE: Therefore, I do compliment the Minister for this that they will not be influenced by what the U.S. tells us about us, but will come to their own conclusion. The information which such a report gives, like knowledge, is usable and should be used and my question is: in so far as the trafficking within the country is concerned, has the Government taken any steps to curb trafficking through the means of marriage? We have centres where this is being done on a large scale, when people from Arab countries come to Miraz, to Aurangabad, to Nanded, marry girls and take them away, and in the same manner, in several other centres in this country, people hunt for brides and they purchase women for the purposes of marriage. (2009: 50)

In response to questions about whether India would develop a new, more comprehensive law on trafficking, the home minister responded that the Ministry of Women and Child Development was working on an amendment to ITPA and that he would wait to see how that developed. This question-and-answer session in the Indian Parliament reveals that there is resistance to US pressure on India's legislation and policy but that the *TIP Reports* do draw attention to the problem and demand some kind of government response. It has become part of the national political debate over how to manage trafficking.

An official in the Home Ministry, interviewed by Ramachandran, expressed similar resistance, saying, "It is our internal problem." This person agreed with the *Reports'* strong criminal justice approach to the problem, but said that the *TIP Reports* are "a stick from above" and that "wielding the stick is *our* job." When asked about the data NGOs provide, the official noted that they can be opportunistic and need to keep an issue alive but that they also do good work. It is clear from India's country narrative in the 2013 *TIP Report* that NGOs have contributed significantly to the text, often complaining about state inaction and complicity with trafficking and state failure to enforce laws and follow through with policies (US Department of State 2013d: 196–98). In the absence of significant information from the government, the *TIP Report*'s narrative presents an NGO perspective and tends to highlight NGO accomplishments alongside state indifference and incapacity.

In interviews with another senior official in the Home Ministry, Ramachandran was told that the designation of India in the Tier 2 Watch List was very arbitrary and that the official had informed the US embassy staff that the interviewee was unhappy about it, mainly because there was not a trafficking problem between the United States and India. Although India has ratified the UN Transnational Organized Crime Convention and the Palermo Protocol, it objects to the US approach. The official said that the Indian government works with the UN, especially the UNODC, in a more collaborative way. As the official argued, India is a "sovereign" and "enlightened" country that had "provisions enshrined in [their] constitution," and they are "making [their] own efforts," following the general line of the Home Ministry. When asked about data collection, this person said that the US embassy had contacted the Home Ministry but that the embassy does not listen to the government — only to NGOs who provide inflated information in order to foster funding. It is the case that several antitrafficking NGOs in India have received funding from the G/TIP office. In 2012, the G/TIP office funded two NGOs in India, Free the Slaves and Shakti Vahini, each for about $500,000 (US Department of State 2012) and in the past has funded other antitrafficking NGOs, such as Apne Aap.

Moreover, the Home Ministry official pointed out that the trafficking situation in India is very complex, with considerable internal migration and women who enter the sex trade through family, neighbor, and friend connections, as well as because of "absurd customs" (perhaps here referring to caste-based work) and organized crime. There are complicating issues such as communities with long traditions of sex work. It is quite complex and could not be "a blanket sort of a thing." The official asked, "Can they understand what the factors are? Uniformity is an obsession in the West, I think — in Europe and the US. They only look at things that way." The official thinks policing is only one approach and is too narrow to encompass the wider problem. In addition to policing, this person advocates approaches such as local council registers and vigilance committees while pointing out that the problem is complicated in India, where most of the trafficking is internal.

Another senior Home Ministry official said in a 2009 interview that trafficking is connected with poverty, social values, and culture, and it is illustrative of society. But this person emphasized the criminal nature of trafficking and the importance of addressing it and pointed to the AHTU scheme, a collaborative project between India and the UNODC through which India has trained ten thousand police officers, prosecutors, and members of the judiciary in five states. The United States has contributed to funding pilot projects for the AHTUs, suggesting that such contributions foster support for the US position, particularly when they build on local initiatives.

Despite this resistance, US pressure through the *TIP Reports* has had an impact on the domestic situation in India, particularly in the way it empowers some perspectives over others. Writing in a collaborative article in 2006, Prabha Kotiswaran argues that the *TIP Reports'* antiprostitution stance and the G/TIP office's funding of only abolitionist NGOs has drawn sharp lines between those who want to abolish sex work and sex trafficking and those who do not take such an absolutist stance (Halley et al. 2006: 370–71). Although reform had been under discussion for the past twenty years, the threat of demotion to the Tier 2 Watch List fostered reform but also drew a sharp line between abolitionists and those ambivalent about this absolutist stance. At the local level, abolitionism fostered closer surveillance of women and girls, ostensibly to prevent their being trafficked into sex work (Kotiswaran 2011a: 7–8). It appears that the US system of ranking and sanctions exerts mostly indirect effects, working through existing organizations and the state and the balance among them.

The *Trafficking in Persons Report* as an Indicator

The *TIP Reports* create a composite indicator by merging a country's performance on several measures into a single tier status. As the authors of the rankings acknowledge, converting a wide array of information into a single score is not easy and is best understood as an art and a matter of judgment rather than a simple product of metrics. As is the case with all composite indicators, tier status provides a powerful, simple assessment that catches the attention of governments and publics. On the other hand, it merges a wide diversity of situations, country conditions, and policies together and can be misleading. Even though India is working on sex trafficking, for example, its tier status is lower because it is not also working on labor trafficking. This nuance disappears in its assignment to a tier. Such simplification can create skepticism and resentment, but it is powerful. It is the tier ranks, rather than the more detailed country narratives, that catch attention and galvanize action.

The *TIP Reports* constitute an example of a unilateral indicator supported by a powerful sponsor. They were far less collaborative in their creation than either of the other two indicators the book examines. They are not based on developing international norms or building cooperative international relationships but instead on the threat of sanctions and the reputational risks of having poor rankings (Chuang 2005–2006; Mattar 2003). The US government decided for itself how to define trafficking and what it considered good practices for controlling trafficking. It established these as the standards against which other countries were to be judged. The TVPA and the *TIP Reports* it created are not the products of international consensus, as the UN Palermo Protocol is, but acts of the US Congress. The US government has supported this indicator with considerable resources, both by funding antitrafficking NGOs around the world, and by exerting foreign-policy pressure. Thus the indicator's success in drawing attention to the problem of trafficking around the world is a combination of its ability to render the problem knowable through reporting and ranking and the institutional support of a powerful country. It has achieved visibility, compliance, and resentment.

Like other indicators, the *TIP Reports* draw on previous templates in their construction of a measurement system. Building on the preexisting framework of a drug trafficking measurement system, they adopt a similar criminal justice approach that holds states accountable for their efforts to prosecute drug traffickers. Since human trafficking is modeled on drug trafficking, there is a tendency to emphasize the agency of the traffickers rather than that of the trafficked goods, or persons. In general, indicators define and measure new problems through the lens of past measurement systems as the genealogical approach makes clear.

Despite the great diversity of situations in which people move into coercive and exploitative labor situations, the *TIP Reports* convert trafficking into a coherent and commensurable phenomenon. They simplify the problem enough to make it visible to nonexperts and have succeeded well in this endeavor. Yet they ignore the myriad paths to labor exploitation and the diverse situations in which victims find themselves. They deny the possibility of consenting to risky options and promote a flat understanding of coercion that fails to recognize how people can and do exercise some agency in the midst of exploitation. The *TIP Reports* assume that all trafficking is hard trafficking—done by organized crime networks — rather than the soft trafficking of family members, relatives, and neighbors, which can include a mixture of coercion and consent (Cheng 2010; Global Alliance against Traffic in Women 2007; Nederstigt and Almeida 2007: 99).

Moreover, the *TIP Reports* interpret trafficking as a dyadic relationship between a trafficker and an innocent and coerced victim while ignoring the structural violence that creates this dyadic relationship. Instead of talking about the lives of poor women and low-status individuals, regional and global economic inequality, or migration regulations that force migrants to travel illegally and increase their vulnerability, the *TIP Reports* define the problem as the product of criminal behavior. They do not touch the forms of inequality based on class, caste, race, and gender that often lie behind patterns of coercion into migration and forced labor.

Yet in order to count and compare, such stripped-down and homogenized categories are essential. If the *TIP Reports* are to compare countries, they have to adopt a uniform template for defining trafficking and analyzing state compliance. The process of commensuration is essential for quantification — its strength as well as its weakness. While such homogenization is essential for rendering trafficking commensurate and constructing a concept that can cross boundaries, it may not provide a good basis for policy.

As is the case with all composite indicators, the *TIP Reports* have an embedded theory of the nature of the problem and its solution. Although they advocate victim/witness protection and prevention and discuss these issues in the country narratives, the *TIP Reports* measure primarily law enforcement efforts and rates of prosecution. The focus of the reports is these numbers and the way they shape tier rankings (see Friman 2010: 105). Instead of measuring the effectiveness of countries' efforts to diminish trafficking, for which there are no adequate data, the reports assess cooperation with the United States in data provision and compliance with US standards for state activities (Friman 2010: 105). Like the narcotics control program, this ranking system does not measure the flows themselves but government efforts and cooperation with the US framework. And just as the phenomenon of trafficking is homogenized, so are the possible solutions.

Conclusions

As a dominant measurement system promoted by a powerful actor and major donor, the *TIP Reports* define the phenomenon of trafficking. Consequently, what trafficking is, is what the US State Department measures: a problem of organized crime, in which a person is forced or tricked into exploitative labor or prostitution by criminal actors. The solution is then, inevitably, a criminal justice one. The police, the state, and businesses are construed as allies of the victim, the sexual desires of clients, often assumed to be deviant individuals, as the cause of their suffering, and the rescue and return to home of victims and the punishment of traffickers as the solution (Chuang 2005–2006: 1703). The proposed criminal justice solution of the *TIP Reports* assumes a reliable, honest, and effective police force and judiciary, even though these are often lacking.

This model could be improved by a broader, more structural analysis of the process of trafficking and its causes and a more nuanced analysis of how trafficking of the kind presented by ethnographic research happens. The present approach ignores the roles of companies seeking cheaper labor, migrants far from home seeking sexual services, lax labor regulations, rigid border controls, the human rights of the victims, and many other factors. It lumps together the person who is sold and tricked with the migrant searching for a better life or a wealthier husband, the child whose parents no longer wish to or can support him or her, the person who borrows heavily to weather a health disaster or family celebration, the single mother seeking money to support her children, and the person trapped in an abusive marriage or hostile family situation. All these people move more or less unwillingly into exploitative labor situations or prostitution, but not necessarily through the agency of organized criminals or through deception or force.

The *TIP Reports'* system of measurement fails to recognize this complexity in the construction of its objects: the trafficker and the trafficked victim. As is characteristic of measurement systems, it focuses on a few core features to make victims commensurate and subtracts the contexts within which these transactions take place. As a result, trafficking is seen as a dyadic exchange between trafficker and victim rather than as a set of social relationships and overarching political, economic, and social structures. By failing to adequately measure the object of intervention, this approach to knowledge will inevitably fail to support nuanced forms of intervention. The ethnographic studies of trafficking and trafficking victims show the limitations of the knowledge provided by the *TIP Reports*, despite their contribution to bringing significant international visibility to the problem.

Human Rights Indicators

Translating Law into Policy

"This will be a frank and constructive dialogue," began the chair of the committee that monitors the International Covenant on Economic, Social, and Cultural Rights (ICESCR) as he opened a hearing to assess Turkey's compliance with this major human rights treaty in May 2011. He was speaking to the six representatives from Turkey who sat together behind a raised desk at the front of an elegant room in the Palais Wilson in Geneva overlooking the lake and the Swiss Alps beyond. The committee used the report Turkey provided to assess its performance in living up to the terms of the treaty it had ratified. During the hearing, committee members grilled the country representatives about how well their country had done in complying with the convention. The eighteen-person committee spent most of the nine hours of the hearing peppering the Turkish delegation with questions, some of which were quite pointed.

Many offered critiques based on the statistics provided in the country report. For example, one member asked, "Why do you have no laws on discrimination against minorities, particularly the Kurdish minority? The Turkish statistical office says that the Kurdish region has a lower proportion of women who work, higher maternal mortality rates, and lower health indicators than the rest of the country." Many asked for more statistics, disaggregated by gender, race, urban versus rural residence, and other possible grounds for discrimination. For example, one expert noted that the report said two-thirds of Turkish households had modern sanitation, but what about special populations, such as the disabled and the elderly? Another expert asked for data on mental health disaggregated by year to see if there had been an increase or a decrease. "Data by themselves we can't monitor," he said. "We need the differentiation."

This hearing is part of a mechanism through which the United Nations assesses compliance with the terms of human rights treaties that countries have ratified. Clearly, numbers are essential to this process. Each major human rights convention is monitored by a committee of experts who examine the extent to which countries are complying with the treaty. The system of human rights conventions developed by the United Nations is a multilateral treaty regime with expert committees authorized to receive periodic performance reports from countries that have ratified the convention. The committees, called treaty bodies, hold hearings to discuss and respond to country reports and issue concluding comments indicating areas of progress and problems yet to be resolved. Since 2006, this system has been augmented by the Universal Periodic Review mechanism of the Human Rights Council (see Charlesworth and Larking 2015), but the conventions and their oversight committees remain the heart of the human rights system. During the 1980s and 1990s, treaty bodies developed their jurisprudence and working methods, gradually claiming more power and a stronger critical voice with relation to the countries — called "states parties" — they were monitoring. For example, since 1992, the Human Rights Committee, which monitors the International Covenant on Civil and Political Rights (ICCPR), has issued concluding observations that sometimes express the committee's "concern" or "deep concern" about state actions (e.g., Kretzmer 2010: 30).

Information is at the heart of this process. The central challenge of human rights monitoring is acquiring accurate information in order to assess compliance and identify failure. Numbers provide a way of assessing performance against the standards set by human rights laws. They promise to make the process of monitoring state compliance more efficient and less costly than a more qualitative examination of the conditions of vulnerable populations. The translation of human rights norms into indicators clarifies and specifies obligations, thus enhancing technologies of accountability. At the same time, this translation shifts human rights from a legal discourse with a broad and flexible vision of justice and rights to a technocratic one of economics and management. Indicators transform abstract legal concepts into specific policy prescriptions. Human rights indicators are one dimension of the dance — or duel — of control over information between treaty bodies and states that defines the human rights monitoring process.

This chapter examines a project of the Office of the High Commissioner for Human Rights (OHCHR) to develop indicators to measure core human rights. Between 2005 and 2012, a committee of experts, including human rights lawyers, development economists, and statisticians, worked together to produce a set of indicators to measure rights such as the right to health and the right to life. This project joined lawyers who wanted to improve compliance with human rights laws with economists who sought to make human rights more understandable outside the legal world. The result was a set of indicators that presented human rights ideas within the framework of economic development. Preliminary versions of this set of indicators were released in 2006 and 2008 (UN International Human Rights Instruments and Office of the High Commissioner for Human Rights 2006; 2008), and the final report and guidelines were published in 2012 (UN Office of the High Commissioner for Human Rights 2012a).

The experts who wrote the indicators thought that framing human rights norms in economic terms would facilitate their circulation across national boundaries and make them more accessible to policy planners. As they argued in the final report, "Policymakers, development and sometimes even human rights practitioners find it difficult to link these concepts with implementation practices" (UN Office of the High Commissioner for Human Rights 2012a: 14). The final report concluded that treaty interpretation would remain a primarily legal exercise, but "its quality can . . . be improved by securing the best possible factual basis for it. Moreover, quantitative indicators can potentially contribute to bridging the human rights discourse and the development policy discourse" (UN Office of the High Commissioner for Human Rights 2012a: 26). The indicators convert broad normative statements about justice and rights into specific, measurable policies and programs. The guidelines, standards, declarations, and recommendations that make up international human rights law are reframed in the language of targets and goals that can be measured.

In order to convert the principles of human rights treaties into indicators, the experts borrowed templates and theories of social change from development planning. They translated human rights standards into numbers, imported public health and management models of assessment, and presented the indicators in single-page grids. By tracing the genealogy of the OHCHR indicators, this chapter shows how they were formed, with what interpretive strategies, and according to which underlying theories of social change. In the long trajectory of indicator development, past measurement systems, frameworks, and theories are used to create new indicators. Here the templates and theories of social change came from development planning and management.

Despite apparent gains in efficiency and effectiveness due to converting the broad standards of human rights treaties into numbers, however, these indicators seem to be a technology in search of an audience.

Measuring Rights?

There are significant debates within the human rights community about the value of indicators for assessing compliance. Many human rights lawyers, activists, and academics hope to add to the specificity of human rights, increase compliance, and enhance state accountability. They also hope to improve the authority and efficiency of the human rights monitoring system. Others argue that identifying human rights violations requires legal judgments, not statistical patterns. It is up to lawyers, not social scientists using numbers, to decide when legal documents such as human rights treaties have been violated (Kalantry et al. 2010: 259).

Theoretically, since human rights are based on universal norms articulated in conventions, they are amenable to standardized measurement and the use of indicators (Green 2001). The treaty bodies are tasked with evaluating state performance against these universal standards. However, in other ways, human rights analysis and monitoring are deeply incompatible with indicators, particularly composite indicators that assign single numbers or ranks to the aggregate performance of a country. Many in the human rights community are skeptical about the value of indicators for measuring human rights. Human rights monitoring focuses on the conditions of the most vulnerable and advocates specific policies and laws to ameliorate those conditions. Thus the analysis is typically historically and contextually specific. In the past, human rights documentation has been largely qualitative and based on legal cases rather than metrics, particularly in the area of civil and political rights (Langford and Fukuda-Parr 2012: 222). Assessing human rights violations depends on a legal analysis of conventions and their terms. Many civil and political rights are very difficult to count and measure. States that engage in widespread torture or extrajudicial killings rarely keep careful records of this behavior; there is also no global consensus on what torture is. Numbers are not determinative. One tortured person is enough; one extrajudicial killing is a violation. There is no need to count and measure.

Nevertheless, over the last thirty years, human rights NGOs, political scientists, and UN agencies have worked to develop tools for measuring human rights, using events data, survey data, standards-based assessments, and administrative data (Landman and Carvalho 2010). Human rights quantification has primarily focused on compliance, but it has also been used for advocacy and for developing social science theories of human rights. There is a growing movement among human rights activists, government donors, NGOs, and development agencies such as the World Bank to develop a human-rights-based approach to development (Kindornay et al. 2012; McInerney-Lankford and Sano 2010).

Since the 1970s and 1980s, academics and NGOs have built several popular indicators for human rights. Freedom House, established in 1941, provides annual measures of "freedom in the world," scoring countries as free, partly free, and not free (www.freedomhouse.org; see Bradley 2015). The Political Terror Scale, adapted from the "political terror" scale in the 1980 *Freedom House Yearbook*, was started at Purdue University in the early 1980s (www.politicalterrorscale.org; Wood and Gibney 2010: 398). The Cingranelli-Richards Human Rights Data Set (CIRI) was initiated in 1994 at the State University of New York at Binghamton (Cingranelli and Richards 2010: 404; Cingranelli-Richards Human Rights Data Set n.d.; see Landman and Carvalho 2010) and terminated in 2014, according to David Richards. The latter two both code data from the annual reports from Amnesty International and the US State Department's *Country Reports on Human Rights Practices*. Both focus on civil and political rights. More recently, Fukuda-Parr, Randolf, and Lawson-Remer have developed the Economic and Social Rights Fulfillment Index to measure economic and social rights. The index combines subscores for six core rights (rights to health, education, food, housing, social security, and decent work) and sums these into an aggregate score. It then produces a measure that links performance to state capacity, recognizing that poorer states can do less for their populations. Thus the index provides a rigorous way to monitor state compliance with the core economic and social rights on the basis of the "progressive realization" principle (Fukuda-Parr 2011: 84; Fukuda-Parr et al. 2009; Fukuda-Parr et al. 2015; Randolf et al. 2010; Randolf and Guyer 2012).

THE PROMISE OF HUMAN RIGHTS INDICATORS

Indicators promise to help with two major challenges facing treaty bodies: acquiring accurate information on state compliance and translating the broad, often vague, terms of the treaty into specific policies, programs, and outcomes that make sense in the particular context and history of a country. Treaty bodies need information on country performance that is reliable, extensive, and applicable to the requirements of the treaty. If governments provide systematic, accurate data on their programs and policies and disaggregated statistics about the conditions of a variety of vulnerable populations, treaty bodies will find it easier to assess compliance. Treaty bodies also look at reports from civil society, called "shadow reports," and hold sessions where national and international NGO representatives can offer information. They receive reports from UN agencies and other intergovernmental bodies, as well as academics and the press. The Committee on the Rights of the Child, for example, receives substantial support from UNICEF and its major international survey, the Multiple Indicator Cluster Survey (MICS). MICS surveys are carried out by UNICEF in conjunction with states in part to assess states' performances with regard to the terms of the Convention on the Rights of the Child (CRC). Nevertheless, there is a continual struggle between the demands for information that a treaty body needs in order to assess performance and the information that a country is able or willing to share.

Indicators offer an appealing solution. Systematized information disaggregated into categories that are important to human rights monitoring, such as gender, race, poverty, and disability, enables committees to see if there is discrimination that states need to address. Data on the number of cases of torture, trafficking victims, and extrajudicial killings are valuable for assessing compliance with civil and political rights. Providing data on a set of preestablished indicators makes the process more streamlined and efficient. It also enhances the authority of the treaty body, since its analysis of a country's human rights performance is based on facts and scientifically generated knowledge. Moreover, indicators specify the terms of human rights treaties. Treaties are often written in broad terms rather than specific requirements. Developing indicators enables a treaty body to set clearer standards for compliance with a convention.

Despite such apparent benefits, the value of indicators is hotly debated by human rights activists and scholars. In 2005, Michael Ignatieff, a leading human rights scholar, bemoaned the lack of attention to measurement systems for human rights compared with burgeoning efforts to measure phenomena such as democracy, governance, corruption, and freedom by organizations such as the World Bank and the UN Development Program (Ignatieff and Desormeau 2005). To promote human rights metrics, he organized a major conference on human rights measurement at Harvard University that brought together fifty-five civil society and academic leaders in the human rights field. Activists at the 2005 conference recognized that numbers and ranks catch greater attention from the media, publics, and policy makers than do narratives. They also observed that indicators contribute to naming and shaming.

Yet some participants at this conference worried about developing a composite human rights index that would provide oversimplified, imprecise measurements and rank countries in ways that could obscure their differing relations to human rights by using a single score (Carr Center for Human Rights Policy 2005: 27–29). Participants expressed concern about the usefulness of a single number for the broad array of human rights; the difficulty of weighting and combining various human rights, given their incommensurability; and the importance of considering the particular circumstances in each country (Holland 2008: 1–2). There have long been criticisms of comparing one kind of violation against another and of merging violations and losing the specificity necessary for action against any particular offense. Some human rights advocates worry about the lack of accurate, valid, and reliable data; the use of inappropriate proxy measures; and the problem of political resistance to ranking among countries (e.g., Barsh 1993; Landman 2004).

Similarly, a major conference in 2011, sponsored by the European Union for Fundamental Rights, advocated using indicators to measure rights in the European Union, stressing their contributions to assessing human rights performance, but worried about data quality, access to information about vulnerable groups, and the lack of standardized, universalized definitions for many concepts, such as disability. They also confronted the difficulty of rendering data from different European countries comparable (Fundamental Rights Agency 2011). In general, human rights activists recognize that aggregation of data more effectively demonstrates the extent of human rights violations than do individual stories but that it inevitably ignores the particular situations of marginalized and vulnerable populations. Debates within the human rights field reflect the trade-off between lumping data to show major effects and splitting data to reveal particular vulnerabilities (Langford and Fukuda-Parr 2012: 232–36).

There are several obstacles to the use of indicators for human rights monitoring. First, since the treaty body system is made up of separate treaties, with committees deeply committed to the full set of obligations under each one, it is difficult to select a small, workable number of indicators and neglect the rest. Second, treaty bodies largely depend on countries to use indicators, even if the treaty body requests them. Third, human rights advocates are reluctant to use the simple, ahistorical, and decontextualized scores produced by composite indicators. Fourth, even when treaty bodies and countries use indicators, treaty bodies lack penalties or rewards for good or bad performance beyond issuing public comments of praise or critique. Fifth, efforts to promote indicators of human rights compliance face resistance from countries concerned about mechanisms that compare and rank them on the basis of their compliance with human rights laws. For example, when the UNDP ranked states on the basis of their human rights performance in the 1991 *Human Development Report*, it came under strong criticism for its methodology and its neglect of cultural difference (Barsh 1993: 87–89; Landman 2004: 923). Since the United Nations, including the treaty bodies, depends on funding by states, it is constrained in adopting strategies that states strongly oppose.

Nevertheless, treaty bodies are increasingly using indicators to specify the obligations of the treaties and encouraging countries to use statistical data in their country reports. They typically prefer counts and ratios to composites, which are more superficial and vulnerable to long, nontransparent interpretive chains. Thus indicators are increasingly advocated and used in human rights monitoring, but not without opposition.

HUMAN RIGHTS MONITORING

Treaties cover a wide range of civil, political, social, economic, and cultural rights, as well as the special situations of vulnerable groups such as racial minorities, women, children, migrants, and the disabled. The fundamental principles of all the treaties are equality, nondiscrimination, and protection of human dignity. A basic tenet of the human rights system is that the rights delineated in these conventions are interconnected and must be considered together. International human rights law is a system of multilateral treaties, in which states commit themselves to the terms of treaties by ratifying them. Most treaties are ratified by 150 or more states out of a total of about 193 states and are monitored by a committee of experts. The first treaty to come into force was the International Convention on the Elimination of all Forms of Racial Discrimination (CERD) in 1969, the treaty body for which was created the same year. The Human Rights Committee, established to monitor the ICCPR, was formed in 1976; the committee to monitor the Convention on the Elimination of all Forms of Discrimination against Women (CEDAW) in 1982; the committees to monitor the Convention against Torture (CAT) and the International Covenant on Economic, Social, and Cultural Rights (ICESCR) in 1987; the committee to monitor the Convention on the Rights of the Child (CRC) in 1990; the committee to monitor the International Convention on Migrant Workers' Rights (ICMWR) in 2004; the committee to monitor the Convention on Rights of Persons with Disabilities (CRPD) in 2009; and the committee to monitor the Convention on Enforced Disappearances in 2011. By 2015, there were nine treaties in force with ten committees in operation, including a subcommittee for the optional protocol to the CAT.

Countries are expected to periodically submit reports detailing their compliance with the treaties they have ratified. For most treaties, reports are due every four years. After countries submit their periodic reports, they appear at a treaty body meeting in New York City or Geneva to present it and answer questions from the committee. Committees consist of ten to twenty-five members who serve as individual experts and do not represent their countries of origin, although they are chosen to be geographically representative. Experts are elected for four-year terms and participate in two- to three-week meetings two or three times a year. They are chosen on the basis of their expertise in the issues of the treaty, receiving expense money but little or no salary. Some are academics, some have civil society experience, and some work for governments, often in their foreign service.

States that ratify human rights conventions consent to their terms but retain sovereignty. They have the option of submitting reservations to terms of the treaty that they do not wish to accept at the time of ratification. Once a country has ratified a treaty, however, it is expected to adopt it into its domestic legal system. This does not always take place. International law lacks some of the direct enforcement capacity of national law, even though it exerts a similar moral and ethical power. The treaty body process is, consequently, a tug of war between the power and influence of the international legal order and the claims to sovereignty of nation-states. Lines of power are ambiguous, and the authority of the treaty body is always subject to question. Sovereign states voluntarily subject themselves to public scrutiny and critique by a small, international group of individuals whose primary commitments are to the treaty itself, yet states sometimes resist this control. Although the exercise is intended to be a "constructive dialogue" or an "interactive dialogue," and the treaty body does not render enforceable judgments, it does criticize states that have a poor human rights record. Yet the treaty body's arsenal is largely persuasion and a country's desire to maintain a good reputation for protecting human rights. Domestic organizations and actors play a critical role in promoting state compliance (Simmons 2009). Even though the hearings themselves are diplomatically courteous and sometimes very detailed and tedious, the sense of opposition is noticeable. The tense contestation over authority and control in the treaty body process is a central feature of monitoring compliance with international human rights law.

Ratifying countries provide a country report that runs anywhere from a few pages to a few hundred pages every two to five years, depending on the treaty. After reading the report and holding a verbal discussion about it, the treaty body issues a statement known as "concluding observations" or "concluding comments" concerning areas in which a country is doing well and areas in which further effort is needed. The comments are then posted on the Internet. In David Kretzmer's study of the development of the Human Rights Committee, he argues that one of the committee's main accomplishments is creating accurate records of state parties' compliance with the ICCPR through this mechanism (Kretzmer 2010: 47). Yet the treaty body is largely dependent on the country to provide information about its performance. The treaty bodies see their task as evaluating compliance with legal standards based on the data presented, not on checking the quality of the data themselves. They look for problems that require state attention, usually focusing on vulnerable and marginal populations, while most countries endeavor to provide the most favorable account of their performances that they can.

These are opposing goals, often leading to distrust between countries and the treaty body (Rosga and Satterthwaite 2009). In order to hold countries accountable, treaty bodies need reliable and extensive information. To avoid scrutiny and criticism, a country may withhold damaging information. Countries may acknowledge problems but offer only vague ideas to address them. Thus acquiring accurate and relevant information is at the heart of the struggle over human rights monitoring. A treaty body cannot compel a country to provide information, but it can undermine the country's reputation as a human-rights-respecting nation. In order to win that reputation, the country has to make some effort to report its activities and conditions. Thus the constructive dialogue is sometimes more akin to a duel. In this delicate dance, the production and analysis of information takes center stage. It is hardly surprising that indicators appeal to at least some treaty body members. Indicators offer a possible solution to the need for accurate information in order to make judgments in this highly contested space. By using apparently objective, scientifically produced statistical data, treaty bodies can enhance their authority in rendering judgments about human rights compliance (Rosga and Satterthwaite 2009: 289–93).

CREATING SPECIFICITY

Indicators translate the vague terms of treaties into specific requirements. For example, the ICESCR articulates a right to adequate food but does not specify how much food, what kind of food, or how it is to be distributed and by whom. Article 11 of the ICESCR defines rights to food, clothing, and housing the following way: "The States Parties to the present Covenant recognize the right of everyone to an adequate standard of living for himself and his family, including adequate food, clothing, and housing, and to the continuous improvement of living conditions" (UN General Assembly 1966). Scholars working to develop indicators for these rights suggest using proxies to measure their implementation, such as daily per-capita supply of calories and other nutritional rates for measuring compliance with the right to food or literacy rates and educational attainment broken down by gender for measuring compliance with the right to education (Landman 2004: 925). While civil and political rights are harder to measure, Landman suggests proxies such as investment in prison and police reform, processing of cases, and funding of the judiciary to assess state commitment to civil and political rights (2004: 926). Obviously, such proxy measurements provide far greater specificity to treaty obligations but only focus on a few measures while neglecting many other dimensions of a given right. Moreover, they depend on what data are available and may not exactly measure what the name of the right suggests.

Over the last thirty years, as the human rights legal system has matured, treaty bodies have constantly grappled with this problem of knowledge. Since the early 1990s, human rights scholars and treaty body members have advocated greater reliance on indicators, primarily in the areas of social, economic, and cultural rights rather than those of civil and political rights. The general reporting guidelines for all treaty bodies list many indicators that countries should include (UN International Human Rights Instruments 2009: 23–25). These cover demographic data; social, economic, and cultural indicators; and indicators on the political system, crime, and the administration of justice. The mandated indicators include widely used measures such as maternal mortality, the proportion of single-parent households and households headed by women, per-capita income, and the incidence of violent deaths and life-threatening crimes reported per one hundred thousand persons. Indicators are to be disaggregated by sex, age, and main population groups (UN International Human Rights Instruments 2009: 23–25).

Many of the treaty bodies routinely request statistical information disaggregated into categories relevant to their convention's mandate, such as gender for the CEDAW and age for the CRC. The committee monitoring the ICESCR asked for indicators in twelve of its twenty-one general comments written between 1989 and 2009. General comments or recommendations are clarifications of the terms of the treaties issued by the treaty bodies.

Health, food, education, and social security are phenomena that have long been subject to measurement, so it makes sense that indicators are important in these areas. Committees working on discrimination against the rights of subgroups such as racial minorities, women, and children have also advocated using indicators. The CRC General Comment 5 asks for indicators, for example (Scheinin 2005: 13). Most of these indicators are simple ratios, such as maternal mortality or rates of school enrollment disaggregated by gender and ethnicity, rather than some composite human rights assessment. The Human Rights Committee that monitors the ICCPR has been far less active in developing indicators and rarely refers to them. Of the thirty-one general comments on the ICCPR, for example, only two ask for statistics (Scheinin 2005: 14).

Some treaty bodies are more enthusiastic about indicators than others. The Committee on Economic, Social, and Cultural Rights has taken the lead on indicator development and promotion, while the Committee on Torture and the Human Rights Committee have been far less interested. Martin Scheinin, who is an international law professor from Finland and is central to the OHCHR indicator process, examined indicator and benchmark references in the general comments and concluding observations of the six major human rights treaties. He showed that three of the treaty bodies — those covering social, economic, and cultural rights; women's rights; and children's rights — have been far more active in the use of indicators than the other three, which deal with civil and political rights, torture, and racial discrimination (Scheinin 2005: 8). My survey of country reports to these treaty bodies, discussed below, showed the same pattern.

Thus establishing indicators for human rights monitoring is attractive but hard. Despite the appeal of using indicators to hold governments accountable and to articulate the universal standards of human rights treaties, it has proved difficult to generate a uniform set of human rights indicators. Moreover, given the lack of political and coercive power of the treaty bodies, it is difficult to compel powerful actors to use indicators, even if they are recommended in the reporting guidelines. Some human rights are more amenable to quantification than others. The rest of this chapter traces the genealogy of an effort to create a universal set of human rights indicators and their uptake by countries and treaty bodies.

The Turn to Human Rights Indicators

THE DEMAND FOR INDICATORS

Given the costs in time and resources of treaty body monitoring and the burden to states of preparing reports and participating in meetings, particularly as the number of treaties grows and the expectations for information increase, both states parties and treaty bodies are eager to find a way to streamline the presentation and analysis of data. Since the system began, problems of cost and efficiency have increased. The first treaty body began its work in 1970, most were formed after 1980, the first meeting of chairpersons of human rights treaty bodies was in 1984, and the chairpersons have held annual meetings since 1994. The problem worsened in the 2000s with the emergence of new conventions and optional protocols.

The problems of time and cost emerged as early as the 1980s. At that time, the secretary general appointed an independent expert, Philip Alston, an Australian human rights lawyer now teaching at New York University Law School, to explore ways of enhancing the long-term effectiveness of treaty bodies. Alston is highly experienced in the human rights system, having worked on the text of the CRC, having served as special rapporteur for extrajudicial executions from 2004 to 2010, and having served as special rapporteur for extreme poverty and human rights beginning in 2014. My conversations with him have been very helpful in understanding the treaty body system. In the late 1980s and early 1990s, he produced a series of reports on the treaty body system, sending the final one to the Commission on Human Rights in 1997. This report documents several problems: reports are overdue or never filed, committees are falling behind in hearing them, the ratification of human rights conventions is still not universal, and additional resources for follow-up and extended meeting times are unavailable. Alston's report describes a backlog of reports so large that countries that report may wait up to three years to have their report heard. During the 1990s, the problem only got worse (Alston 1996: 12–13). Alston concluded that the treaty body system in its form at that time was "unsustainable" (1996: 28). A subsequent report also highlighted problems of a lack of ratification by many countries, large numbers of reservations by those who did ratify, and overdue or missing reports (Bayefsky 2001).

These problems have inspired a series of reform proposals.[1] Although many of these difficulties could be resolved by increasing resources for the treaty body system, such as more meeting time and additional rapporteurs or staff to engage in follow-up, a lack of resources continues to plague the system. Developing indicators was only one of many approaches to strengthening human rights monitoring. By the early 2010s, efforts at treaty body reform focused on harmonization among the treaty bodies and developing a common core document that could be submitted to several treaty bodies. In 2009, High Commissioner Navi Pillay initiated a five-year reform process that included a series of meetings, a report by the High Commissioner in 2012, and a discussion in the General Assembly in 2014. In April 2014, the General Assembly passed a resolution that addressed problems of the costs of document translation and interpretation services, a lack of meeting time and staff, and backlogs of reports. Some countries complained about the expansion of treaty obligations through general comments during this discussion. The resolution affirmed the importance of treaty body independence, increased meeting time and staff, and established limits on document length (Broecker and O'Flaherty 2014; O'Flaherty 2014: 5; UN General Assembly 2014).

At the same time as issues of cost and time have arisen for treaty bodies, the burden on ratifying countries of preparing periodic reports has increased with the addition of two new treaties, more ratifications, and more extensive requests for information from treaty bodies. Reporting guidelines for each treaty delineate a wide range of issues that reports need to address. Treaty bodies continue to offer careful, thoughtful analysis of individual country reports, preparing sets of questions in advance on each country report targeted to the particular situation of that country and its human rights issues. The general approach of treaty bodies is to gather information specific to a country and its government and evaluate it against the rather broad standards articulated in the treaty and the somewhat more specific issues raised in general comments. The treaty body process assesses the actions of states in light of their specific histories, situations, capacities and resources, and past efforts.

Indicators are thought to offer a solution to some of these persistent problems of overload, underreporting, and the cost of a particularized monitoring system. An indicator-based process could increase the efficiency and speed of processing and minimize the burden on states of preparing reports. Instead of producing long narrative texts, countries could simply indicate how they perform on the treaty's indicators and monitor their own performance. The treaty bodies could read a short text bristling with indicators that would assess state performance along a series of agreed-upon indicators that would allow them to evaluate how the country had performed in comparison to its last report. They are clearly valuable in determining to what extent countries have fulfilled their obligations in the field of social, economic, and cultural rights, as well as the rights of particular vulnerable groups, such as women, children, minorities, and persons with disabilities. In the initial report on the OHCHR human rights indicators that was submitted to the treaty body chairs in 2006, its authors, Rajeev Malhotra and Nicolas Fasel, argued that quantitative indicators could help streamline the process, enhance its transparency, make it more effective, reduce the reporting burden, improve follow-up to the committee's recommendations and general comments, and increase accountability (UN International Human Rights Instruments and Office of the High Commissioner for Human Rights 2006: 2).

Indeed, since the mid-2000s, human rights advocates' interest in creating standardized international indicators has grown (Welling 2008: 937). Advocates say that if states had to produce standardized data, they would tend to examine their own practices more fully. With greater transparency and public awareness of rights, there would be more public pressure on states to reform government behavior (Welling 2008: 947). If indicators made state-to-state or over-time comparisons easier, states would be pressured to conform to human rights norms and to produce better data. Standardized data sets would make all these comparisons more straightforward, simplifying the work of treaty bodies and making it appear more objective and scientific (Welling 2008: 940–42). Given these potential benefits, treaty body leaders asked the OHCHR to develop a set of indicators for human rights. In 2005, the OHCHR initiated a project of developing indicators for human rights treaties.

PAST EFFORTS TO CREATE HUMAN RIGHTS INDICATORS

Although the OHCHR initiative was the first attempt to establish a general framework for human rights indicators applicable to many rights (Malhotra and Fasel 2005), efforts to develop indicators for particular human rights stretch back to the 1980s (Welling 2008: 938 and interviews). Interest in developing human rights indicators accelerated in the 1990s, providing a platform for the OHCHR project. In 1993 — in preparation for the 1993 Vienna Conference on Human Rights — a major conference sought to develop "appropriate indicators to measure achievements in the progressive realization of economic, social, and cultural rights," inspired by a 1990 recommendation from the first special rapporteur on economic, social, and cultural rights, Danilo Turk (UN Secretariat 1993: 6). The conference identified several useful roles for indicators: to measure progressive realization, to develop a method of determining difficulties or problems encountered by states, and to "assist with the development of 'core contents' of economic, social, and cultural rights" (UN Secretariat 1993: 8). Indicators could also assist in revealing the extent to which rights were and were not enjoyed in practice and "in providing a means to measure and compare performance of individual countries" (UN Secretariat 1993: 8). Some thought that indicators should focus not just on development, for which they were already in widespread use, but also on the obligations of states to protect, respect, and fulfill human rights (UN Secretariat 1993: 9). Some also hoped that indicators could address the lack of clarity of human rights concepts and build bridges between human-rights-based indicators and development-based indicators (UN Secretariat 1993: 9).

However, Katerina Tomaševski argued that human rights indicators differ from development ones in their emphasis on disaggregation to reveal discrimination against disadvantaged and vulnerable groups (Tomaševski in Chapman 2007b: 126; see also Chapman 2007a: 159). Some hoped to capture "real life" with only four or five indicators, while others worried about what issues would be left out. "Extreme caution was expressed concerning the search for magic indicators as well as quantitative fetishism" (UN Secretariat 1993: 30). Statistics were juxtaposed to judgment, with the worry that their use would exclude judgment.

Clearly, the conference grappled with the key trade-off in indicator production: the fewer and less disaggregated the indicators, the easier they are to use, but the less effective they are in showing inequality, difference, and exclusion. Moreover, the fewer the indicators, the fewer dimensions of a right are included. A recurring issue was how narrowly to define the problem and to what extent larger social forces were relevant. At the conference, one participant would suggest a narrow measure and others would object that it was not broad enough and did not take into account structural factors or discrimination. The seminar concluded that there needed to be more conceptual work first in order to identify and clarify the content of various rights and obligations (UN Secretariat 1993). Twenty years later, despite considerable work on clarifying rights and developing indicators, the fundamental trade-off between a narrow and a holistic view of rights remains far from settled.

Although the goal of the conference was to increase the visibility of social, economic, and cultural rights, it rejected the use of the most visible form of indicators: the composite, ranked index. A composite indicator produces simple, packaged information that draws attention to an issue but condenses a series of measures into one score or rank in a way that obscures inequalities among groups and blurs the constituent elements. The conference report noted that "considerable concern was expressed about UNDP's Human Development Index and its Human Freedom Index which were seen as arbitrary in the criteria upon which they are based and largely inconsistent with the indivisibility and interdependence of rights under human rights law" (UN Secretariat 1993: 36, para. 174).

During the 1980s and early 1990s, treaty bodies started to encourage states to create indicators and benchmarks for themselves. Instead of developing standardized, universal indicators and benchmarks, this approach charges countries with setting their own standards. It offers states some autonomy. In its first general comment in 1989, the ICESCR advocated this approach in its reporting guidelines:

A fifth objective is to provide a basis on which the State party itself, as well as the Committee, can effectively evaluate the extent to which progress has been made towards the realization of the obligations contained in the Covenant. For this purpose, it may be useful for States to identify specific benchmarks or goals against which their performance in a given area can be assessed. Thus, for example, it is generally agreed that it is important to set specific goals with respect to the reduction of infant mortality, the extent of vaccination of children, the intake of calories per person, the number of persons per health-care provider, etc. In many of these areas, global benchmarks are of limited use, whereas national or other more specific benchmarks can provide an extremely valuable indication of progress. (UN Committee on Economic, Social, and Cultural Rights 1989)

Virtually all ICESCR general comments between 1998 and 2009 on topics such as the rights to health, education, food, and social security asked countries to set benchmarks for themselves. The CRC similarly asks countries to develop indicators to monitor the implementation of treaty rights, while the CEDAW, CERD, and Human Rights Committee ask states to use statistics but do not consider this part of their human rights obligations (Rosga and Satterthwaite 2009: 275–76, n. 79).

In the late 1990s, human rights monitoring began to shift from country-created indicators and benchmarks to a more standardized system. In 1998, as a newly elected member of the ICESCR, Paul Hunt organized a day of discussion on the right to education during which he advocated standardized indicators (Scheinin 2005: 9; see also Hunt 1998). Hunt is a British human rights law professor who has worked in New Zealand and the United Kingdom and served as the special rapporteur on the right to health from 2002 to 2008. He wanted to create universal indicators for assessing and comparing countries and their performances over time based on treaty obligations rather than the specific local conditions of countries. In this model, first expressed in General Comment 14 (UN Committee on Economic, Social, and Cultural Rights 2000) on the right to health, the international community creates indicators, and states parties set appropriate benchmarks for themselves. General Comment 15 on the right to water (2002) takes a similar approach. Although primarily intended to assess country progress over time, benchmarking does allow comparison across countries. It represents a step toward universal categories rather than only national ones. Paul Hunt, as special rapporteur on the right to health, took the further step of developing universal indicators for the right to health (Hunt 2003a).

In 2000, at the annual meeting of the chairpersons of the human rights treaty bodies, the need for indicators, especially civil and political rights indicators, emerged clearly. The report noted the "lack of clear, objective and measurable criteria for assessing compliance with international human rights standards" (UN International Human Rights Instruments 2000: 6). It said that conceptualizing human rights indicators was of great interest to a wide variety of institutions, particularly development agencies, including the UNDP. An expert seminar on indicators for civil and political rights, held in September 1999, included special rapporteurs to the Human Rights Commission and treaty body members from the CEDAW, CERD, and CAT. The report concluded with a recommendation that OHCHR organize a 2001 workshop to identify progressive developmental benchmarks and indicators related to the right to education (UN International Human Rights Instruments 2000: 9). The subsequent 2001 meeting of the treaty body chairpersons reiterated the call for developing indicators and asked the OHCHR to take the lead, particularly in developing indicators for civil and political rights (UN Human Rights Treaty Bodies 2001: para. B3).

THE OFFICE OF THE HIGH COMMISSIONER FOR HUMAN RIGHTS INDICATOR PROJECT

Thus, by 2000, there were increasing demands for indicators by the treaty bodies, as well as growing pressures on the efficiency of the treaty body system, and the idea of universal indicators was in play. Although the 1993 Vienna conference had called for a series of expert seminars to develop indicators and benchmarks for human rights, little was done until an initial meeting in Turku, Finland, in 2005. This conference, organized by Martin Scheinin, was cosponsored by the OHCHR and Åbo Akademi University and was supported by the Finnish Ministry for Foreign Affairs. It was a seminar in the Nordic Network in Human Rights Research Program and was attended by a cosmopolitan group of human rights law professors and academics from Europe and the United States, many of whom had already worked together and had experience with treaty bodies. The background paper was written by Rajeev Malhotra and Nicolas Fasel, economists with backgrounds in statistics who were working for OHCHR (2005). The OHCHR subsequently created an informal expert group on indicators, called the Human Rights Indicators Expert Group, to develop standardized indicators (Chapman 2007b: 121–22). It included many of the same people who attended the Turku meeting. The group met six times between 2005 and 2009. The OHCHR staff, consisting of Malhotra and Fasel, drafted the indicators and used the expert group to peer-review its concepts, methodology, and choice of illustrative indicators (UN International Human Rights Instruments and Office of the High Commissioner for Human Rights 2008: 15). I attended the last of the initial six planning meetings in 2009. There was another meeting on the guidelines in 2010, and the final guidelines were issued in 2012 (UN Office of the High Commissioner for Human Rights 2012a).

The goal of the OHCHR project was to "build a structured, common and consistent approach for elaborating indicators across all rights, covering the different human rights treaties" (UN International Human Rights Instruments and Office of the High Commissioner for Human Rights 2008: 7). The OHCHR described its goals as streamlining the treaty body process, making it more transparent and effective, reducing reporting burdens, and reinforcing state accountability (UN International Human Rights Instruments and Office of the High Commissioner for Human Rights 2006: paras. 2, 3). While the initial purpose was to improve compliance, as Scheinin, who originated the project, told me when I interviewed him in 2013, by the time the final report was released, it claimed simply to provide a set of tools that countries could use in reporting; countries were free to pick and choose which indicators to use and were able develop their own country-specific indicators. This retreat from a universal set of measures of compliance to a voluntary tool kit may be in response to countries' resistance to being measured and ranked.

The leadership of this project came largely from human rights law professors and economists from Finland, Denmark, Ireland, and Germany, as well as a political scientist and an ethicist from the United States. Neither of the OHCHR professional staffers, Malhotra and Fasel, had a background in human rights. Malhotra is a development economist from India and Fasel is an economist and statistician from Switzerland. The leaders of the group had all served on the ICESCR committee or the Human Rights Committee, and some had also been appointed as special rapporteurs by the Human Rights Council. The project was chaired by Martin Scheinin, who originated the meeting in Turku, Finland, and attended most, but not all, meetings. Paul Hunt and Eibe Riedel, for a time vice chair of the ICESCR, played critical roles, as did Audrey Chapman and Hans-Otto Sano. Hunt attended the initial meeting; Riedel was at most of them. I interviewed Nicolas Fasel, Eibe Riedel, Hans-Otto Sano, and Martin Scheinin and had more informal discussions with Audrey Chapman, Michael O'Flaherty, and Rajeev Malhotra, along with other participants, about the process.

The two-day meeting I attended in April 2009 in Geneva included twenty participants in addition to several representatives from UN agencies and the OHCHR, most of whom stayed for short periods of time. There were representatives from the national human rights institutions in Uganda and the Philippines and a CERD treaty body member from Guatemala, but the rest were Europeans and Americans, along with a few UN staff members. The core group was European men. There were two members from the ICESCR committee; two members from the Human Rights Committee, which monitors the ICCPR; and one member apiece from the monitoring committees of the CERD, CEDAW, and CRC.

The focus of this meeting was fine-tuning the indicators of violence against women and nondiscrimination. Only small changes were made: the framework was clearly settled, and the group was tasked only with tinkering with the details. Larger questions of framework and structure were not open for debate. Several experts, including the chair, worried that the indicators were too numerous, that they needed to be simplified, and that there were too many on each page, but these concerns wrought no change in the final product. A few said, to no avail, that the structure-process-outcome framework was difficult to use. Some found the requirement that all the indicators for one human right fit on a single page to be overly constraining. This restriction sometimes produced a fairly unreadable congestion of words. Some of the experts told me that they were concerned that these indicators were too complicated, that the treaty bodies would not use them, and that they would gather dust on a shelf. Other experts resisted any effort to simplify the indicators. Some argued that they were useful because they laid out a series of steps that countries should follow in making structural changes and following designated processes in order to improve their human rights situations. However, some of the process and outcome indicators overlapped, and there were debates about where they fit. What was a measure of process for one right could have been a measure of outcome for another.

Many of the treaty body members at this expert group meeting appeared to be ambivalent. Although the project was designed to support treaty body monitoring, when queried whether their treaty committee supported the indicators, members said they could not speak for their committees and denied that they were representing them. The CRC representative said that his committee was developing its own indicators on early child development. None seemed enthusiastic, nor did any of them participate actively in the discussions. Only a few of those attending were government representatives, statisticians from national statistical offices, or representatives from national human rights institutions. Very few came from Africa or Asia. Insofar as there was discussion about the availability of relevant data, it was assumed that national human rights institutions would pressure national statistical offices to gather it. Although a rep-

resentative of the UNSD was invited and came to other meetings, he did not
attend this one.

Indeed, at times it seemed as though the human rights indicator project
was a technology in search of an audience, a tool kit without a clientele. The
major users, the treaty bodies, seemed to be rather lukewarm consumers of
this new technology on the basis of both their participation at the meeting
and the responses from the committees to the presentation of the overall project. The OHCHR itself was one of the most enthusiastic supporters. A member of the Human Rights Committee told me that the OHCHR was working
hard to promote indicators, partly for cost-saving purposes. Perhaps the most
important audiences for the OHCHR indicators were development economists, public health planners, and policy makers—groups that often do not
fully understand human rights. The final report emphasized the contribution
of indicators to helping these groups understand the apparently arcane field of
human rights (UN Office of the High Commissioner for Human Rights 2012a).

There are three technologies used by the OHCHR indicators that render
them more accessible to economic and policy audiences. First, they convert
human rights laws into numbers. Second, they replace the respect-protect-
fulfill framework developed by human rights lawyers in the 1980s with a
structure-process-outcome template used in public health and development.
Third, they array the indicators on simple one-page grids, a mode of presentation commonly used in development planning. Thus the OHCHR indicators
construct human rights in a form that is recognizable to development planners, public health experts, and policy makers, and they define human rights
within these expert discourses rather than that of the law. This might account
for some of the ambivalence of human rights actors. The next section discusses
these three technologies.

Technologies of the Office of the High Commissioner for Human Rights Indicators

THE STRUCTURE-PROCESS-OUTCOME FRAMEWORK

During the 1980s, the early years of the treaty body system, several prominent
human rights lawyers developed a framework for assessing human rights compliance based on the categories "respect," "protect," and "fulfill." In the 2000s,
a new framework, using the categories "structure," "process," and "outcome,"
was developed alongside and, to some extent, in place of the older framework.
The new framework subtly shifted the assessment of human rights perfor-

mance from one based on state obligations to one that specified a series of steps that would produce human rights outcomes. Thus it presumed a model of social change based less on state regulation and more on development.

The first framework was developed by a subcommittee of the International Law Association that included several prominent human rights lawyers concerned about social and economic rights, particularly the right to food. It included G. J. H. Van Hoof, Asbjørn Eide, and Philip Alston. In 1984, Van Hoof advocated four levels of state obligations (Van Hoof 1984: 106), a proposal reshaped by Eide into a three-level typology: the duty to respect, the duty to protect, and the duty to facilitate or fulfill human rights (Eide 1987). States were obligated to respect the human rights of their citizens, protect these rights against the activities of third parties, and fulfill their obligations to citizens so that they could enjoy and promote these rights. An edited collection by Alston and Tomaševski elaborated on this framework with relation to the right to food (Alston and Tomaševski 1984; Shue 1984: 85; Tomaševski 1984). Here "respect" means noninterference by states with existing access to adequate food. "Protect" describes the duty to ensure that enterprises and individuals do not deprive individuals of the right to food. "Fulfill" refers to a positive duty to facilitate and provide, to actively promote, and to strengthen people's "access to and utilization of resources and means to ensure their livelihood, including food security" (Narula 2006: 707–8, citing Eide 1987: paras. 112–14; quote from UN Committee on Economic, Social, and Cultural Rights 1999: para. 15). This framework was also used in 2000 by the ICESCR treaty body for the right to health in General Comment 14:

> The right to health, like all human rights, imposes three types or levels of obligations on States parties: the obligations to respect, protect and fulfill. In turn, the obligation to fulfill contains obligations to facilitate, provide and promote. The obligation to respect requires States to refrain from interfering directly or indirectly with the enjoyment of the right to health. The obligation to protect requires States to take measures that prevent third parties from interfering with article 12 guarantees. Finally, the obligation to fulfill requires States to adopt appropriate legislative, administrative, budgetary, judicial, promotional and other measures towards the full realization of the right to health. (UN Committee on Economic, Social, and Cultural Rights 2000: para. 33)

This framework focuses on legal obligations rather than government policies or quantifiable outcomes. It clearly comes out of the legal tradition and was developed to delineate the variety of legal obligations of states. It was used often at the World Conference on Human Rights in Vienna in 1993 and is still a dominant framework in human rights analysis, appearing, for example, in a new proposal for sexual and reproductive health (Roseman 2010) and in a slightly revised version for business and human rights guidelines (UN Human Rights Council 2011). Paul Hunt argues that this framework is particularly useful to sharpen legal analysis of the right to health in national political and legal systems (Hunt 2003a: 35). It appears frequently in country reports and human rights documents and is used widely by UNFPA, UNICEF, WHO, and OHCHR.

However, at the first meeting of the Human Rights Indicators Expert Group in Finland in 2005, they decided to use a new measurement-friendly framework for human rights monitoring, which ultimately became the structure-process-outcome model. It was originally discussed at the 1993 conference but was not developed.[2] At the 2005 meeting, Malhotra and Fasel advocated the new framework (2005). It was drawn in part from the public health field and was proposed for the human right to health by Hunt in 2006 in his capacity as special rapporteur on the right to health, following earlier advocacy for indicators (Hunt 2003b: 10). He defined the concepts as follows:

> 54. Structural indicators address whether or not key structures and mechanisms that are necessary for, or conducive to, the realization of right to health, are in place. [This includes treaties, laws, and policies and basic institutional mechanisms including regulatory agencies.]
>
> 55. Process indicators measure programmes, activities and interventions. They measure, as it were, State effort . . . Such process indicators can help to predict health outcomes.
>
> 56. Outcome indicators measure the impact of programmes, activities and interventions on health status and related issues. Outcome indicators include maternal mortality, child mortality, HIV prevalence rates, and the percentage of women who know about contraceptive methods. (Hunt 2006a: 14–15)

Structural indicators, which refer to questions such as whether a country has ratified a particular human rights treaty, have yes-or-no answers, while process and outcome indicators have values and can be used to measure change over time. Hunt acknowledged in this report that although it is sometimes possible to link structural and process indicators with outcomes, outcomes are often the result of multiple factors.

Hunt developed this approach further in a 2006 report (Hunt 2006b) as

184

well as in an article in the prominent medical journal *The Lancet* (Backman et al. 2008; Hunt 2006b). He justifies using the structure-process-outcome model because "in the health literature, these categories and labels appear to be widely understood—for example, they are the terms routinely used by the WHO Department of Essential Drugs and Medicines Policy" (Hunt 2006a: 7). He views his right to health indicators as a way to professionalize health rights advocacy (Backman et al. 2008). This framework has a long history in public health. It is found in various WHO documents from the 1990s onward, usually in relation to measurement and evaluation or the creation of indicators to evaluate specific health issues. For example, in Hunt's first mention of the structure-process-outcome framework (Hunt 2003a), he cites a 1999 WHO manual called *Indicators for Monitoring National Drug Policies*. Hunt says, "The Special Rapporteur suggests that, to begin with, special attention is devoted to the following categories of right to health indicators: structural indicators, process indicators and outcome indicators. While there is no unanimity in the health literature, these categories and labels appear to be widely understood— for example, they are the terms routinely used by the WHO Department of Essential Drugs and Medicines Policy" (Hunt 2003a: 7, para. 15).

The genealogy of this framework in public health reaches back at least to the 1950s and 1960s, when a similar approach was used to measure the quality of medical care, to rank hospitals in New York City (Makover 1951), and to measure the quality of medical care in the United States (Gruskin and Ferguson 2009; Donabedian 1966). This approach also has a history in economic development. Development planning requires action plans, which include a catalogue of measures, a timeline of activities and milestones, and indicators that show whether the objectives have been accomplished— all organized in a tabular fashion to show how activities will unfold over time (see Rottenburg 2009: 37–42.) These plans are organized around a narrative of progress such that development and the transformation toward modernity will be accomplished by following this path (Rottenburg 2009: 80). As with the human rights indicators, there is an assumption that carrying out a set of activities will inevitably move a country toward desired outcomes. Both the public health and human rights approaches' uses of the template share an assumption of means and ends: if certain conditions are fulfilled and certain processes are carried out, certain results will follow. Development planning makes similar assumptions. Although the creators of the OHCHR indicators claim that process and outcome indicators have a cause-and-effect relationship (UN International Human Rights Instruments and Office of the High Commissioner for Human Rights 2008: 11), the template presumes, but does not prove, this relationship (Rosga and Satterthwaite 2009: 296–97).

BUILDING THE INDICATORS

Each right was divided not only into structure-process-outcome categories but also into attributes that describe the right's specific dimensions and contexts. The use of attributes was recommended by Martin Scheinin, a human rights lawyer who was a member of the Human Rights Committee at the time. For example, the right to work was divided into four attributes: access to decent and productive work; just and safe working conditions; training, skill upgrading, and professional development; and protection from forced labor and unemployment (UN Office of the High Commissioner for Human Rights 2012a: 194). These attributes differentiate the right and provide context. In an interview in 2013, Scheinin said that the attributes were the most important part of the indicators for him, while the structure-process-outcome framework and the one-page tables were promoted by Malhotra. These categories reflect the difference between a legal approach and an economic one, with attributes referring to legal categories and the structural, process, and outcome categories to economic and developmental ones. According to Audrey Chapman—who served as rapporteur for the 1993 conference and was also a core member of the Human Rights Indicators Expert Group—at the 2005 meeting, they first identified a small number of attributes for each human right to be measured and then selected indicators for structural, process, and outcome measures (Chapman 2007a: 122).

At the second meeting, in March 2006, the group developed illustrative indicators for four human rights using this approach: the right to life, the right to judicial review of detention (the right to liberty), the right to adequate food, and the right to health (UN International Human Rights Instruments and Office of the High Commissioner for Human Rights 2006: 17–21). Two were civil/political rights, and two were economic, social, and cultural rights. Eibe Riedel told me that they began with the Universal Declaration of Human Rights, a basic point of consensus, in selecting rights for indicator development. They also wanted to integrate the rights in the two major human rights treaties: the ICCPR and the ICESCR.

In four subsequent meetings, the expert group developed indicators for eight more human rights, half civil/political and half economic/social/cultural, as well as two cross-cutting rights, violence against women and nondiscrimination. In addition to the first four, the other eight human rights were the right not to be tortured, the right to participate in public affairs, the right to education, the right to adequate housing, the right to social security, the right to work, the right to freedom of opinion and expression, and the right to a fair trial (UN International Human Rights Instruments and Office of the High

Commissioner for Human Rights 2008: 26–33). Each right was examined separately. The indicators included whether a treaty had been ratified; counts, such as the number of people on death row; and ratios, such as the proportion of law enforcement officers formally investigated for physical or nonphysical abuse or crime (including torture and disproportionate use of force) during the reporting period.[3]

The 2008 report from the Human Rights Indicators Expert Group to the chairs of the treaty bodies said that the new framework translated the "narrative on the normative content of human rights . . . into a few characteristic attributes and a configuration of structural, process and outcome indicators" (UN International Human Rights Instruments and Office of the High Commissioner for Human Rights 2008: 19). It claimed that these indicators were not intended to be applied across all countries, regardless of their level of development, nor used for cross-country comparisons. It emphasized flexibility in the use of these indicators: "Indeed, the framework allows a balance between the use of a core set of human rights indicators that may be universally relevant and at the same time retains the flexibility of a more detailed and focused assessment on certain attributes of the relevant human rights, depending on the requirements of a particular situation" (2008: 19–20).

Thus the OHCHR human rights indicators served to translate human rights concepts into terms and formats accessible to development economists and policy planners. The final report concluded that treaty interpretation would remain a primarily legal exercise, but noted, "Its quality can however be improved by securing the best possible factual basis for it. Moreover, quantitative indicators can potentially contribute to bridging the human rights discourse and the development policy discourse" (UN Office of the High Commissioner for Human Rights 2012a: 26). The report noted that the categories of structure, process, and outcome were familiar to UN agencies and donors who wanted to use human rights standards to guide their assistance programs.

The OHCHR indicator project builds on efforts to bring human rights approaches to development. Hans-Otto Sano, an economic historian and senior researcher at the Danish Institute for Human Rights, as well as one of the core members of the OHCHR indicator project, was seconded to the World Bank by the Nordic Trust Fund to develop a human-rights-based approach to development (McInerney-Lankford and Sano 2010). This approach to development considers the impact of development on human rights and integrates human rights into development policy (McInerney-Lankford and Sano 2013: 2). It seeks to incorporate questions of social justice and vulnerable populations into development. Human-rights-based development emphasizes principles of participation, accountability, equality, nondiscrimination, transparency, and empowerment (Gready 2008; Sano n.d.). It imagines people as key actors in their own development rather than as passive recipients, emphasizes empowerment and inclusion of all stakeholders in the planning process, and promotes locally owned processes.

While there are clearly overlaps between development and human rights promotion, there are also significant differences (see Alston 2005a; 2005b; Alston and Robinson 2005; Chapman 2007a; Fukuda-Parr 2011; McInerney-Lankford and Sano 2010: 27–44). Development focuses on improving averages, while human rights assessment focuses on the situations of the marginalized and vulnerable. Rosga and Satterthwaite argue that rights-based monitoring of development projects differs from monitoring compliance with human rights treaties in that the former assesses the extent to which a development project has enhanced human rights, while the latter assesses the extent to which a state has complied with its duties under the legal standard of the treaty (Rosga and Satterthwaite 2009: 300). Martin Scheinin points out that the treaty body process is a legal one in which an established set of facts is the basis for an assessment of performance in terms of the legal obligations of a treaty. He argues that this is a complex process and cannot be reduced to the direct use of empirical data through qualitative and quantitative indicators; instead, it requires knowledge of applicable treaty provisions and practices of interpreting treaties (Scheinin 2005: 2). He said in an interview in 2013 that his main concern when he started on the project was damage control. He was concerned about creating lists of items to be checked off as a mode of monitoring. Data do not replace legal judgment, in his view, but provide the basis for judgment.

In sum, the translation of legal norms into measurements and the importation of the structure-process-outcome framework from health and management to human rights draw development and human rights closer together. Not only does this translation redefine legal norms as numbers and stages of development, but it also creates bridges between human rights and statistical modes of thinking, which are sometimes lacking. In several discussions with statisticians at the UNSD and other international statistical agencies, I was told that they do not really like working in the field of human rights, which is seen as too political and some of its terms, such as "decent work," as too vague to measure. According to one statistician, the worlds of statistics and law are very different, and it is hard to get human rights activists and statisticians to talk to each other. Another statistician from an international agency, whom I met at a conference in New York City, said that statisticians run away when they hear about human rights because they seem too political. A third statistician said they find them scary and that it is not easy to get statisticians to work with human rights. Indeed, the much celebrated Fundamental Principles of Official Statistics, renewed by the UNSC in 2014, emphasize the autonomy of official statistics from political influence — an enduring threat to the independence, objectivity, and professionalism of official statisticians.

At the same time, the adoption of the structure-process-outcome framework shifts the conception of human rights monitoring from a focus on measuring the attainment of rights toward assessing government efforts that are presumed to attain these rights for their residents. To some extent, this shift is a product of the demands of measurement itself. It is easier and less expensive to report and measure government programs than residents' overall level of enjoyment of human rights in a country. A state can more easily count the number of domestic violence shelters than the proportion of women who have been abused. Yet as Rosga and Satterthwaite point out, particular government efforts may not produce the anticipated outcomes, and which efforts produce which outcomes varies greatly in different kinds of societies (2009: 296–97).

It is a central argument of this book that the frameworks, or templates, by which information is organized have powerful if implicit roles in structuring knowledge. Templates, such as the respect-protect-fulfill template, carry embedded theories that are not necessarily made explicit. For example, that framework presumes that the role of the state is as much to avoid impinging on rights and to prevent others from doing so as it is to create the conditions for those rights' fulfillment. It incorporates ideas of negative rights along with those of positive rights and imagines states as responsible for both restraint and the provision of rights. It brings civil/political and economic/social/cultural rights together. However, the terms are often vague and not readily quantifiable.

In contrast, the new structure-process-outcome template incorporates assumptions about development and social change, suggesting that the creation of certain state institutions and laws and the implementation of particular state policies will produce a specific outcome: the increased enjoyment of human rights by the general public as well as particular vulnerable populations. Like current development thinking, it emphasizes the role of institutions in improving the living conditions of populations. It presumes a relatively developed society with an effective state. Unlike social science understandings of social structure and process, "structure" refers to laws and institutions rather than social and political structures, while "process" means government programs rather than mechanisms of social change. Thus the template converts theoretical concepts into countable entities but also changes their meanings.

The move toward measurement could increase the focus on human rights out-side the legal community, but it could also, as Koskenniemi warns, domesticate and tame them so that they become merely one consideration in development projects rather than a trump card (2010).

THE INDICATOR TABLES: THE DEVELOPMENT GRID

Another way that the OHCHR indicators reflect their close ties to develop-ment thinking is their presentation in a grid or table. The project produced one-page diagrams for twelve human rights and two cross-cutting ones for nondiscrimination and violence against women. There was a strong commit-ment to restricting the list of indicators to a single page, even if this required a very small font and terse descriptions of the indicators. Each right is pre-sented as series of specific obligations, with rows defined as structure, process, and outcome and columns defined as attributes. In order to incorporate the human rights concern with discrimination, along the bottom of each sheet is written the requirement that all indicators should be disaggregated by gender, race, ethnicity, and so forth. The metadata sheets that explain how to use the indicator matrices say, for example, that data on reported cases of forced evic-tions should be disaggregated by "sex," "age" (if under eighteen), "economic and social situation," "ethnicity," "minority," "indigenous," "color," "language," "religion," "political or other opinion," "national or social origin," "migrant," "disability," "sexual orientation," "marital and family status," and "place of res-idence" (i.e., rural vs. urban; UN Office of the High Commissioner for Human Rights 2012a: 160). Data are not often available at such levels of disaggregation, of course, and producing such extensive disaggregation is expensive. Disaggre-gated data are essential to uncover discrimination and human rights violations of vulnerable groups, yet here it is presented as an addendum to the overall framework.

Table 7.1 on the right to health provides a good illustration of the approach. The right is divided into five attributes, each representing a particular issue in the field: sexual and reproductive health; child mortality and health care; natural and occupational environment; prevention, treatment, and control of diseases; and accessibility to health facilities and essential medicines. Although the chart format requires structural, process, and outcome variables for each attribute, the structural indicators usually run across all the attributes, as do some of the process and outcome indicators. This format requires outcome measures for each attribute, even though some can be measured far more read-ily than others. In contrast, Hunt's earlier efforts to produce indicators for this

TABLE 7.1. *Illustrative indicators on the right to the enjoyment of the highest attainable standard of physical and mental health (Universal Declaration of Human Rights, art. 25)*

	Sexual and reproductive health	Child mortality and health care	Natural and occupational environment	Prevention, treatment and control of diseases	Accessibility to health facilities and essential medicines
Structural	• International human rights treaties relevant to the right to the enjoyment of the highest attainable standard of physical and mental health (right to health) ratified by the State • Date of entry into force and coverage of the right to health in the constitution or other forms of superior law • Date of entry into force and coverage of domestic laws for implementing the right to health, including a law prohibiting female genital mutilation • Number of registered and/or active NGOs (per 100,000 persons) involved in the promotion and protection of the right to health • Estimated proportions of births, deaths and marriages recorded through vital registration systems				
	• Time frame and coverage of national policy on sexual and reproductive health • Time frame and coverage of national policy on abortion and foetal sex determination	• Time frame and coverage of national policy on child health and nutrition		• Time frame and coverage of national policy on physical and mental health • Time frame and coverage of national policy for persons with disabilities • Time frame and coverage of national policy on medicines, including list of essential medicines, measures for generic substitution	
Process	• Proportion of received complaints on the right to health investigated and adjudicated by the national human rights institution, human rights ombudsperson or other mechanisms and the proportion of these responded to effectively by the Government • Net official development assistance for the promotion of the health sector received or provided as a proportion of public expenditure on health or gross national income*				

- Proportion of births attended by skilled health personnel*
- Antenatal care coverage (at least one visit and at least four visits)*
- Increase in proportion of women of reproductive age using, or whose partner is using, contraception (CPR)*
- Unmet need for family planning*
- Medical terminations of pregnancy as a proportion of live births
- Proportion of reported cases of genital mutilation, rape and other violence restricting women's sexual and reproductive freedom responded to effectively by the Government

- Proportion of schoolchildren educated on health and nutrition issues
- Proportion of children covered under programme for regular medical check-ups in the reporting period
- Proportion of infants exclusively breastfed during the first 6 months
- Proportion of children covered under public nutrition supplement programmes
- Proportion of children immunized against vaccine-preventable diseases (e.g., measles*)

- Proportion of targeted population that was extended access to an improved drinking water source*
- Proportion of targeted population that was extended access to improved sanitation*
- CO_2 emissions per capita*
- Number of cases of deterioration of water sources brought to justice
- Proportion of population or households living or working in or near hazardous conditions rehabilitated
- Proportion of driving licences withdrawn for breaches of road rules
- Number of prosecutions under domestic law on natural or workplace environment

- Proportion of population covered under awareness-raising programmes on transmission of diseases (e.g., HIV/AIDS*)
- Proportion of population (above age 1) immunized against vaccine-preventable diseases
- Proportion of population applying effective preventive measures against diseases (e.g., HIV/AIDS, malaria*)
- Proportion of disease cases detected and cured (e.g., tuberculosis*)
- Proportion of population abusing substances, such as drugs, chemical and psychoactive substances, brought under specialized treatment
- Proportion of mental health facilities inspected in the reporting period

- Per capita government expenditure on primary health care and medicines (Improvement in)
- Density of medical and paramedical personnel, hospital beds and other primary health-care facilities
- Proportion of population that was extended access to affordable health care, including essential drugs,* on a sustainable basis
- Average availability and median consumer price ratio of 30 selected essential medicines in public and private health facilities
- Proportion of people covered by health insurance
- Rate of refusal of medical consultations, by target group (discrimination testing surveys)
- Proportion of persons with disabilities accessing assistive devices
- Share of public expenditure on essential medicines met through international aid

continued

TABLE 7.1. *Continued*

	Sexual and reproductive health	Child mortality and health care	Natural and occupational environment	Prevention, treatment and control of diseases	Accessibility to health facilities and essential medicines
Outcome	• Proportion of live births with low birthweight • Perinatal mortality rate • Maternal mortality ratio*	• Infant and under-five mortality rates* • Proportion of underweight children under five years of age*	• Prevalence of deaths, injuries, diseases and disabilities caused by unsafe natural and occupational environment	• Death rate associated with and prevalence of communicable and non-communicable diseases (e.g., HIV/AIDS, malaria, tuberculosis*) • Proportion of persons abusing harmful substances • Life expectancy at birth or age 1 and health-adjusted life expectancy • Suicide rates	

Source: UN Office of the High Commissioner for Human Rights 2012a: 90. http://www.ohchr.org/Documents/Publications/Human_rights_indicators_en.pdf

All indicators should be disaggregated by prohibited grounds of discrimination, as applicable and reflected in metadata sheets.

* MDG-related indicators

right listed a long series of attributes on the left side of the chart and used the columns to specify structure, process, and outcome (2006a). The OHCHR tables lose some flexibility by placing the attributes along the top as columns and the structure-process-outcome categories down the side as rows and by presenting it in a single page, which could not be reprinted exactly here.

The entire table on the right to health includes eleven structural indicators, thirty-two process indicators, and ten outcome indicators: a total of fifty-three indicators. One of the challenges of the format, which emerged clearly in the expert group meeting I attended, is determining which indicators are structural ones, which are process ones, and which are outcome ones. For example, the table on the right to health includes "time frame and coverage of national policy on sexual and reproductive health" as a structural indicator, along with national policies on child health and nutrition, physical and mental health, persons with disabilities, and medicines. Structural variables are primarily legal, including ratification of relevant conventions and domestic laws, but in the case of the right to health, they also include national policies and the number of NGOs per capita involved in the promotion of the right to health.

Indicators must refer to countable phenomena, including yes-or-no responses to treaty ratification. For process and outcome indicators, there was an effort to use measures that might be available from either international data collection or national or civil society statistics. Many were drawn from the set of indicators related to the Millennium Development Goals (MDGs), which were relatively available. For example, the outcome measures proposed for sexual and reproductive health — "proportion of live births with low birthweight" and "maternal mortality ratio" — are widely used in development and public health. However, many of the measures seem difficult to collect, such as "proportion of reported cases of genital mutilation, rape and other violence restricting women's sexual and reproductive freedom responded to effectively by the government." Despite the appearance of objectivity, there are clearly interpretive dimensions to many of these indicators, as in the reference above to an "effective" response by the government.

The underlying assumption of the grid is that if the structural and process indicators are followed, then the outcome indicators will improve. Yet in practice, there is often no clear causal relationship between the process and the outcome measures, as Rosga and Satterthwaite point out (2009). For example, the process indicators for child mortality and health care are the extent of nutrition education for children, medical checkups, breastfeeding, the availability of public nutrition programs, and immunization rates. The outcome variables are infant and under-five mortality rates and the proportion of underweight

194

children under five. While the process steps could improve child mortality and weight, there are other strategies that might be more effective depending on local conditions, such as providing access to subsistence farmland or stemming the sale of agricultural land to international investors. Moreover, the proposed strategies do not take into account situations where the problem of child nutrition is the result of severe food shortages or inequalities in the distribution of food. Under these conditions, the interventions necessary to improve child mortality and health are different, and the recommended ones may not help. The templates developed by the OHCHR process assume a state that has the capacity to carry out programs as well as a society in which inequalities based on class, gender, religion, and region do not affect child health. It does not consider how "son preference" could diminish the feeding and care of girl children, for example, or how marginal or indigenous groups might be excluded from government benefits and be disproportionately poor. These larger systemic factors are ignored.

Thus a drawback of the structure-process-outcome grid is that it prescribes a standard set of actions to improve a problem, yet these may not be the right acts for a particular country. They may be more appropriate for advanced, industrialized states than resource-poor ones. Since outcome data are generally harder to acquire than process data, there is a risk that countries will focus on implementing programs without knowing whether they are the most effective given their circumstances. It is also not easy to distinguish between indicators that measure conduct (process) and those that measure results (outcomes). Some process measures could stand as outcomes. The designers of these indicators acknowledge that the process indicator for one right can be an outcome indicator for another (UN International Human Rights Instruments and Office of the High Commissioner for Human Rights 2006: 8). For example, some of the process indicators for the right to health, such as the "proportion of births attended by skilled health personnel," could be seen as outcomes — as enjoyments of the right — regardless of their effects on maternal mortality rates or underweight children (table 7.1).

Moreover, because of the focus on measurable inputs and outputs, more systemic features of society are not included. For example, there is no discussion of government policies toward population size overall. There is an assumption that the interventions and institutions that will contribute to the enjoyment of the right to health come from states and involve the provision of state services. There is, in other words, an implicit assumption that improvement depends on state action and that states have the resources and the capacity to provide health care services, nutrition programs, breastfeeding training, and so forth.

Finally, the focus on specific rights rather than on particular treaties makes these indicators less useful to treaty bodies, which typically work through their treaty article by article, but may well serve the development community better as it seeks to understand what actions constitute compliance with human rights laws (see Kalantry et al. 2010: 274).

Clearly, the tables are designed to specify state obligations. As a tool for monitoring state compliance with human rights treaty obligations, this approach makes sense. Yet the demands of measurement and the availability of data restrict the theoretical model of social change embedded in the table. Rather than addressing forms of inequality produced by racism, differences between rural and urban residence, patriarchal kinship systems, dependence on international investment, or social norms concerning gender, the tables articulate a model of social change in which increasing state services to the population at large is assumed to benefit the entire population. They pay little attention to the need for broader social change, reducing social inequality, or targeting particular vulnerable communities. This is a model of development, not human rights.

In sum, the creators of the OHCHR indicators grappled with the challenge of converting broad standards into specific measures that would be easy to use and circulate widely among countries by importing frameworks and templates from economic development and public health, arguing that this approach would make human rights more understandable to the development community. They carried out this transformation in three ways. First, they converted human rights obligations into measurable entities. Second, they shifted from the respect-protect-fulfill framework to the structure-process-outcome framework, highlighting the trajectory of development in producing human rights outcomes. Third, they used single-page templates that quickly offered countries a guide on what they needed to do to fulfill their obligations. Thus they subtly shifted the indicators from a legal frame to a development one. The use of indicators facilitates a closer relationship between human rights and development, but whether this will improve development planning and enhance human rights compliance or subordinate legal rights to development and undermine their role as trump cards in cases of abuse is open to debate.

THE FINAL GUIDELINES AND THE UN LAUNCH

The final report from the OHCHR project says that one goal of the project was to make human rights more understandable to the development and policy communities (UN Office of the High Commissioner for Human Rights

2012a: 2). This perspective was emphasized at the report's UN launch in New York City on May 10, 2013, which I attended along with an audience of about 150 in the elegant UN ECOSOC chamber. High Commissioner for Human Rights Navi Pillay gave a speech supporting the indicators, saying that they would help implement human rights and would be useful for including human rights in the post-2015 revision of the MDGs. Noting that in the current MDGs, "we treasured what we measured," she argued that it would be better to "measure what we treasure." Development and human rights do not always go well together, she said, but statistics help bridge the gap. She also made clear that the indicators were not to be used for ranking or to replace judicial decision making but to construct a framework useful for each country to assess itself.

Her talk was followed by statements of support from Finland and Mexico, each noting their early role in the process and subsequent investment in it. Mexico, for example, worked with the OHCHR to develop indicators for several rights, such as the right to physical and mental health, the right to a fair trial, the right to a life free of violence, and the right to a clean environment, while Finland emphasized its sponsorship of the initial 2005 conference. This was followed by a panel of experts. The chair emphasized the contribution of indicators in reinforcing objectivity and universality, as well as strengthening local and national governments. Rajeev Malhotra participated via video conferencing from India, where he is now a professor at the Jindal School of Government and Public Policy. He noted that this is an important time for the indicators as the new, post-2015 MDGs are being developed. His vision of human rights is that they are not just about protecting legal rights but also about putting them into policy. For human rights to influence policy, he thinks, they need to be less legalistic and more concrete, specific, and accessible to others. It is necessary to operationalize them, to provide benchmarks, and to streamline the reporting process and make it more efficient to ease the reporting burden. In the chair's summary of Malhotra's talk, he said that Malhotra's key point was that the language of rights needed to be more concrete and practical and that it was necessary to turn legal issues into numbers to make them more accessible to larger audiences.

One of the panelists said that indicators translate legal terms into broader ways of thinking and a language that policy makers can hear—the language of state management and statisticians. The chair pointed out that it was new for statisticians and human rights activists to talk to each other and that Malhotra was a person who was able to bridge policy and statistics. With twenty-five years of experience as a development economist, he taught statistics to the OHCHR and, in turn, picked up some human rights language. (He has also worked for the Finance Ministry in India.) Another speaker pointed out that evidence-based human rights indicators make contributions to public policy, which he contrasted to using human rights in a "denunciatory mode." However, this speaker also noted that there was a risk of reducing human rights indicators to a technocratic approach.

Several speakers noted that the original version of the MDGs did not take human rights standards into account and that they wanted the post-2015 version to be founded on states' human rights obligations. Human rights metrics have an important role to play here. Speakers noted that they could increase accountability, deal with disparities such as access to water and sanitation, put more emphasis on targets and time frames that take human rights into account, and focus on available resources, rates of progress, and the contributions of developed countries to global development. However, the speakers also pointed to the risk that what would be measured would be what could be measured and that what could not be measured would be ignored. They thought it was important for national statistical offices to measure more. The most important contribution of the indicators, according to the panel, is that they provide a new language for human rights that is accessible to wider audiences of policy makers and development economists. Some speakers expressed concern that quantitative measures might lead to neglect of qualitative ones.

According to the speakers, the structure-process-outcome framework is a major contribution of the project. Many discussed the importance of civil society's adoption of this framework and gave examples of countries and organizations that were using parts of it and adapting them to the particular issues in various places. The final report, *Human Rights Indicators: A Guide to Measurement and Implementation*, was published in a 174-page book in Spanish and English, reflecting the enthusiasm in Latin America and Europe. It was distributed at the launch and was also made available online (UN Office of the High Commissioner for Human Rights 2012a).

Thus by translating human rights into a development framework, the OHCHR project blurs the distinction between monitoring human rights compliance and promoting human-rights-based development. In contrast to human-rights-based development, which seeks to introduce human rights principles such as participation and bottom-up planning into development planning, these indicators focus on introducing development principles such as the use of numerical indicators, models of developmental change, and structured tables that imply causal relationships between actions and outcomes into human rights monitoring. The OHCHR indicators re-present human rights less as a legal project and more as a dimension of good governance and development. While this translation clearly increases the legibility of human rights to these other fields, it strays from the distinctive logic of a legal system that sets firm standards of right and wrong against which actions can be judged. Instead of human-rights-based development, these techniques produce development-based human rights.

Governance Effects

Once an indicator regime is created, the challenge is to persuade others to use it and take it seriously. This requires powerful actors to adopt the template and invest in connecting data to the model. The ability of any indicator to achieve this recognition depends in part on the power of the institution that creates and promotes it. Well-known indicators, such as the UNDP's HDI or the Worldwide Governance Indicators originally developed at the World Bank, are backed by powerful agencies, while the *TIP Reports* have the sanctions and rewards of the United States behind them. Unlike many centralized, coordinated indicators, however, the OHCHR framework is a collaborative, negotiated, multicountry project. Creating the OHCHR indicators required negotiation among all treaty bodies, which are resolutely independent and committed to their own conventions. The institutional basis for the OHCHR indicators is weaker, and its ability to force its categories and practices on those that are governed is far less. The use of these indicators is a matter of choice by the countries that are being governed. The only sanction attached to nonuse or noncompliance is criticism in the concluding comments of the treaty bodies. Despite the desire of some of the proponents of human rights indicators to develop a set of standardized, universal indicators, in the end, the OHCHR indicators are no more unified than the treaty bodies themselves or the countries they seek to monitor.

SELLING THE INDICATORS

The OHCHR staff has worked hard to connect with countries interested in using its indicators. According to Nicolas Fasel, this is a more bottom-up process than many other indicator initiatives. In contrast to the UNDP and the World Bank, which simply create indicators and use them to measure and rank countries, Fasel says he spends considerable time working with countries. Sometimes he talks to a government official in the national statistical office or finance ministry, but most often he talks to the national commission on human rights. People approach him for help in deciding which indicators to focus on and how to develop their approach to indicators. OHCHR staffers hold workshops and provide technical assistance when countries request it. The OHCHR ran workshops in Uganda and New Delhi in 2007; in Nepal, Columbia, and Azerbaijan in 2008; and in Kenya and Ecuador in 2009. It also held meetings about its indicators with the Council of Europe in 2009 and with Brazil, the United Kingdom, and Mexico in 2010.

Some of these workshops with regional, subregional, and national stakeholders were designed as validation exercises. The meetings were intended to assess whether the indicators reflected the way human rights were understood in different parts of the world. They were also intended to disseminate knowledge about the indicators and persuade countries to use them. For example, the New Delhi meeting was attended by policy makers; representatives from national human rights institutions and statistical agencies; and some civil society representatives from twelve countries in the region (Sharma et al. 2007: 4). The general approach, followed in this as well as other meetings was to ask participants to come up with attributes and indicators for a particular human right (Sharma et al. 2007: 11–15). After a session of brainstorming, they were presented with the tables of attributes and indicators developed by the OHCHR. The OHCHR staff noted "a striking consistency" between the attributes and indicators identified by the participants and those identified by the OHCHR, which the participants "endorsed." The OHCHR staff took this experience as validation of the framework and indicators (UN International Human Rights Instruments and Office of the High Commissioner for Human Rights 2008: 16). Thus the exercise served to inform and engage the stakeholders rather than to facilitate collaboration in constructing the indicators, although the team did make some changes in response to the feedback. The organizers argue that the indicators are simply a tool kit that can be selectively adapted to a particular context; they do not need substantial revision in response to these meetings. The meetings served to validate the approach and the choice of indicators rather than to reformulate them to fit within the region more closely.

The indicators have been particularly influential in Latin America and Europe. Guatemala was the first to use the indicators for reporting, in 2009, and Brazil, Kenya, Mexico, Nepal, Sweden, Ecuador, and the United Kingdom have also used elements of them (UN Economic and Social Council 2011: para. 27; UN Office of the High Commissioner for Human Rights 2012a; 2012b). Johannes Waldmueller's recent anthropological study in Ecuador reported the country's enthusiastic adoption of the human rights indicators (Waldmueller 2014). The Inter-American Commission on Human Rights adapted the OHCHR framework for its proposed guidelines for reporting on economic, social, and cultural rights in 2008 (Inter-American Commission on Human Rights 2008: paras. 29–33). The OHCHR indicators' framework was used to measure progress in the implementation of fundamental rights in the European Union at the second annual meeting of the EU Agency for Fundamental Rights (FRA) in 2011 in Vienna (Fundamental Rights Agency 2011). The UK Equality and Human Rights Commission introduced a "Human Rights Measurement Framework" in 2012 based on the OHCHR indicators, substantially revised for the conditions in England, Scotland, and Wales (Vizard 2012). The Human Rights Commissioner for the Council of Europe stressed the value of the OHCHR approach in a statement in 2009 (Vizard 2012: 241).

In 2011, the High Commissioner for Human Rights reported on the use of this indicator system for economic, social, and cultural rights to the Economic and Social Council of the United Nations, noting its adoption by countries such as Nepal, Ecuador, and Kenya and its use in developing indicators on poverty by the UNDP, on sexual and reproductive health by the WHO, and on global food and nutrition security by the High-level Task Force on the Global Food Security Crisis (UN Economic and Social Council 2011: paras. 27, 29). The report also noted that members of the Human Rights Council encourage the use of indicators in the universal periodic review process (UN Economic and Social Council 2011: para. 44).

Overall, however, the OHCHR has not been pushing the indicators very hard, according to some of the experts I interviewed. In comparison to the funds and political pressure exerted by the United States in support of its trafficking indicators, discussed in chapters 5 and 6, the push behind the OHCHR indicators has been quite limited. For example, the 2014 General Assembly resolution on reform of the treaty body process did not even mention the use of indicators or quantification (Broecker and O'Flaherty 2014; O'Flaherty 2014: 5; UN General Assembly 2014).

INDICATOR UPTAKE BY TREATY BODIES AND
REPORTING COUNTRIES

Although the treaty bodies endorsed the OHCHR framework in 2008 (UN Economic and Social Council 2011: para. 1), the uptake of these indicators by treaty bodies has been limited. Some treaty bodies have added the OHCHR indicators to their reporting guidelines, suggesting that countries use them in preparing their periodic reports. They are mentioned in the ICESCR and CRPD guidelines for 2009 (UN Committee on Economic, Social, and Cultural Rights 2009: 3) and the ICCPR guidelines for 2010 (UN Human Rights Council 2010: 4). However, I heard no discussion of these indicators at the ICESCR hearings I visited in May 2011 and was told by an expert member of the Human Rights Committee whom I interviewed that indicators did not come up at all during the meeting in March 2011. Many treaty body members have legal or diplomatic backgrounds and are not necessarily comfortable with statistical data analysis. Gauthier de Beco notes that in general the enthusiasm for human rights indicators seems to be greater among academics than among practitioners and that most human rights indicator sets have never been applied (de Beco 2013: 3). He attributes this failure to use indicators mostly to their complexity, which is a problem for the OHCHR indicators as well. Another difficulty is the organization of the indicators. Treaty bodies monitor compliance by moving through their treaties article by article, while the OHCHR indicators are organized by rights, which are not closely tied to particular treaties or articles. Consequently, the scheme is not easily adapted to monitoring treaties.

The leaders of the project and OHCHR staff made presentations to several of the treaty bodies. The ICESCR treaty body was the most enthusiastic, followed by the CEDAW treaty body, but a person who attended both presentations said that the overall responses of both were quite lukewarm. The CAT committee was not particularly interested. The CERD and CRC committees were accepting of the approach. I observed the presentation of a different indicator model to the CRC committee in June 2010 in which about one-third of the experts asked questions, but the rest seemed disengaged. Those experts who expressed interest were people with advanced training in the social sciences and government bureaucrats familiar with statistical data. When Martin Scheinin and Nicolas Fasel presented the OHCHR indicators to the Human Rights Committee in July 2009, the committee was split between those who were enthusiastic about the project and those who opposed it on the grounds that the indicators might lead to country ranking, even though the OHCHR presenters claimed it would not. A press report from the UN Office in Geneva described the committee's response as concerned about making the indicators more user friendly and about their lack of fit with issues such as enforced disappearances and legal changes (UN Office in Geneva 2009). Ranking emerged as a major concern:

> It would be possible to rank countries in their implementation of a specific right, several Experts noted. That could then be compared to other rankings as done by Freedom House or Transparency International. Was such a ranking envisaged? Experts noted that such a ranking by the United Nations was especially sensitive. This data could be used to allocate World Bank funds, which

was problematic. Experts also feared that such indicators would be abused to get rid of human rights treaty bodies. . . .

Concluding the briefing, Mr. Scheinin and Mr. Fasel said that there was no intention of comparing countries, although technically it could be done. Countries should rather use those indicators as benchmarks. As to costs, the indicators should not be more expensive than producing other statistical information. It was true that they could be used to other means, as for the attribution of development aid, but that was beyond the scope of the human rights treaty bodies anyway. (UN Office in Geneva 2009)

There was clearly some ambivalence in the Human Rights Committee. In general, treaty bodies are committed to an intensive, particularized process that uses statistics as useful data but does not readily give way to a standardized assessment on the basis of agreed-upon indicators.

UPTAKE BY COUNTRIES

When countries prepare their periodic reports to the various treaty bodies, they are encouraged to use indicators. In order to assess how country reports use indicators, my research assistant Amy Field counted how often the word "indicator" was used in all country reports to the six major treaty bodies between 2007 and 2011, excluding uses of the term in titles or tables. Counting the number and kinds of references to indicators is only a rough way to assess the importance of quantitative data within a country and the issues for which it is considered relevant, however. Country reports differ in part depending on who writes them, whether government officials, national consultants, or international consultants, so that they reveal not simply national enthusiasm or antipathy for statistics but significant difference by treaty. On average, these 365 country reports included 4.6 references to indicators, but there was an above-average number of references to indicators in reports to the ICESCR, CRC, and CEDAW treaty bodies and a below-average number of references in reports to the ICCPR and CAT treaty bodies. Surprisingly, CERD reports also had low indicator usage, perhaps because many countries did not gather data by race. Measuring racial discrimination requires creating categories of race and ethnicity and finding ways to count the population in these terms. It is possible that countries' reluctance to carry out surveys of their racial composition contributed to this low rate of indicator use (see Clark 2009; 2015).[4] The ICCPR and CAT treaty bodies focus more strongly on legal issues and are less concerned with the number of violations. Statistics are more available on social and economic rights and on women and children than on the frequency of torture or civil rights violations.

A qualitative content analysis of 528 country reports to the six major human rights treaties from 2007 to 2013[5] showed that the indicators mentioned in these reports were primarily counts and ratios of basic social and demographic information rather than the full range of indicators that the OHCHR project advocates. They were almost entirely economic, health, and educational measures, such as poverty rates, school enrollment numbers, maternal and infant mortality rates, labor market characteristics, employment levels, and gender equality ratios. Many referred to the MDGs and the UNDP human development indicators, such as the HDI. Developing countries use more indicators than developed countries, suggesting that the use of indicators is fostered by interactions with international organizations and donors. Particularly among relatively poor, donor-dependent countries such as those of sub-Saharan Africa, country reports refer to the HDI and the MDGs and rely on data produced by the MICS or the DHS. There are frequent references to donor-initiated programs and statistics. Donors and UN agencies sometimes also supply the consultants who write the reports.

Richer countries with more sophisticated statistical systems, such as European countries and India, tend to use fewer indicators in their reports.[6] For example, the statistics-rich countries of Germany and Australia used only six and three indicators respectively in their recent country reports to the CRC treaty body, while Togo provided twenty-three. In reports to the CEDAW treaty body, Benin referred to indicators eleven times, including references to both access to water and gender, listing the many donors who helped with this problem. On the other hand, Chile referred to indicators only twice, even though it has an advanced statistical system, and India mentioned no indicators at all. Richer countries may strive for autonomy to achieve some escape from being observed and counted, and they may feel less of a need to show that they are modern. Despite efforts to have countries set benchmarks for themselves (Riedel 2011), there were few references to benchmarks.

At least in the short run, the OHCHR indicators have not provided the hoped-for streamlining or standardization of the monitoring process. However, the structure-process-outcome template has become generally accepted and widely disseminated (de Beco 2013: 2). It was used to produce indicators for the rights to health, education, and water, among others (de Beco 2013; Hunt 2003a; Kalantry et al. 2010). Rajeev Malhotra used the framework to create indicators for the right to development but referred to "criteria" rather than "indicators" because of countries' resistance to indicators, according to Maria

Green and Susan Randolf, two of the experts who developed the framework (UN Working Group on the Right to Development 2010). The African Commission on Human and Peoples' Rights added the framework to its reporting guidelines for economic, social, and cultural rights in 2010 (African Commission on Human and Peoples' Rights 2010: 15). A project to produce indicators for early child development, sponsored by academics at the University of British Columbia, used this framework (Vaghri, Arkadas, and Early Childhood Rights Indicators Group 2009; Vaghri et al. 2011), as did an expert group developing indicators for indigenous peoples (UN ILO, UN OHCHR, SPFII 2010). An organization of indigenous Latin American women produced a set of indicators for indigenous people at the Permanent Forum in 2009 using this template. In his survey of human rights indicators for business, de Felice advocates using this framework, translated into policy, process, and outcome indicators (2015). Even though the framework as a whole struggles for recognition, this template travels well.

Conclusions

Unlike many other indicators, those of the OHCHR were international and collaborative. They built on the expertise of a small group of human rights lawyers, academics, development economists, and treaty body experts, mostly from the global North. The disciplines of human rights law and development economics shaped this indicator regime. The indicators introduced a new framework into the human rights field that was designed to highlight objectively measurable phenomena, to emphasize cause and effect relationships, and to "help demystify the notion of human rights and take the human rights discourse beyond the confines of legal and justice sector discussions" (UN International Human Rights Instruments and Office of the High Commissioner for Human Rights 2008: 7, 11). The stated goal of the creators was to facilitate mainstreaming human rights in policy making and development implementation (2008: 7).

Clearly, a major goal was to translate human rights into terms compatible with development rather than only law and justice. The core strategy in achieving this translation was converting human rights obligations into numbers. Adding the structure-process-outcome template to the more legalistic respect-protect-fulfill framework also contributed to the shift, as did representing the indicators on a single-page grid. The indicators succeeded in transforming human rights measures into patterns of data gathering and assessment familiar to development economics and public health. Both of these academic disciplines are embedded in large international bureaucracies, such as the WHO, the UNDP, and the World Bank, that have been generating indicators and measurements for a long time. Development economics provided the framework for the HDI and the MDGs, and public health did the same for such key indicators as maternal mortality and life expectancy. Finally, and perhaps most important, the OHCHR indicators build on a theory of human rights that is widely accepted in development thinking that the rule of law, good governance, and state accountability promote development and the general well-being of a population.

However, the hope that indicators could streamline the process of human rights regulation, increase accountability, deal with a need for accurate data disaggregated to expose discrimination, and develop specific dimensions of human rights obligations seems to be as yet unfulfilled. Their complexity remains a challenge. Indeed, at the national validation exercises, there was "initial skepticism that was expressed by some of the participants at the beginning of the workshop regarding the apparent complexity of the conceptual framework adopted for the work on human rights indicators" (UN International Human Rights Instruments and Office of the High Commissioner for Human Rights 2008: 16). As Malhotra and Fasel acknowledge, these consultations underlined the need to simplify the conceptual framework or at least improve its communication and accessibility (UN International Human Rights Instruments and Office of the High Commissioner for Human Rights 2008: 17).

Several factors contributed to this complexity: fear of focusing on too few issues and neglecting some, avoiding ranking, and concerns about oversimplifying and standardizing. Despite the widespread acceptance of the MDGs, scholars point to the fact that they have the aforementioned drawbacks (see Fukuda-Parr and Yamin 2014; 2015; Yamin and Falb 2012: 222). Moreover, the MDGs pay little attention to inequality; some scholars have suggested indicators that incorporate this issue (Winkler et al. 2015). In addition, because treaty body experts are committed to their particular treaty and to preserving a holistic, country-specific approach, their support for standardized indicators was limited. Despite the benefits of indicators in terms of efficiency of data processing, access to more reliable information, and ability to assess change over time, the human rights community has generally resisted quantification and ranking. Ranking is not only too simplified but also politically unpalatable to countries. Ironically, naming and shaming is a crucial element of the power of human rights, so it is perhaps understandable that countries resist it and treaty body members hesitate to use it. The OHCHR indicators compromised by producing a large number of indicators and viewing them as a tool kit — a set of possible measures among which countries can pick and choose — and by refusing to rank.

Ironically, this fragmented approach undermines the power of the indicators themselves. The most successful indicators tell a simple story using numbers and rankings, often depicted in colorful maps. Those that draw attention to an issue are big, bold, and well-funded. They tend to be highly simplifying composites. The attempts at complexity and multidimensionality embedded in the OHCHR indicators make them more useful for thinking about human rights compliance but less effective in influencing wider publics. This is the inevitable indicator trade-off between lumping data for maximum effect and splitting them for greater accuracy.

Are these effective indicators? From the perspective of presenting simple data that appeal to the general public, the answer is no. What makes indicators successful in general is their capacity to synthesize complex situations and present simplified accounts based on numerical data. They depend on a clear theory embedded in the indicator. These indicators lack a theory beyond the presumption that passing certain laws and enacting particular government programs will lead to specific outcomes. The proponents of the OHCHR indicators refuse to rank and compare or to present simplistic and potentially misleading representations. Yet it is such composite indicators' simplification, decontextualization, and ranking that catch public attention. While avoiding these pitfalls, the indicator project has produced tables that are not very effective in streamlining, monitoring, or bringing issues to public attention.

On the other hand, these complicated indicators may well appeal to experts and policy makers in the fields of development and health. They are more collaborative, multinational, and multidisciplinary than the *TIP Reports* or even the HDI or MDGs. They were born from a more negotiative process and resist linear scoring, highly targeted goals, and superficial assessments of complex situations. Ironically, it is their effort to be more true to the nature of human rights thinking that has made them less accessible as indicators. Perhaps as public disillusionment with composite indicators builds, more complex metrics such as these will increase in popularity. It depends on what happens to the cultural enthusiasm for this technology and whether public trust in its claims to make a complex world knowable through "indicator culture" — technical rationality, a pragmatic approach to measurement, and the magic of numbers — grows along with support for evidence-based governance and skepticism about political debate. If so, the human rights indicators may yet grow in popularity and influence.

CHAPTER EIGHT

Conclusions

Comparing the three indicator projects makes clear the value of a genealogical approach to understanding the knowledge an indicator creates and its governance effects. It opens up the circumstances of each one's creation, templates and formats, and underling theory. Each measurement system constructs a theory of social life and strategies for change, but the theory of each is embedded in the way data are collected, arranged, and presented. The theory of the UNSC's indicators of violence against women is that violence is a product of particular kinds of interpersonal relationships and that understanding the frequency, type, and severity of violence requires identifying victim-perpetrator relationships. Acts of violence are defined dyadically, while the social context — norms of violence, everyday practices, and gendered identities and power — is absent. The *Trafficking in Persons Reports* theorize trafficking as a process in which innocent victims, mostly poor and from developing countries, are coerced into exploitative labor against their will. Like drugs, trafficked persons are simply transported without agency or choice. The trafficker alone is responsible for recruitment into exploitative labor and deserves punishment, while victims need to be rescued and sent home. The human rights indicators link human rights compliance with development, fashioning a development-based human rights approach that assumes that government policies and programs that enhance development will also improve human rights compliance. This approach shifts the legal frame of analysis and judgment to a managerial one that sets quantitative standards and seeks to make states responsible for complying with them.

Intriguingly, all these theories assign responsibility for violations to an individual or the state rather than to systemic inequalities or structural violence. They do not include analyses of the roles of larger economic, political, and social structures or patterns of inequality and violence or theories that would suggest different solutions that address underlying patterns of inequality. The UNSC's indicators of violence against women frame acts of violence as the product of particular dyadic relationships with partners or strangers rather than as the product of poverty, migration, racial exclusion, or a social context that tolerates such violence. The *TIP Reports'* trafficking indicators imagine the problem as being caused by criminal traffickers rather than the pressures of violent marriages, poor food and housing, family obligations, long-term indebtedness, or even the desire for travel and modernity that shape the path into exploitative labor. The OHCHR's human rights indicators locate the source of problems in the failure of governments to provide policies that support battered women, maternal health care, or effective policing rather than in capitalist relations of production, environmental degradation, global supply chains, or corrupt governments.

In each of these cases, the theory is expressed through the measurement system. Like the HDI, which reinforced the capabilities approach, the *TIP Reports'* ranking system supports the focus on prosecuting traffickers, the indicators of violence against women focus on the risks posed by partners, and the human rights indicators name the government actions necessary for better human rights outcomes. Thus the indicators and the knowledge they create reinforce the theory they embody.

Indicator Genealogies

What do these genealogies tell us about the social, political, economic, and cultural factors that create quantified knowledge? All three cases are clearly the products of particular institutions, political and economic contexts, cultural preferences for quantification, and agendas of reform and management. In each case, a specific set of actors, institutional supporters, and theories produce the indicators. The expertise of these actors and the availability of data shape the way they categorize and analyze information to develop an indicator. The politics of indicators are visible in the way categories are constructed, decisions are made about what to count, and concepts are defined as measurable. The knowledge they provide is inevitably interpreted through their expertise and experience. Counts and ratios are interpretive but are less so than composites. Composite indicators are potentially the most influential and also the most problematic because of their long interpretive chains. The genealogical, ethnographic approach foregrounds the actors, the institutions, the processes of theoretical development, and the temporality of the process. It indicates how quantified measures acquire authority and influence, supported by the power of numbers and the role of expertise and experience with measurement.

The genealogical analysis of indicator development and dissemination as a temporal process shows how and for whom these forms of knowledge become stable over time and why contestation over their frameworks and knowledge construction becomes increasingly difficult. As we have seen, models and templates may be imported from other domains, just as human trafficking indicators imported those of drug trafficking models and the OHCHR indicators imported development frameworks. Importing models facilitates communication with other domains: in the trafficking case, with criminal justice, and in the human rights case, with development economics.

The tendency to follow established paths is a product of the mechanisms of data inertia and expertise inertia. Data inertia occurs because reliance on existing data constrains what can be measured, and new issues require either the use of existing data as proxies or the expensive collection of new data. Expertise inertia is the result of using existing models and templates for new problems and the practice of endowing those who have professional expertise and past experience in measurement with the responsibility for designing new measurement systems. Both forms of inertia explain how measurement systems build on past work and why they are difficult to change. They also explain why experts from countries with a history of statistical work tend to dominate the creation of indicators and why it is hard for ordinary people to influence the shape and content of measurement systems.

While the creators of this form of knowledge are well aware of the pragmatic compromises required by measurement categorization and data quality, when quantified knowledge is presented, it makes claims to objectivity and science, offering a form of knowledge that is technically reliable and useful for decision making. The social context within which an indicator is created and its political dimensions are rarely presented. The tenets of "indicator culture" render such knowledge pragmatically useful, while the public presentation of information without qualification inhibits deeper investigation and critique. As we have seen, however, struggles among groups with different ideas of what should be counted are central to the development of indicators. There were tensions between the legal and economic models for the OHCHR indicators and the feminist, human rights, criminal justice, and statistical approaches to surveying violence against women. The *TIP Reports'* approach to measuring trafficking contrasts with those of the Global Slavery Index and the International Labour Organization. Although these struggles shape the way categories are formed and counted, the link between politics and the knowledge that indicators present often disappears from public discourse.

Despite the quiet power that indicators exercise in their creation of knowledge and in their influence on governance, some people, organizations, and countries resist. Researchers challenge the adequacy of data or the frameworks of analysis, as the gender equality and human rights group did of the UNSC indicators. The *TIP Reports* have been substantially criticized by researchers within the antitrafficking community for thin data and an overemphasis on prosecution. Those who are measured sometimes resist, both in the way knowledge is constructed and in the way data are gathered, although this book has not been able to explore resistance at the level of data collection or analysis. Countries clearly rejected being ranked by the human rights indicators, and the treaty bodies themselves showed limited enthusiasm for the model.

The Institutional Framework

Comparing these three indicators suggests significant differences in the institutional conditions of their creation and in the level of support they receive. Two were formed by international institutions. The human rights indicators were developed through an international process in which representatives of several countries took part, and it was sponsored by the United Nations. Similarly, the violence-against-women indicators were an initiative of the UN General Assembly, although as in the previous case, not all countries were able to participate equally. The US *TIP Reports*, in contrast, constitute a unilateral action by one country that set its own standards and judges all other countries by these standards. It is both the least collaborative and the best resourced indicator. The OHCHR encourages countries to use its human rights indicators but seems not to be investing heavily in their promotion or dissemination beyond publishing guidelines for reporting to treaty bodies and supporting workshops. The UNSC has also invested in the publication of indicators and guidelines, but it expects that national statistical offices, under pressure from the UN General Assembly and its resolutions about measuring violence against women, will use their own resources to carry out the surveys. The *TIP Reports*, in contrast, have had strong support from the US government in the country's foreign policy and its funding for organizations carrying out its mandate.

These differences in institutional support are correlated with impact. The *TIP Reports* are generally credited with bringing significant attention to the problem of trafficking, while the human rights indicators have had relatively little uptake by the treaty bodies, their intended users. There have already been about ten surveys of violence against women using the UNSC's guidelines in some way, but these are done by local statistical offices rather than the UNSC itself. The UNSD intends to do a meta-analysis of them with other national and international surveys of violence against women to reveal the global pattern of violence against women but recognizes that the data are scattered and not necessarily comparable. Neither of these two indicators has had the impact of the *TIP Reports*. Although both are far newer, and therefore may gain influence over time, they lack the support of the *TIP Reports*. The comparison suggests that a powerful parent organization willing to invest resources substantially improves the governance potential of an indicator. At the same time, a multiauthored indicator such as the OHCHR's indicator system is less able to develop a coherent underlying narrative and measurement system.

Impact also varies with the nature of the indicator itself. Only the *TIP Reports* use composite scores and ranking—the techniques that are most successful in presenting a substantial amount of information in a way that is simple to understand and affects reputations. The OHCHR indicators resist both composites and ranking, and their indicator grids are complicated and hard to use. The violence-against-women-survey approach has struggled with the issue of how narrowly to define the problem. One survey using this model presents data on the percentage of women physically and sexually abused, thus using ratios that are readily understandable and easy to compare with other countries, but it took a narrow definition of violence against women (Secretariat of the Pacific Community 2010). A composite indicator on violence against women that would permit global ranking has yet to be developed, although in a talk at the CSW meeting, the Friends of the Chair chairperson from Mexico suggested it as a goal. In sum, a comparison of these three cases suggests that the indicators that make the greatest impact are ones with strong institutional support and funding, a coherent and attractive narrative, and a composite indicator that allows for ranking.

Although I have not discussed the aesthetics of presentation and the process of dissemination, many prominent indicators are displayed in colorful, interactive websites, often with world maps that paint the good countries green and the bad ones red, following the familiar traffic-light model. As Edward Tufte pointed out (2001), the aesthetics of presenting quantitative data is highly complex and, to be effective, must be carefully thought through. The *TIP Reports* include colored maps depicting tier status, with green for Tier 1 and red for Tier 3, along with pictures of trafficked victims and boxed short stories about their lives. In contrast, the OHCHR indicators are presented in dense and difficult grids with no guidance about how to make the data accessible and engaging. The violence-against-women survey mentioned above uses a simple but accessible bar chart to present ratio data on the prevalence of physical and sexual violence (Secretariat of the Pacific Community 2010: 3). For an indicator to be persuasive and widely used, it needs to be presented in a way that is easy to understand and that uses familiar color codes and maps. All these factors enhance the power of indicators to create global knowledge. As this book argues, quantification represents a technology of producing knowledge that has the capacity to shape decisions and governance that is open to whatever organizations or individuals can harness its power. As this comparison suggests, however, it is not equally open to all.

Producing Commensurability

This book has traced the development of indicators over the last three decades in order to understand the political, social, and cultural processes by which they are created. It shows that quantifying social phenomena requires translating things understood in idiosyncratic, systemic, or situational terms into things that can be counted. In making them commensurable, they must be viewed as, in some ways, the same, pulled away from their embeddedness in a holistic cultural and political context. Some features can be considered; others must be ignored. As we have seen, this process inevitably leads to simplification and decontextualization. Yet such simplification is inescapable. In order to quantify social life, different things must be made equivalent, categories for comparison have to be constructed, and things have to be classified into these categories. As the genealogies of indicators showed, there are three steps.

First, it is necessary to *create equivalence* across individual differences. This requires finding a commonality or some shared trait among individuals and ignoring differences. To compare the frequency of violence against women in different societies, for example, it was necessary to establish equivalence across a wide range of forms of conflict involving women, which could include insults, sexual assault, rape, humiliation, slicing car tires, attacking pets and children, intimidation, blows, threats, harassment, injuries, and withholding financial support. These are very different actions with differing meanings within a relationship, and they produce quite different experiences. But it is necessary to see them all as manifestations of the same thing in order to count them. It is essential to construct a way to make distinct, individual acts equivalent as instances of a single concept of violence against women. The survey accomplished this by focusing on specific acts of physical or sexual violence.

Alain Desrosieres describes the process of creating equivalence as one that "allows a large number of events to be recorded and summarized according to standard norms." These spaces of equivalence were, he argues, practical before they were cognitive, thus emphasizing the pragmatic nature of the process (1998: 10). Through creating spaces of equivalence, random, unpredictable individual behaviors are converted into averages and become regular and predictable through the statistical summary of these acts (1998: 10). Once this construction is accepted, as it was in the case of the idea of the "average man," it becomes a real thing (1998: 11). We have traced this process in relation to violence against women and trafficking, both of which are broad and multifaceted concepts. Those tasked with counting them have focused on a relatively narrow range of behaviors, such as the act of physical or sexual violence or recruitment into exploitative labor, to define the concept. Similarly, the OHCHR indicators convert broad obligations, such as the right to health, into narrow, measurable concepts, such as the proportion of live births with low birth weights.

The second step in making social life commensurable is to *develop categories and classifications*. Categories must be organized according to a system of classifications so that things belong in one class or another. Categories are ideally mutually exclusive and all-encompassing. They cannot be too numerous for purposes of encoding and analysis or even, as Bowker and Star point out in their analysis of the international system of recording causes of death, too numerous to fit on a form (1999). Categories require the creation of boundaries. These may be arbitrary divisions along a continuum, such as measurements of severity of violence, or boundaries that reflect apparently distinct categories, such as gender. One approach, similar to the Linnaean classification system, assumes that it is possible to create theoretical spaces by specifying criteria that reflect the way groups occur, while the other sees a multidimensional continuum with nominal cuts and assumes that the categories exist in the imagination (Desrosieres 1998: 242). In the example of measuring violence against women, it can be done either way. Violence can be categorized using distinct legal categories such as rape, assault, harassment, or threats, or it can be divided into categories of more or less severe violence, drawing boundaries across a continuum. These systems of classification make it possible to designate an action as falling into one category or another.

Classifications may begin by using local categories but, over time, may move to more generic ones in order to facilitate comparison. For example, Bowker and Star described how the international system of classifying causes of death replaced local conceptions of disease with more generic terms that were able to cross boundaries (1999). However, local classifications may also become global, as they did in the violence-against-women survey. Here the experts used local categories developed in the United States and Europe to build global categories for physical and sexual violence and controlling behavior. From this set of categories, a new one was constructed for severe violence, the boundaries for which were drawn by experts. The *TIP Reports* constructed the categories of trafficking victims, prosecutions, convictions, and laws passed, based on US experience with criminalizing violence against women.

The creation of categories requires significant interpretive work. As we have seen, they are shaped by preexisting categories and theoretical concerns. Debates recur in the history of statistical classifications about "a sacrifice of inessential perceptions; the choice of pertinent variables; how to construct classes of equivalence; and last, the historicity of discontinuities" (Desrosieres 1998: 239). The categories inevitably lump disparate things together under a label, thus constituting a single concept. Moreover, each category has to be usable in all countries and locations. Categories must all refer to the same thing, even though that thing is manifested differently in different places. In order to understand the politics of categories, it is essential to examine the process of their creation and the actors, interests, networks, and templates that together constitute the expertise to draw up comparative categories, as the genealogies of indicators presented here attempt to do.

The third step in commensuration is to *encode*: to classify individual phenomena into one or another category. Encoding requires slotting a case into a particular category. It is, in Desrosieres's view, generally seen as a technical or practical problem solved by practitioners rather than theoreticians. Thus, through these social, political, and technical processes, things that are seen as objective are measured, and others become accepted as measurable over time: they become real, not just constructs. As Desrosieres puts it, at some point, collective objects or aggregates of individuals can come to "hold," to be accepted as real, at least for a while: "When the actors can rely on objects thus constructed, and these objects resist the tests intended to destroy them, aggregates do exist — at least during the period and in the domain in which these practices and tests succeed" (1998: 101). In other words, if these aggregates work in practice, they will be accepted in theory. Once they are accepted, they come to seem real.

These three processes are, of course, deeply interpretive, driven by theories and past experience with measurement. For example, feminists who worked on the violence-against-women survey wanted a description of the extent and severity of violence against women that was as inclusive and full as possible. They wished to avoid nondisclosure or situations in which women would fail to report violence. They designed the survey instrument to ask the questions in several ways and thought about how to make the interview situation safe and private. The concerns of the UNSC statisticians were less about nondisclosure and more about developing logical statistical categories. Surveys of domestic violence carried out by criminal justice institutions put greater emphasis on whether victims called the police and whether the police responded adequately to their calls. In the end, surveys are also driven by measurement problems, data availability, and cost. Any data collection process must consider what can be measured for how much money.

The demands of classification and encoding feed into what gets measured and counted. Encoding loops back and shapes both equivalence and classification, since the need to sort and classify determines what categories are usable and what forms of equivalence will work. In the case of violence against women, the demands of encoding led to an emphasis on apparently objective phenomena, such as acts, rather than apparently subjective ones, such as fear. This meant that acts and injuries were counted, while battered women's feelings about their experiences were not. The UNECE questionnaire asked interviewees about whether they feared their partners or were afraid for their lives, as well as about their states of well-being, but these questions were not in the original UNSC list of indicators. Measures of a more general sense of fear, vulnerability, and uneasiness are hard to use because it is difficult to sort them into categories and encode them. Consequently, surveys of violence against women resort to measures that bypass this problem, such as the nature of the violent act. Instead of measuring women's experience, they measure whether women are slapped, hit, choked, or assaulted with a gun. These acts are relatively easy to classify; how women feel about them is harder to classify and may not be measured at all.

The demand for commensurable categories means that local systems of knowledge cannot be incorporated into the quantification system. Those with local knowledge of the surveyed populations rarely participate in indicator construction, and even if representatives of countries without statistical expertise are around the planning table, they have less influence on the shape of categories. More fundamentally, vernacular understandings of violence against women, of trafficking, and of what constitutes a violation of the right to health have to be translated into global categories that will travel across lines of culture, class, and region. In a global survey, these categories must traverse borders and social lines without losing their shared meanings. This creates a paradox: they need to be translated into local terms in order to measure local ideas and behaviors accurately, but they need to retain their universal meanings in order to make comparisons possible across these borders. Therefore, the categories must refer to the same thing, manifested differently in different places. The efforts of the Friends of the Chair committee to define "severe physical violence" show the challenges of constructing a universal category out of a culturally varied set of categories developed for national and local surveys. In order to make global comparisons, categories need to be commensurable across countries, regions, settings (i.e., urban vs. rural), and a vast array of social and cultural formations.

The creation of categories that can travel occurs in what Richard Rottenburg calls "the technical game," based on his research in the field of development planning. The technical game is "perceived to be independent of social and cultural frames of reference." Technologies of representation and inscription produce the facts of this domain (Rottenburg 2012; see also Rottenburg 2009). He argues that recourse to the technical game is unavoidable in epistemologically heterogeneous zones such as development projects. The technical language constitutes a "metacode" that assumes that reality can be represented without distortion alongside distinct cultural codes. The metacode is, of course, also culturally situated but pragmatically treated as universal in order to make it possible to act (Rottenburg 2012). In a similar way, systems of measurement are clearly products of distinct national histories, yet they circulate globally as technologies distinct from their national origins with their claims of providing culture-free, nonlocalized knowledge.

Another effect of the development of commensurable categories is the homogenization of diverse phenomena. This is clearly the case with both violence against women and trafficking: the highly diverse set of activities, practices, motivations, and contexts of the activities that are labeled by these terms cannot be included in the system of quantification. In order to paint a big picture of the phenomenon, the little picture is blurred, and people's experiences are set aside. Yet it is precisely this kind of qualitative, situated, culturally framed knowledge that is essential to understanding trafficking and violence against women—in other words, the kind of knowledge that ethnography can provide.

Making Better Indicators

Not all indicators are equally misleading and superficial, of course. Although the demands of commensuration inevitably lead to decontextualization and homogenization, indicators that are created along with qualitative information can develop more accurate and locally relevant categories for comparison.

There are several ways that indicators can be made less misleading and distorting. They all involve some democratization of the creation and production of indicators. It is important to engage a wider range of people — particularly those who are the targets of measurement — in the construction of indicators as a way to resist expertise inertia. Increasing public discussion and debate during the early stages of making indicators, while their terms are still open to contestation, would make them more democratic by allowing changes before they become settled and taken for granted. As we have seen, when more parties are involved in creating indicators, they are more complex and difficult to use, but they are also better at reflecting the diversity of the social experiences they are measuring. Initial qualitative research would improve translations of local categories into global ones and incorporate more local meanings. Doing qualitative research within the populations that are to be measured to determine more accurate category construction and encoding would provide better guidance about what can be measured and how it should be categorized. The process of commensuration means that the translation will never be without slippage, but it could be less distorting.

Greater reliance on counts and ratios rather than composites would diminish distortion, since they require less interpretive work than composites and are less vulnerable to the twists produced by long interpretive chains. Avoiding speculative numbers and weak proxies is also important. A proliferation of indicators at the local, national, and regional, as well as global, levels challenges the hegemony of any one indicator in establishing the truth of a phenomenon. Finally, providing clearer warnings about the limitations of indicators, the problems of missing and inadequate data, weak proxies, the generalization inherent in commensuration, and the loss of structural and systemic knowledge could improve indicator literacy. None of these strategies — democratizing production, initial qualitative research, reliance on counts and ratios, developing multiple competing indicators, or providing more warnings — eliminates the need for interpretation in the creation of indicators, but they suggest forms of collaboration with qualitative forms of knowledge that would strengthen both. While quantitative data clearly benefit from linkages with qualitative information, qualitative data used alone are also problematic. Absence of quantitative data risks relying on simple narratives taken out of context that do not represent wider patterns. Although there is division within the social sciences concerning the relative emphasis on these two forms of knowledge, it is clear that both are important and that working together, they provide more accurate and comprehensive analyses.

Despite the advantages of a democratically produced, qualitatively informed, and accurately presented mode of indicator production, such measurement systems may not be effective within the highly competitive ecology of indicators. Those that generate public and policy attention tend to be simple; ranked; presented in visually appealing ways, such as color-coded maps; expressive of popular values, such as freedom or the rule of law; and consonant with familiar hierarchies that place the wealthy countries of the global North at the top. As we have seen, indicators are often the means by which institutions promote particular ideologies and policies, such as antitrafficking, rather than social science attempts to understand the social world.

Governance by Indicators

Quantification is a technology of control, but whether it is reformist or authoritarian depends on who has harnessed its power and for what purposes. In the cases in this book, it has been mobilized for reform agendas. The premise of the violence-against-women indicators is that reducing the problem requires identifying its scope and provenience. The OHCHR project recognizes the problem of information in assessing countries' compliance with human rights treaties and seeks, through quantification, to develop specific, countable obligations to improve state behavior. The *TIP Reports* clearly seek to ameliorate the problem of trafficking. Like human rights work in general, the assumption underlying all three projects is that providing knowledge of abuses will contribute to ending them. These are all agendas of reform, but as we have seen, their power depends on institutional resources and support.

One of the challenges of using quantification as a mode of reform is the difficulty of counting and measuring broad social phenomena such as justice, fear, fairness, corruption, freedom, democracy, and the rule of law. There are now efforts to measure these ideas, such as the World Justice Project's Rule of Law Index, but it is difficult. In order to reduce such concepts, including human rights treaties, to measurable entities, they must be made narrower and more specific. This work of narrowing and specifying comes at the cost of recognizing interdependence and a holistic perspective. Fukuda-Parr and Yamin make this point with reference to the MDGs (Fukuda-Parr and Yamin 2015). Their "Power of Numbers" project provides eleven case studies of MDG indicators that together show that the use of quantitative indicators for the MDGs drew valuable attention to some issues but, at the same time, distorted development planning by narrowing the focus to a few features; ignoring the interconnections among them; failing to measure difficult concepts, such as vulnerability; and taking a reductionist approach to development. For example, instead of the broad, transformative approach of the Beijing Platform for Action, gender equality was defined narrowly in terms of gender equality in primary and secondary education. Sexual and reproductive health and rights were narrowed to maternal health (Fukuda-Parr and Yamin 2014: 7).

Fukuda-Parr and Yamin conclude that numerical target setting is a poor methodology for articulating the international agenda of a complex phenomenon such as sustainable, inclusive development. The simplification, reification, and abstraction of quantification in the MDGs created perverse effects that detracted from the conception of human-rights- and people-centered approaches to development (Fukuda-Parr and Yamin 2014: 11). Moreover, the MDG regime put great demands on the capacity of statistical offices of African countries, sometimes straining the limited resources of these offices and impeding further data analysis (Jerven 2013: 96).

Under the evidence-based regime of governance, it is necessary to be counted to be recognized. Quantification makes issues visible and reveals the extent and scope of a problem. But things that are more easily counted and more often counted tend to be those counted in the future, while those that have not been counted or are hard to quantify tend to be neglected and thus disappear from view. This shows another dimension of the power of quantification: measurement makes things visible, while the unmeasured disappear. It is easier to count what has already been counted, while the unfamiliar escapes quantification. For example, in our study of a pilot test for a children's rights indicator in Tanzania, Summer Wood and I found that data on familiar topics such as birth registration and breast feeding were far more available than those on unfamiliar human rights topics such as children's right to play (Merry and Wood 2015). Counting something makes it visible and subject to intervention and reform, but the failure to count the unfamiliar or hard to quantify, such as women's unpaid labor, children's right to play, or the justice contribution of a legal aid center, banishes it to the world of the unnoticed and the disappeared.

The use of quantification in governance is an improvement over private decision making, but it may also displace public judgment into private settings where experts design measurement systems that have judgments embedded in them. Moreover, the construction of measurement systems is often not open to public discussion or debate. Although there was public discussion of the UNSC indicators, for example, it was in the more private setting of the closed Friends of the Chair meeting that indicators of female genital cutting, psychological violence, and economic violence were added back in. The consultants who brought the more feminist, gender equality perspective into the UNSC violence-against-women guidelines worked in the even more private sphere of consultancy contracts and informal editing. Transparency is important for indicators as well as for those they seek to govern.

The Rise of "Indicator Culture"

The recent enthusiasm for quantification builds on a two-hundred-year movement toward a new way of knowing populations. With the nineteenth-century birth of statistics and its new forms of knowledge based on practices of commensuration and the search for regular patterns in the midst of apparently random events, governments acquired new tools for managing populations, both at home and in colonial territories. This use of evidence enhanced state control, but as this information became more publicly available, it also opened up political decision making to public scrutiny. Statistics are now seen as basic to holding states accountable to their citizens and to their human rights obligations. This book supports the argument that the availability of quantitative data increases state accountability but cautions that at the technical level, the production of this kind of knowledge is not so open or transparent. It is shaped, as we have seen, by ideology, inertia, social and political influence, inadequate data, and the pragmatic compromises that poor data require. Not all that should be counted is counted, nor does counting itself necessarily provide an accurate picture of a situation or its explanation.

The tendencies toward individualization, homogenization, and universalization inherent in the process of finding equivalence, developing categories, and encoding cases produce knowledge that is quite different from that which is generated by analyses of local systems of meaning and action or studies of individual behavior in terms of larger structural contexts of inequality and violence. It differs from knowledge produced by studies that analyze the interdependence of structures and actions. From a quantitative perspective, trafficking is the number of vulnerable people forced by a trafficker to do exploitative work; from a qualitative or systemic perspective, it is what happens when a particular poor woman travels to town to gather wages to help her family, finds that factory work pays too little, tries to work in a bar, and is pressured into doing sex work in order to keep her job. These are different forms of knowledge; both are valuable, but both are partial.

Democratic indicator creation, the incorporation of qualitative knowledge into indicator production, and increased indicator literacy offer ways to offset the growing reliance on quantification (see Merry 2011). This means a turn from the current enthusiasm for numerical data as clear descriptors of the world, now abetted by the enthusiasm for big data, toward a more skeptical understanding of what this information does and does not provide. The taken-for-granted use of scales and quantities, such as grades for school children and rankings for universities and colleges, are already recognized as producing unintended and often undesirable side effects. The conjunction of qualitative and quantitative forms of knowledge avoids the distortion of using either numerical or case-study data alone (Haltom and McCann 2004). By qualitative information, I am referring not to the generic narratives in boxes or the faceless pictures without context favored by the *TIP Reports* but to contextualized, historicized accounts of particular situations located within larger structures and patterns.

I argued at the beginning of the book that we are seeing the rise of what could be called "indicator culture": a set of techniques and practices of knowledge production that has acquired a significant level of public trust and acceptance. Both in policy circles and in the general public, there is a faith that numbers and scores can provide secure knowledge of a world that seems unknowable. Indeed, these three cases promise to provide valuable and hard-to-acquire information on how much trafficking is taking place and where, how often and in what ways women experience violence, and to what extent countries are abiding by their human rights commitments. In this era of quantitative enthusiasm, we use data to define problems and construct solutions to them. The answers they offer are seductive: a quick reading of which countries have low levels of health, education, and income; which ones are not working against trafficking; where women are most likely to be beaten; which countries are the worst human rights violators. Indicators seductively promise to provide guidance through a complex world.

But as we have seen, it is essential to also develop microethnographic studies and qualitative knowledge of people, social situations, and their larger structural contexts to counter the homogenization and stripping away of the social world inherent in quantification. Without that, one misses critical dimensions of the texture of social life and reinterprets the lives of nonelites around the world through the lens of the cosmopolitan experts who design indicators and their concepts of social problems and interventions — for example, assuming that police are a solution to violence instead of challenging the idea that violence is discipline meted out by males, who are understood as superior to females. Quantification has a great deal to contribute to global knowledge and governance, but it is important to resist its seductive claim to truth and to recognize it as only one form of knowledge with its own distinctive limitations. The narrative ethnographic account provides an important complement to quantification. We rely on numbers alone at our peril.

Notes

Chapter Three

1. There was a similar workshop in Bangkok in September 2010, organized by the UN Economic and Social Commission for Asia and the Pacific (UNESCAP), on strengthening national capacities to measure violence against women (UN Economic and Social Commission for Asia and the Pacific 2011: 7).

Chapter Seven

1. Alston's report included several suggestions, including providing more assistance to states in preparing reports, submitting consolidated reports for more than one treaty body, and consolidating the treaty bodies (Alston 1996: 26–28). The secretary general's second reform report in 2002 called on treaty bodies to develop a more coordinated approach and to allow each state to produce a single report for the full range of human rights treaties it had signed. In his 2005 report, *In Larger Freedom*, the secretary general emphasized the need to strengthen the monitoring, implementation, and visibility of the treaty body system and called for harmonized guidelines on reporting so that the treaty bodies could function as a unified system (UN Secretary General 2005: 38). In 2006, Louise Arbour, the high commissioner for human rights, proposed a more radical solution: creating a unified standing treaty body instead of the then seven separate treaty bodies (UN Secretariat 2006). At that point, the problem of overdue reports and the backlog of unheard reports was even worse than in the late 1990s. As of February 2006, only 8 of the 194 states that had ratified one or more treaties were up to date with their reports, and the remaining 186 states owed 1,442 reports (UN Secretariat 2006: 7). However, if these reports were presented as required, the treaty bodies would not be able to hear them for years. The high commissioner noted that the treaty body system faced several problems: an inconsistency in working methods and reporting guidelines among the committees, a lack of visibility in the treaty body process, a lack of authority of the committees, a lack of information with which to assess compliance,

an absence of follow-up, the need for greater efficiency in processing reports, and increasing costs of the system in the face of limited resources. After detailing these difficulties, the high commissioner for human rights proposed the creation of a single, unified treaty body. This proposal encountered strong resistance by treaty bodies and has been dropped. But the problem continues. In 2010, a report by the Open Society Justice Initiative pointed out the low levels of compliance with treaty body recommendations and individual complaints (Baluarte and DeVos 2010). In 2012, two-thirds of country reports for all treaty bodies were more than a year overdue, and problems with backlogs continued (Broecker and O'Flaherty 2014: 7).

2. The 1993 version viewed indicators at three levels: "(a) at the level of inputs or (legal) conditions; (b) at the level of throughputs or activities, together with (a), also referred to as process indicators; (c) at the level of outputs or outcomes, also referred to as impact indicators, which measure the actual results." (UN Secretariat 1993: 14, para. 47).

3. Once the indicator sheets were more or less finalized, the OHCHR team worked on developing guidelines for their use, called metadata sheets. These defined more carefully each indicator along with its rationale, method of computation, source, periodicity, and disaggregation (see UN International Human Rights Instruments and Office of the High Commissioner for Human Rights 2008: 34–48). The project of producing metadata sheets, about one page per indicator, for the five hundred or so indicators was ongoing in 2011 and was expected to reach completion in 2012, although the final report included metadata sheets for only sixteen indicators (UN Office of the High Commissioner for Human Rights 2012: 141–67).

4. Of the thirty-eight CERD reports between 2011 and 2013, only 60 percent referred to indicators at all, and those were primarily health and educational statistics that were not often disaggregated by ethnicity. Two countries — Venezuela (Venezuela 2013) and Slovakia (Slovakia 2013) — directly addressed the problem of how to develop indicators for ethnic identity.

5. This includes 365 reports from 2007 to 2011 and 163 from the CRC, CEDAW, CESCR, and CERD from 2011 to 2013.

6. Data by region support this argument. The highest average reference to indicators comes from Latin American and Middle Eastern countries, which included an average of 6 indicators per report between 2007 and 2011, followed by the Pacific (including Australia and New Zealand) at 4.7, Eastern Europe at 4.6, Asia at 4.2, Africa at 4.0, and Western Europe at a surprisingly low 2.6. This regional variation again suggests the importance of internationally generated indicators rather than national ones. Considering the treaty bodies separately, even stronger regional variations appear. For 2008–2011, CESCR country reports varied from 14.8 indicator mentions in Latin America to 12.2 in Eastern Europe to 6 in the Pacific to 5.3 in the Middle East to 4.8 in Asia to 4.5 in Western Europe to 3.8 in Africa. In contrast, the CCPR country reports for the same time period ranged from 6 in the Pacific to 4.2 in Africa to 2.8 in the Middle East to 2.1 in Latin America to 2 in Asia to 1.9 in Eastern Europe to 1.7 in Western Europe.

References

African Commission on Human and Peoples' Rights. 2010. *Principles and Guidelines on the Implementation of Economic, Social and Cultural Rights in the African Charter on Human and Peoples' Rights*. 48th session, November. http://www.escr-net.org/resources_more /resources_more_show.htm?doc_id=1599552.

Agustin, Laura Maria. 2007. *Sex at the Margins: Migration, Labour Markets, and the Rescue Industry*. London: Zed.

Ali Mollah, Md. Shahjahan. 2009. *Status of Statistics Pertaining to Violence against Women in the Context of Bangladesh*. UN Statistical Commission. ESA/STAT/AC.193/6. http://unstats.un.org/unsd/demographic/meetings/vaw/docs/Paper6.pdf.

Alston, Philip. 1996. *Final Report on Enhancing the Long-Term Effectiveness of the United Nations Human Rights Treaty System*. UN Office of the High Commissioner for Human Rights. E/CN.4/1997/74. http://www.unhchr.ch/Huridocda/Huridoca.nsf/(Symbol)/E.CN.4.1997.74 .En?OpenDocument.

———. 2005a. "Richard Lillich Memorial Lecture: Promoting the Accountability of Members of the New UN Human Rights Council." *Journal of Transnational Law and Policy* 15: 49–96.

———. 2005b. "Ships Passing in the Night: The Current State of the Human Rights and Development Debate Seen through the Lens of the Millennium Development Goals." *Human Rights Quarterly* 27: 755–829.

Alston, Philip, and Katarina Tomaševski. 1984. *The Right to Food: Towards a System for Supervising States' Compliance with the Right to Food*. Leiden, Netherlands: Martinus Nijhoff.

Alston, Philip, and Mary Robinson, eds. 2005. *Human Rights and Development: Towards Mutual Reinforcement*. Oxford: Oxford University Press.

Amnesty International. 2001. *Broken Bodies, Shattered Minds: Torture and Ill-Treatment of Women*. London: Amnesty International.

———. 2003. "Women's Rights Are Human Rights." http://www.amnestyusa.org /stopviolence/about.html.

Andreas, Peter, and Kelly M. Greenhill, eds. 2010. *Sex, Drugs, and Body Counts: The Politics of Numbers in Global Crime and Conflict*. Ithaca, NY: Cornell University Press.

Asdal, Kristin, Brita Brenna, and Ingunn Moser, eds. 2007. *Technoscience: The Politics of Interventions*. Oslo: Oslo Academic Press, Unipub Norway.

Backman, Gunilla, Paul Hunt, Rajat Khosala, Camilla Jaramillo-Strouss, Belachew Mekuria Fikre, Caroline Rumble, David Pevalin, et al. 2008. "Health Systems and the Right to Health: An Assessment of 194 Countries." *Lancet* 372(9655): 2047–85.

Bales, Kevin. 2003. "International Labor Standards: Quality of Information and Measures of Progress in Combating Forced Labor." *Comparative Labor Law and Policy Journal* 24: 321–54.

———. 2004. "Slavery and the Human Right to Evil." *Journal of Human Rights* 3(1): 55–63.

———. 2005. "The Challenge of Measuring Slavery." In *Understanding Global Slavery: A Reader*, pp. 87–112. Berkeley: University of California Press.

———. 2012. *Disposable People: New Slavery in the Global Economy*, 3rd edition. Berkeley: University of California Press.

Ballestero, Andrea S. 2012. "Transparency Short-Circuited: Laughter and Numbers in Costa Rican Water Politics." *Polar: Political and Legal Anthropology Review* 35(2): 223–41.

Baluarte, David C., and Christian M. DeVos. 2010. *From Judgment to Justice: Implementing International and Regional Human Rights Decisions*. Open Society Justice Initiative, Open Society Foundation, New York, November. http://www.opensocietyfoundations.org/reports/judgment-justice-implementing-international-and-regional-human-rights-decisions.

Barsh, Russel Lawrence. 1993. "Measuring Human Rights: Problems of Methodology and Purpose." *Human Rights Quarterly* 15(1): 87–121.

Bayefsky, Anne F. 2001. *The UN Human Rights Treaty System: Universality at the Crossroads*. Ardsley, NY: Transnational.

Berman, Jacqueline. 2005–2006. "The Left, the Right, and the Prostitute: The Making of U.S. Antitrafficking in Persons Policy." *Tulane Journal of International and Comparative Law* 14: 269–93.

Bernstein, Elizabeth. 2007. "Sexual Politics of the New Abolitionism: Imagery and Activism in Contemporary Anti-Trafficking Campaigns." *Differences: Journal of Feminist Cultural Studies* 18(3): 128–51.

———. 2010. "Militarized Humanitarianism Meets Carceral Feminism: The Politics of Sex, Rights, and Freedom in Contemporary Anti-Trafficking Campaigns." Special issue on "Feminists Theorize International Political Economy," Kate Bedford and Shirin Rai, guest eds., *Signs: Journal of Women in Culture and Society* 36(1): 45–71.

———. 2012. "Carceral Politics as Gender Justice? The 'Traffic in Women' and Neoliberal Circuits of Crime, Sex, and Rights." *Theory and Society* 41(3): 233–59.

Bowker, Geoffrey C., and Susan Leigh Star. 1999. *Sorting Things Out: Classification and Its Consequences*. Cambridge, MA: MIT Press.

Bradley, Christopher G. 2015. "International Organizations and the Production of Indicators: The Case of Freedom House." In *The Quiet Power of Indicators: Measuring Governance, Corruption, and Rule of Law*, chapter 2. Sally Engle Merry, Kevin Davis, and Benedict Kingsbury, eds. Cambridge: Cambridge University Press.

Brennan, Denise. 2014. *Life Interrupted: Trafficking into Forced Labor in the United States*. Durham, NC: Duke University Press.

Broecker, Christen, and Michael O'Flaherty. 2014. *The Outcome of the General Assembly's Treaty Body Strengthening Process: An Important Milestone on a Longer Journey*. Policy brief, Universal Rights Group. http://www.universal-rights.org/urg-policy-reports/the-outcome-of-the-general-assemblys-treaty-body-strengthening-process-an-important-milestone-on-a-longer-journey.

Bunch, Charlotte. 1990. "Women's Rights as Human Rights: Toward a Re-Vision of Human Rights." *Human Rights Quarterly* 12: 489–98.

Callon, Michel. 2007. "Some Elements of a Sociology of Translation: Domestication of the Scallops and the Fishermen of St. Brieuc Bay." In *Technoscience: The Politics of Interventions*, pp. 57–78. Kristin Asdal, Brita Brenna, and Ingunn Moser, eds. Bergen, Norway: Fagbokforlaget.

Carr Center for Human Rights Policy. 2005. *Measurement and Human Rights: Tracking Progress, Assessing Impact.* A Carr Center Project Report, Kennedy School, Harvard University, summer. http://carrcenter.hks.harvard.edu/files/carrcenter/files/measurement _2005report.pdf.

Chapman, Audrey R. 2007a. "Development of Indicators for Economic, Social and Cultural Rights: The Rights to Education, Participation in Cultural Life and Access to the Benefits of Science." In *Human Rights in Education, Science and Culture: Legal Developments and Challenges*, pp. 111–53. Yvonne Dondersa and Vladimir Volodin, eds. Paris: UNESCO.

———. 2007b. "The Status of Efforts to Monitor Economic, Social, and Cultural Rights." In *Economic Rights: Conceptual, Measurement, and Policy Issues*, pp. 143–65. Shareen Hertel and Lanse Minkler, eds. Cambridge: Cambridge University Press.

Charlesworth, Hilary, and Emma Larking, eds. 2015. *Human Rights and the Universal Periodic Review: Rituals and Ritualism.* Cambridge: Cambridge University Press.

Cheng, Sealing. 2008. "The Traffic in 'Trafficked Filipinas': Sexual Harm, Violence, and Victims' Voices." In *Violence and Gender in the Globalized World: The Intimate and the Extimate*, pp. 141–56. Sanja Bahun-Radunovic and V. G. Julie Rajan, eds. Farnham, UK: Ashgate.

———. 2010. *On the Move for Love: Migrant Entertainers and the US Military in South Korea.* Philadelphia: University of Pennsylvania Press.

Chuang, Janie. 2005–2006. "The United States as Global Sheriff: Using Unilateral Sanctions to Combat Global Trafficking." *Michigan Journal of International Law* 27: 437–94.

———. 2010. "Rescuing Trafficking from Ideological Capture: Prostitution Reform and Anti-Trafficking Law and Policy." *University of Pennsylvania Law Review* 158: 1655–728.

———. 2014. "Exploitation Creep and the Unmaking of Human Trafficking Law." *American Journal of International Law* 108: 609–49.

Cingranelli, David L., and David L. Richards. 2010. "The Cingranelli and Richards Human Rights Data Project." *Human Rights Quarterly* 32(2): 401–24.

Cingranelli-Richards Human Rights Data Set. n.d. http://www.humanrightsdata.com.

Clark, Joshua. 2009. "Classification, Enumeration, and Indigenous Rights: The Case of El Salvador's 2007 Census." Paper delivered at the Pacific Coast Council on Latin American Studies Annual Conference, Torrance, CA, November.

———. 2015. "Numbers as Knowledge and Practice: Disaggregated Data in the Reporting Process of the Committee on the Elimination of Racial Discrimination." In *Fifty Years of ICERD: A Living Instrument.* David Keane and Annapurna Waughray, eds. Manchester, UK: Manchester University Press (forthcoming).

Coalition against Trafficking in Women. 2015. http://www.catwinternational.org.

Cohn, Bernard S. 1990. *An Anthropologist among the Historians and Other Essays.* Delhi: Oxford University Press.

———. 1996. *Colonialism and Its Forms of Knowledge: The British in India.* Princeton, NJ: Princeton University Press.

Comaroff, Jean, and John L. Comaroff. 2006. "Figuring Crime: Quantifacts and the Production of the Un/Real." *Public Culture* 18(1): 209–46.

Connors, Jane. 1996. "General Human Rights Instruments and their Relevance to Women." In *Advancing the Human Rights of Women: Using International Human Rights Standards in*

Domestic Litigation, pp. 27–39. Andrew Byrnes, Jane Connors, and Lum Bik, eds. London: The Commonwealth Secretariat.

Cook, Rebecca. J. 1994a. *Human Rights of Women: National and International Perspectives*. Philadelphia: University of Pennsylvania Press.

———. 1994b. "State Responsibility for Violations of Women's Human Rights." *Harvard Human Rights Journal* 7: 125–75.

Cooley, Alexander, and Jack Snyder, eds. 2015. *Ranking the World: Grading States as a Tool of Global Governance*. Cambridge: Cambridge University Press.

Dauer, Sheila. 2014. "Introduction: Anthropological Approaches to Gender-Based Violence." Special issue on "Anthropological Approaches to Gender-Based Violence and Human Rights," *Gender, Development, and Globalization Program*, Michigan State University, Center for Gender in Global Context, June. Working paper 304. http://gencen.isp .msu.edu/documents/Working_Papers/WP304.pdf.

Davis, Kevin E., Angelina Fisher, Benedict Kingsbury, and Sally Engle Merry, eds. 2012. *Governance by Indicators: Global Power through Quantification and Rankings*. Oxford: Oxford University Press.

Davis, Kevin E., Benedict Kingsbury, and Sally Engle Merry. 2012. "Indicators as a Technology of Global Governance." *Law and Society Review* 46(1): 71–104.

de Beco, Gautier. 2013. "Human Rights Indicators: From Theoretical Debate to Practical Application." *Journal of Human Rights Practice* 5(2): 380–97.

de Burca, Grainne. 2010. "New Governance and Experimentalism: An Introduction." *Wisconsin Law Review* 2: 227–38.

de Felice, Damiano. 2015. "Business and Human Rights Indicators to Measure the Corporate Responsibility to Respect: Challenges and Opportunities." *Human Rights Quarterly* 37(2): 511–55.

Demographic and Health Surveys. 2006. "Demographic and Health Surveys Domestic Violence Module." http://dhsprogram.com/pubs/pdf/DHSQMP/domestic_violence_module .pdf.pdf.

———. 2014. "Demographic and Health Surveys" (homepage). http://www.icfi.com/insights /projects/research-and-evaluation/demographic-and-health-surveys.

Desrosieres, Alain. 1998. *The Politics of Large Numbers: A History of Statistical Reasoning*. Camille Naish, trans. Cambridge, MA: Harvard University Press.

Donabedian, Avedis. 1966. "Evaluating the Quality of Medical Care." *Milbank Memorial Fund Quarterly* 44: 166–206.

Eide, Asbjørn. 1987. *The Right to Adequate Food as a Human Right*. UN Economic and Social Council, Subcommittee on Prevention of Discrimination and Protection of Minorities, July 7. E/CN.4/Sub.2/1987/23.

Erturk, Yakin. 2008a. "The Due Diligence Standard: What Does It Entail for Women's Rights?" In *Due Diligence and Its Application to Protect Women from Violence*, pp. 27–46. Carin Benninger-Budel, ed. Leiden, Netherlands: Martinus Nijhoff.

———. 2008b. "Report of the Special Rapporteur on Violence against Women, Its Causes and Consequences, the Next Step: Developing Transnational Indicators on Violence against Women" (addendum). In *Promotion and Protection of all Human Rights, Civil, Political, Economic, Social and Cultural, Including the Right to Development*. Human Rights Council, 7th session, February 25. A/HRC/7/6/Add.5.

———. 2008c. "Report of the Special Rapporteur on Violence against Women, Its Causes and Consequences, Yakin Erturk: Indicators on Violence against Women and State Response." In *Promotion and Protection of all Human Rights, Civil, Political, Economic, Social and Cultural, Including the Right to Development*. Human Rights Council, 7th session, January 29. A/HRC/7/6.

Espeland, Wendy Nelson, and Michael Sauder. 2007. "Rankings and Reactivity: How Public Measures Recreate Social Worlds." *American Journal of Sociology* 113(1): 1–40.

Espeland, Wendy Nelson, and Mitchell L. Stevens. 1998. "Commensuration as a Social Process." *Annual Review of Sociology* 24: 313–43.

——. 2008. "A Sociology of Quantification." *European Journal of Sociology* 49(3): 401–36.

Farley, Melissa, Ann Cotton, Jacqueline Lynne, Sybille Zumbeck, Frida Spiwak, Maria E. Reyes, Dinorah Alvarez, and Ufuk Sezgin. 2003. "Prostitution and Trafficking in Nine Countries: An Update on Violence and Posttraumatic Stress Disorder." *Journal of Trauma Practice* 3(3–4): 33–74.

Feingold, David A. 2010. "Trafficking in Numbers: The Social Construction of Human Trafficking Data." In *Sex, Drugs, and Body Counts: The Politics of Numbers in Global Crime and Conflict*, pp. 46–75. Peter Andreas and Kelly M. Greenhill, eds. Ithaca, NY: Cornell University Press.

Foucault, Michel. 1979. *Discipline and Punish: The Birth of the Prison.* New York: Vintage.

——. 1991. "Governmentality." In *The Foucault Effect: Studies in Governmentality*, pp. 87–105. Graham Burchell, Colin Gordon, Peter Miller, eds. Chicago: University of Chicago Press.

Friedman, Elisabeth. 1995. "Women's Human Rights: The Emergence of a Movement." In *Women's Rights, Human Rights: International Feminist Perspectives*, pp. 18–35. Julie Peters and Andrea Wolper, eds. New York: Routledge.

Friman, H. Richard. 2010. "Numbers and Certification: Assessing Foreign Compliance in Combating Narcotics and Human Trafficking." In *Sex, Drugs, and Body Counts: The Politics of Numbers in Global Crime and Conflict*, pp. 75–110. Peter Andreas and Kelly M. Greenhill, eds. Ithaca, NY: Cornell University Press.

Fukuda-Parr, Sakiko. 2011. "The Metrics of Human Rights: Complementarities of the Human Development and Capabilities Approach." *Journal of Human Development and Capabilities* 12(1): 73–89.

Fukuda-Parr, Sakiko, and Alicia Ely Yamin, guest eds. 2014. "The Power of Numbers: A Critical Review of Millennium Development Goal Targets for Human Development and Human Rights." Special Issue on "Millennium Development Goals," *Journal of Human Development and Capabilities* 15(2–3): 1–13.

——. 2015. *The MDGs, Capabilities, and Human Rights: The Power of Numbers to Shape Agendas.* New York: Routledge.

Fukuda-Parr, Sakiko, Terra Lawson-Remer, and Susan Randolf. 2009. "An Index of Economic and Social Rights Fulfillment: Concept and Methodology." *Journal of Human Rights* 8(3): 195–221.

——. 2015. *Fulfilling Social and Economic Rights.* Oxford: Oxford University Press.

Fundamental Rights Agency. 2011. "FRA Symposium Report: Using Indicators to Measure Fundamental Rights in the EU: Challenges and Solutions." Conference paper, Second Annual FRA Symposium, European Agency for Fundamental Rights, Vienna, Austria, May 12–13. http://fra.europa.eu/en/publication/2012/fra-symposium-report-using-indicators-measure-fundamental-rights-eu-challenges-and.

Gallagher, Anne. 2001. "Book Review: *Trafficking in Persons Report (Department of State, United States of America, July 2000)*." *Human Rights Quarterly* 23: 1135–41.

——. 2009. "Human Rights and Human Trafficking: Quagmire or Firm Ground? A Response to James Hathaway." *Virginia Journal of International Law* 49: 789–848.

——. 2011. "Improving the Effectiveness of the International Law of Human Trafficking: A Vision for the Future of the U.S. Trafficking in Persons Reports." *Human Rights Review* 12(3): 381–400.

——. 2012. *Abuse of a Position of Vulnerability and Other "Means" within the Definition of Trafficking in Persons* (issue paper). Vienna, Austria: UN Office of Drugs and Crime.

Gallagher, Anne, and Elaine Pearson. 2010. "The High Cost of Freedom: A Legal and Policy Analysis of Shelter Detention for Victims of Trafficking." *Human Rights Quarterly* 32: 73–114.

Gallagher, Anne T., and Janie Chuang. 2012. "The Use of Indicators to Measure Government Responses to Human Trafficking." In *Governance by Indicators: Global Power through Quantification and Rankings*, pp. 317–43. Kevin E. Davis, Angelina Fisher, Benedict Kingsbury, and Sally Engle Merry, eds. Oxford: Oxford University Press.

Gallagher, Anne, and Paul Holmes. 2008. "Developing an Effective Criminal Justice Response to Human Trafficking: Lessons from the Front Line." *International Criminal Justice Review* 18: 318–43. http://icj.sagepub.com/content/18/3/318.

Gallagher, Anne T., and Rebecca Surtees. 2012. "Measuring the Success of Counter-Trafficking Interventions in the Criminal Justice Sector: Who Decides—and How?" *Anti-Trafficking Review* 1: 10–30. http://works.bepress.com/anne_gallagher/21.

Global Alliance against Traffic in Women. 2007. *Collateral Damage: The Impact of Anti-Trafficking Measures on Human Rights around the World*. Bangkok, Thailand: Global Alliance against Traffic in Women.

———. 2015. "Global Alliance against Traffic in Women" (homepage). http://www.gaatw.org.

Goonesekere, Savatri. 2004. "Introduction: Indicators for Monitoring Implementation of CEDAW." In *CEDAW Indicators for South Asia: An Initiative*, pp. 7–13. New Delhi, India: UNIFEM South Asia Regional Office, Centre for Women's Research.

Gready, P. 2008. "Rights-Based Approaches to Development: What Is the Value-Added?" *Development in Practice* 18(6): 735–47.

Green, Maria. 2001. "What We Talk about When We Talk about Indicators: Current Approaches to Human Rights Measurement." *Human Rights Quarterly* 23: 1062–97.

Gruskin, S., and L. Ferguson. 2009. "Using Indicators to Determine the Contribution of Human Rights to Public Health Efforts." *Bulletin of the World Health Organization* 87: 714–19. http://www.who.int/bulletin/volumes/87/9/08-058321/en/print.html.

Guinn, David E. 2008. "Defining the Problem of Trafficking: The Interplay of US Law, Donor, and NGO Engagement and the Local Context in Latin America." *Human Rights Quarterly* 30(1): 119–45.

Gulati, Girish J. 2011. "News Frames and Story Triggers in the Media's Coverage of Human Trafficking." *Human Rights Review* 12: 363–79.

Hacking, Ian. 1990. *The Taming of Chance*. Cambridge: Cambridge University Press.

Halley, Janet, Prabha Kotiswaran, Hila Shamir, and Chantal Thomas. 2006. "From the International to the Local in Feminist Legal Responses to Rape, Prostitution/Sex Work, and Sex Trafficking: Four Studies in Contemporary Governance Feminism." *Harvard Journal of Law and Gender* 29(2): 335–423.

Halliday, Terence C., and Gregory Shaffer. 2015. "Researching Transnational Legal Orders." In *Transnational Legal Orders*, pp. 475–528. Terence C. Halliday and Gregory Shaffer, eds. New York: Cambridge University Press.

Halliday, Terence C., and Pavel Osinsky. 2006. "Globalization of Law." *Annual Review of Sociology* 32: 447–70.

Haltom, William, and Michael McCann. 2004. *Distorting the Law: Politics, Media, and the Litigation Crisis*. Chicago: University of Chicago Press.

Hannan, Carolyn. 2009. "Launch of the Secretary General's Database on Violence against Women." Statement by the director of the UN Division for the Advancement of Women, March 5. http://www.un.org/womenwatch/daw/statements/speech2009/2009%20Launch%20VAW%20database%20at%20CSW.pdf.

Hathaway, James C. 2008–2009. "The Human Rights Quagmire of 'Human Trafficking.'" *Virginia Journal of International Law* 49: 1–59.

Haynes, Dina Francesca. 2006–2007. "(Not) Found Chained to a Bed in a Brothel: Conceptual, Legal, and Procedural Failures to Fulfill the Promise of the Trafficking Victims Protection Act." *Georgetown Immigration Law Journal* 21: 337–81.

———. 2009. "Exploitation Nation: The Thin and Grey Legal Lines between Trafficked Persons and Abused Migrant Laborers." *Notre Dame Journal of Law, Ethics, and Public Policy* 23: 1–71.

Holland, Sean. 2008. "Ranking Rights: Problems and Prospects for a Quantitative Global Human Rights Index." In *MHR Issue Papers*, vol. 1, no. 4, Carr Center for Human Rights Policy, Kennedy School, Harvard University, August. http://carrcenter.hks.harvard.edu/publications.

Huckerby, Jayne. 2007. "United States of America (USA)." In *Collateral Damage: The Impact of Anti-Trafficking Measures on Human Rights around the World*, pp. 230–56. Bangkok, Thailand: Global Alliance against Traffic in Women.

Hunt, Paul. 1998. "State Obligations, Indicators, Benchmarks and the Right to Education." Background paper for the UN Committee on Economic, Social, and Cultural Rights, Geneva, Switzerland, November 30. E/C.12/1998/11. http://daccess-dds-ny.un.org/doc/UNDOC/GEN/G98/168/83/PDF/G9816883.pdf?OpenElement.

———. 2003a. *Report of the Special Rapporteur on the Right of Everyone to the Enjoyment of the Highest Attainable Standard of Physical and Mental Health*. UN General Assembly, New York City, October 10. A/58/427. http://daccess-dds-ny.un.org/doc/UNDOC/GEN/N03/564/69/PDF/N0356469.pdf?OpenElement.

———. 2003b. *The Right of Everyone to the Enjoyment of the Highest Attainable Standard of Physical and Mental Health*. Report to the Commission on Human Rights, 59th session, Geneva, Switzerland, February 13. E/CN.4/2003/58. http://daccess-dds-ny.un.org/doc/UNDOC/GEN/G03/109/79/PDF/G0310979.pdf?OpenElement.

———. 2006a. "Economic, Social and Cultural Rights." In *Report of the Special Rapporteur on the Right of Everyone to the Enjoyment of the Highest Attainable Standard of Physical and Mental Health*. UN Commission on Human Rights, 62nd session, March 3. E/CN.4/2006/48.

———. 2006b. "The Human Right to the Highest Attainable Standard of Health: New Opportunities and Challenges." *Transactions of the Royal Society of Tropical Medicine and Hygiene* 100: 603–7.

Ignatieff, Michael, and Kate Desormeau. 2005. "Measurement and Human Rights: An Introduction." In *Measurement and Human Rights: Tracking Progress, Assessing Impact*. A Carr Center Project Report, Kennedy School, Harvard University, summer. http://www.ksg.harvard.edu/cchrp/mhr/publications/index.php.

Igo, Sarah E. 2007. *The Averaged American: Surveys, Citizens, and the Making of a Mass Public*. Cambridge, MA: Harvard University Press.

India. 2009. *Parliamentary Record for 08.07.2009*. A/KGG-HMS/11:00.

Inter-American Commission on Human Rights. 2008. *Guidelines for Preparation of Progress Indicators in the Area of Economic, Social and Cultural Rights*. July 19. OEA/Ser.L/V/II.132/Doc.14/Rev.1.

International Institute for Population Sciences and Macro International. 2007. *National Family Health Survey (NFHS-3), 2005–06: India*, vol. 1. Mumbai: International Institute for Population Sciences. http://dhsprogram.com/pubs/pdf/FRIND3/FRIND3-Vol1AndVol2.pdf.

———. 2008. *ILO Action against Trafficking in Human Beings*. Geneva, Switzerland: International Labour Office. http://www.ilo.org/wcmsp5/groups/public/@ed_norm/@declaration/documents/publication/wcms_090356.pdf.

———. 2009. *Operational Indicators of Trafficking in Human Beings: Results from a Delphi Survey Implemented by the ILO and the European Union*. Geneva, Switzerland: International Labour

Office. http://www.ilo.org/wcmsp5/groups/public/@ed_norm/@declaration/documents/publication/wcms_105023.pdf.

Jerven, Morten. 2013. *Poor Numbers: How We Are Misled by African Development Statistics and What to Do about It*. Ithaca, NY: Cornell University Press.

Johnson, Holly, Natalia Ollus, and Sami Nevala. 2008. *Violence against Women: An International Perspective*. New York: Springer Science.

Kalantry, Sital, Jocelyn E. Getget, and Steven Arrigg Koh. 2010. "Enhancing Enforcement of Economic, Social and Cultural Rights Using Indicators: A Focus on the Right to Education in the ICESCR." *Human Rights Quarterly* 32(2): 253–310.

Kangaspunta, Kristina. 2003. "Mapping the Inhuman Trade: Preliminary Findings of the Database on Trafficking in Human Beings." *Forum on Crime and Society, UN Office on Drugs and Crime* 3(1–2): 81–103.

Kapur, Ratna. 2007. "India." In *Collateral Damage: The Impact of Anti-Trafficking Measures on Human Rights around the World*, pp. 114–42. Bangkok, Thailand: Global Alliance against Traffic in Women.

Kaufmann, Daniel, and Aart Kraay. 2007. "Governance Indicators: Where Are We, Where Should We Be Going?" World Bank, Washington, DC. Policy research working paper 4370.

Keck, Margaret E., and Kathryn Sikkink. 1998. *Activists beyond Borders: Advocacy Networks in International Politics*. Ithaca, NY: Cornell University Press.

Kelley, Judith G., and Beth A. Simmons. 2015. "Politics by Number: Indicators as Social Pressure in International Relations." *American Journal of Political Science* 59: 55–70.

Kindornay, Shannon, James Ron, and Charli Carpenter. 2012. "Rights-Based Approaches to Development: Implications for NGOs." *Human Rights Quarterly* 34(2): 472–506.

Koskenniemi, Martti. 2010. "Human Rights Mainstreaming as a Strategy for Institutional Power." *Humanity: An International Journal of Human Rights, Humanitarianism, and Development* 1(1): 47–58.

Kotiswaran, Prabha. 2008. "Born unto Brothels: Toward a Legal Ethnography of Sex Work in an Indian Red-Light Area." *Law and Social Inquiry* 33(3): 579–629.

———. 2011a. *Dangerous Sex, Invisible Labor: Sex Work and the Law in India*. Princeton, NJ: Princeton University Press.

———. 2011b. "Introduction." In *Sex Work*, pp. xi–lxii. Prabha Kotiswaran, ed. New Delhi, India: Women Unlimited.

Kretzmer, David. 2010. "The UN Human Rights Committee and International Human Rights Monitoring." Paper delivered at the IILJ International Legal Theory Colloquium, New York University School of Law, New York, spring.

Laczko, Frank, and Marco A. Gramegna. 2003. "Developing Better Indicators of Human Trafficking." *Brown Journal of World Affairs* 10: 179.

Landman, Todd. 2004. "Measuring Human Rights: Principle, Practice, and Policy." *Human Rights Quarterly* 26: 906–31.

Landman, Todd, and Edzia Carvalho. 2010. *Measuring Human Rights*. New York: Routledge.

Langford, Malcolm, and Sakiko Fukuda-Parr. 2012. "The Turn to Metrics." *Nordic Journal of Human Rights* 30(3): 222–38.

Latour, Bruno. 1987. *Science in Action: How to Follow Scientists and Engineers through Society*. Cambridge, MA: Harvard University Press.

———. 2005. *Reassembling the Social: An Introduction to Actor-Network-Theory*. Oxford: Oxford University Press.

Levitt, Peggy, and Sally Engle Merry. 2009. "Vernacularization on the Ground: Local Uses of Global Women's Rights in Peru, China, India and the United States." *Global Networks* 9(4): 441–61.

Makover, H. B. 1951. "The Quality of Medical Care: Methodological Survey of the Medical

Groups Associated with the Health Insurance Plan of New York." *American Journal of Public Health* 41: 824–32.

Malby, Steven, and Anna Alvazzi del Frate. 2007. "Indicators, Crime, and Violence against Women: Supporting Paper 3." Paper submitted by UNODC to the Expert Group Meeting on Indicators to Measure Violence against Women, co-organized by the UNDAW, UNECE, and UNSD, Geneva, Switzerland, October 8–10.

Malhotra, Rajeev, and Nicolas Fasel. 2005. "Quantitative Human Rights Indicators: A Survey of Major Initiatives." Background paper for the UN Expert Meeting on Human Rights Indicators, Turku, Finland, March 10–13. Document on file with author.

March, James G., and Herbert A. Simon. 1958. *Organizations*. New York: Wiley.

Markon, Jerry. 2007. "Human Trafficking Evokes Outrage, Little Evidence." *Washington Post*. http://www.washingtonpost.com/wp-dyn/content/article/2007/09/22/AR2007092201401.html.

Mattar, Mohamed Y. 2003. "Monitoring the Status of Severe Forms of Trafficking in Foreign Countries: Sanctions under the US Trafficking Victims Protection Act." *Brown Journal of World Affairs* 10(1): 159–78.

Maurer, Bill. 2005. *Mutual Life, Limited: Islamic Banking, Alternative Currencies, Lateral Reason*. Princeton, NJ: Princeton University Press.

McInerney-Lankford, Siobhan, and Hans-Otto Sano. 2010. *Human Rights Indicators in Development: An Introduction*. Washington, DC: World Bank.

——. 2013. "Human Rights Indicators in Development: Definitions, Relevance and Application." Manuscript on file with author.

Merry, Sally Engle. 1995. "Gender Violence and Legally Engendered Selves." *Identities: Global Studies in Culture and Power* 2: 49–73.

——. 2006a. *Human Rights and Gender Violence: Translating International Law into Local Justice*. Chicago: University of Chicago Press.

——. 2006b. "Transnational Human Rights and Local Activism: Mapping the Middle." *American Anthropologist* 108(1): 38–51.

——. 2009. *Gender Violence: A Cultural Perspective*. Malden, MA: Wiley Blackwell.

——. 2011. "Measuring the World: Indicators, Human Rights, and Global Governance." Special issue on "Corporate Lives: New Perspectives on the Social Life of the Corporate Form," Damani Partridge, Marina Welker, and Rebecca Hardin, guest eds. Wenner-Gren Symposium Series. *Current Anthropology* 52(suppl. 3): S83–S95.

——. 2014. "Global Legal Pluralism and the Temporality of Soft Law." Special Issue on "Temporalities of Law," *Journal of Legal Pluralism and Unofficial Law* 46(1): 108–22.

——. 2015. "Human Rights Monitoring, State Compliance, and the Problem of Information." In *Studying Law Globally: New Legal Realist Perspectives*, vol. 2. Heinz Klug and Sally Engle Merry, eds. Cambridge: Cambridge University Press.

Merry, Sally Engle, Kevin Davis, and Benedict Kingsbury, eds. 2015. *The Quiet Power of Indicators: Measuring Governance, Corruption, and Rule of Law*. Cambridge: Cambridge University Press.

Merry, Sally Engle, Peggy Levitt, Mihaela Serban Rosen, and Diana H. Yoon. 2010. "Law from Below: Women's Human Rights and Social Movements in New York City." *Law and Society Review* 44(1): 101–28.

Merry, Sally Engle, and Summer Wood. 2015. "Quantification and the Paradox of Measurement: Translating Children's Rights in Tanzania." *Current Anthropology* 56(2): 205–29.

Merry, Sally Engle, and Susan Coutin. 2014. "Technologies of Truth in the Anthropology of Conflict." *American Ethnologist* 41(1): 1–16.

Miller, Peter, and Nikolas Rose. 1990. "Governing Economic Life." *Economy and Society* 19(1): 1–31.

Mitchell, Timothy. 2002. *Rule of Experts: Egypt, Techno-Politics, Modernity*. Berkeley: University of California Press.

Molland, Sverre. 2012. *The Perfect Business? Anti-trafficking and the Sex Trade along the Mekong*. Honolulu: University of Hawai'i Press.

Montgomery, Heather. 2001. *Modern Babylon? Prostituting Children in Thailand*. New York: Berghahn.

Monzini, Paola. 2005. *Sex Traffic: Prostitution, Crime and Exploitation*. London: Zed.

Musto, Jennifer Lynne. 2011. *Institutionalizing Protection, Professionalizing Victim Management: Explorations of Multi-Professional Anti-Trafficking Efforts in the Netherlands and the United States*. PhD dissertation in Women's Studies, University of California, Los Angeles.

Narula, Smita. 2006. "The Right to Food: Holding Global Actors Accountable under International Law." *Columbia Journal of Transnational Law* 44(3): 691–800.

Nederstigt, Frans, and Luciana Campello R. Almeida. 2007. "Brazil." In *Collateral Damage: The Impact of Anti-Trafficking Measures on Human Rights around the World*, pp. 87–114. Bangkok, Thailand: Global Alliance against Traffic in Women.

Nelken, David. 2011. "Human Trafficking and Legal Culture." *Israel Law Review* 43: 479–513.

Nevala, S. 2005. *The International Violence against Women Surveys*. Geneva, Switzerland: European Institute for Crime Prevention and Control.

O'Flaherty, Michael. 2014. "The UN General Assembly and the Strengthening of the United Nations Human Rights Treaty Body System." Universal Rights Group Blog. February 23. http://www.universal-rights.org/blog/the-un-general-assembly-and-the-strengthening-the-united-nations-human-rights-treaty-body-system.

O'Malley, Pat. 1999. "Governmentality and the Risk Society." *Economy and Society* 28: 138–48.

Patterson, Orlando. 2012. "Trafficking, Gender, and Slavery: Past and Present." In *The Legal Understanding of Slavery: From the Historical to the Contemporary*, pp. 1–52. Jean Allain, ed. Oxford: Oxford University Press.

Pearson, Elaine. 2007. "Australia." In *Collateral Damage: The Impact of Anti-Trafficking Measures on Human Rights around the World*, pp. 28–61. Bangkok, Thailand: Global Alliance against Traffic in Women.

Poovey, Mary. 1998. *A History of the Modern Fact: Problems of Knowledge in the Sciences of Wealth and Society*. Chicago: University of Chicago Press.

Porter, Theodore M. 1995. *Trust in Numbers: The Pursuit of Objectivity in Science and Public Life*. Princeton, NJ: Princeton University Press.

Power, Michael. 1999. *The Audit Society: Rituals of Verification*. Oxford: Oxford University Press.

———. 2004. "Counting, Control and Calculation: Reflections on Measuring and Management." *Human Relations* 57(6): 765–83.

Randeria, Shalini. 2006. "Entangled Histories of Uneven Modernities: Civil Society, Caste Solidarities and Legal Pluralism in Post-Colonial India." In *Civil Society—Berlin Perspectives*, pp. 213–42. John Keane, ed. Cambridge: Cambridge University Press.

Randolf, Susan, and Patrick Guyer. 2012. "Tracking the Historical Evolution of States' Compliance with their Economic and Social Rights Obligations of Result: Insights from the Historical SERF Index." *Nordic Journal of Human Rights* 30(3): 297–323.

Randolf, Susan, Sakiko Fukuda-Parr, and Terra Lawson-Remer. 2010. "Economic and Social Rights Fulfillment Index: Country Scores and Rankings." *Journal of Human Rights* 9(3): 230–61.

Report of the Secretary General. 1995. *From Nairobi to Beijing: Second Review and Appraisal of the Implementation of the Nairobi Forward-Looking Strategies for the Advancement of Women*. 2nd session, March 15–19. E/CN.6/1999/PC/3.

Riedel, Eibe. 2011. "New Bearings in Social Rights? The Communications Procedure under the ICESCR." In *From Bilateralism to Community Interest: Essays in Honour of Judge Bruno Simma*, pp. 547–89. Ulrich Festenrath, Rudolf Geiger, Daniel-Erasmus Khan, Andreas Paulus, Sabine von Shorlemer, and Christoph Vedder, eds. Oxford: Oxford University Press.

Rittich, Kerry. 2014. "Governing by Measuring: The Millennium Development Goals in Global Governance." In *Law in Transition: Human Rights, Development and Transitional Justice*, pp. 165–85. Ruth Buchanan and Peer Zumbansen, eds. Oxford: Hart.

Rose, Nikolas. 1989. *Governing the Soul: The Shaping of the Private Self.* London: Routledge.

———. 1991. "Governing by Numbers: Figuring Out Democracy." *Accounting Organizations and Society* 16(7): 673–92.

———. 1996. "The Death of the Social? Re-figuring the territory of government." *Economy and Society* 25: 327–56.

———. 1999. *Predicaments of Freedom.* Cambridge: Cambridge University Press.

Roseman, Mindie. 2010. "Revised Background Document for Proposed CESCR General Comment on Sexual and Reproductive Health," October 20. Manuscript on file with author.

Rosga, Ann Janette, and Margaret L. Satterthwaite. 2009. "The Trust in Indicators: Measuring Human Rights." *Berkeley Journal of International Law* 27(2): 253–315.

Rottenburg, Richard. 2009. *Far-Fetched Facts: A Parable of Development Aid.* Allison Brown and Tom Lampert, trans. Cambridge, MA: MIT Press.

———. 2012. "On Juridico-Political Foundations of Meta-Codes." In *The Globalization of Knowledge in History*, pp. 483–500. Jürgen Renn, ed. Berlin: Max Planck Research Library for the History and Development of Knowledge.

Sano, Hans-Otto. n.d. "Human Rights and Development: Human Rights Principles and Their Indicators." Manuscript on file with author.

Scheinin, Martin. 2005. "Use of Indicators by Human Rights Treaty Bodies — Experiences and Potentials." Background Paper for the UN Expert Meeting on Human Rights Indicators, Turku, Finland, March 11–13. Manuscript on file with author.

Schmitt, Robert C. 1968. *Demographic Statistics of Hawai'i: 1778–1965.* Honolulu: University of Hawai'i Press.

Schneider, Elizabeth M. 2004. "Transnational Law as a Domestic Resource: Thoughts on the Case of Women's Rights." *New England Law Review* 38(3): 689–724.

Schuler, Margaret, ed. 1992. *Freedom from Violence: Women's Strategies from around the World.* New York: UNIFEM.

Schweber, Libby. 2006. *Disciplining Statistics: Demography and Vital Statistics in France and England, 1830–1885.* Durham, NC: Duke University Press.

Secretariat of the Pacific Community. 2010. *Kiribati Family Health and Support Study: A Study on Violence against Women and Children.* Report to the Ministry of Internal and Social Affairs and Statistics Division, Bairiki, Tarawa, Republic of Kiribati.

Sen, Amartya. 1999. *Development as Freedom.* New York: Knopf.

———. 2005. "Foreword." In *Readings in Human Development: Concepts, Measures and Policies for a Development Paradigm*, pp. vii–xiii. Sakiko Fukuda-Parr and A. K. Shiva Kumar, eds. New Delhi, India: Oxford University Press.

Shamir, Hila. 2012. "A Labor Paradigm for Human Trafficking." *UCLA Law Review* 60: 76–136.

Sharma, Aruna, Rajeev Malhotra, and Alak N. Sharma. 2007. *Report on Asian Sub-Regional Workshop: Using Indicators to Promote and Monitor the Implementation of Human Rights.* Report to the Institute of Human Development, Delhi, and National Human Rights Commission of India, Office of the High Commissioner for Human Rights, New Delhi, India, July 26–28.

Sharma, Nandita. 2005. "Anti-Trafficking Rhetoric and the Making of a Global Apartheid."
NSWA Journal 17(3): 88–111.

Shore, Cris, and Susan Wright. 1999. "Audit Culture and Anthropology: Neo-Liberalism in
British Higher Education." *Journal of the Royal Anthropological Institute* 5(4): 557–75.

———. 2000. "Coercive Accountability: The Rise of Audit Culture in Higher Education." In
Audit Cultures, pp. 57–90. Marilyn Strathern, ed. London: Routledge.

———. 2015. "Audit Culture Revisited: Rankings, Ratings, and the Reassembling of Society."
Current Anthropology 56(3): 421–44.

Shue, Henry. 1984. "The Interdependence of Duties." In *The Right to Food*, pp. 83–95. Philip
Alston and Katerina Tomaševski, eds. Leiden, Netherlands: Martinus Nijhoff.

Simmons, Beth A. 2009. *Mobilizing for Human Rights: International Law in Domestic Politics*.
Cambridge: Cambridge University Press.

Simon, William H. 2004. "Toyota Jurisprudence: Legal Theory and Rolling Rule Regimes."
In *Columbia Public Law and Legal Theory Working Papers*. Working paper 0479.
http://lsr.nellco.org/columbia_pllt/0479.

Slovakia. 2013. *Reports Submitted by States Parties under Article 9 of the Convention: Ninth and
Tenth Periodic Reports of States Parties Due in 2012: Slovakia*. Country report to the Committee on the Elimination of Racial Discrimination, August 27. CERD/C/SVK/9–10.

Soderlund, Gretchen. 2005. "Running from the Rescuers: New US Crusades against Sex
Trafficking and the Rhetoric of Abolition." *NSWA Journal* 17(3): 64–87.

Special Issue on "Violence Against Women." 2005. *Statistical Journal of the United Nations Economic Commission for Europe* 22(3–4).

Stanton, Elizabeth A. 2007. "The Human Development Index: A History." Political Economy Research Institute, University of Massachusetts, Amherst. Working paper 127.

Star, Susan Leigh, and James R. Griesemer. 1999. "Institutional Ecology, 'Translations,' and
Boundary Objects: Amateurs and Professionals in Berkeley's Museum of Vertebrate
Zoology, 1907–39." In *The Science Studies Reader*, pp. 505–24. Mario Biagioli, ed. New
York: Routledge.

Strathern, Marilyn, ed. 2000. *Audit Cultures: Anthropological Studies in Accountability, Ethics,
and the Academy*. London: Routledge.

Straus, M. A. 1979. "Measuring Intrafamily Conflict and Violence: The Conflict Tactic (CT)
Scales." *Journal of Marriage and Family* 41(1): 75–88.

Tomaševski, Katarina. 1984. "Human Rights Indicators: The Right to Food as a Test Case."
In *The Right to Food*, pp. 135–67. P. Alston and K. Tomaševski, eds. Leiden, Netherlands:
Martinus Nijhoff.

Tufte, Edward R. 2001. *The Visual Display of Quantitative Information*, 2nd edition. Cheshire,
CT: Graphics Press.

Turku Report. 2005. *Report of Turku Expert Meeting on Human Rights Indicators*. Institute for
Human Rights, Åbo Akademi University, Turku, Finland, March 10–13. Document on file
with author.

UN Commission on the Status of Women. 2007. *Issues Paper*. Joint Parallel Event with the
UN Statistical Commission and the UN Commission on the Status of Women, 51st
session, March 1.

———. 2008a. *Joint Dialogue on Indicators to Measure Violence against Women*. Moderator's
summary, 52nd session, 39th session of the UN Statistical Commission, February 28.
Manuscript on file with author.

———. 2008b. *Proposals for a Multi-Year Programme of Work for the Period 2010–2014 of the Commission on the Status of Women: Report of the Secretary-General*. 53rd session, March 2–13. E/
CN.6/2009/3.

UN Committee on Economic, Social, and Cultural Rights. 1989. *Reporting by States Parties*.

General comment 1, February 24. http://tbinternet.ohchr.org/_layouts/treatybodyexternal /Download.aspx?symbolno=INT%2fCESCR%2fGEC%2f4756&Lang=en.

——. 1999. "The Right to Adequate Food." In *The International Covenant on Economic, Social and Cultural Rights*. General comment 12, article 11, May 12. E/C.12/1999/5.

——. 2000. "The Right to the Highest Attainable Standard of Health." In *The International Covenant on Economic, Social and Cultural Rights*. General comment 14, article 12, August 11. E/C.12/2000/4.

——. 2009. *Guidelines on Treaty-Specific Documents to Be Submitted by States Parties under Articles 16 and 17 of the International Covenant on Economic, Social, and Cultural Rights*. March 24. E/C.12/2008/2.

UN Committee on the Rights of the Child. 2010. *Treaty-Specific Guidelines Regarding the Form and Content of Periodic Reports to Be Submitted by States Parties under Article 44, Paragraph 1(b), of the Convention on the Rights of the Child*. November 23. CRC/C/58/Rev.2.

UN Department of Economic and Social Affairs. 2009. *The World's Women 2005: Progress in Statistics*. New York: United Nations.

UN Development Group. 2003. "The Human Rights-Based Approach to Development Cooperation: Towards a Common Understanding among UN Agencies." http://www .undg.org/content/programming_reference_guide_(undaf)/un_country_programming _principles/human_rights-based_approach_to_development_programming_(hrba).

UN Development Programme. 2000. "Using Indicators for Human Rights Accountability." In *Human Development Report 2000: Human Rights and Human Development*, pp. 89–111. New York: UN Publications. http://hdr.undp.org/sites/default/files/reports/261/hdr _2000_en.pdf.

——. 2010a. "History of the Human Development Report." http://hdr.undp.org/en /humandev/reports.

——. 2010b. *Report on Statistics of Human Development: Note by the Secretary-General*. December 7. E/CN.3/2011/15.

UN Development Programme Executive Board. 2011. *Executive Board Resolution 2011/11*. June 16. DP/2011/32.

UN Division for the Advancement of Women. 2005. *Violence against Women: A Statistical Overview, Challenges and Gaps in Data Collection and Methodology and Approaches for Overcoming Them*. Report of the expert group meeting organized in collaboration with the UN Economic Commission for Europe and World Health Organization, Geneva, Switzerland, April 11–14. http://www.un.org/womenwatch/daw/egm/vaw-stat-2005/index .html.

——. 2007. *Expert Group Meeting on Indicators to Measure Violence against Women*. Report of the expert group meeting organized in collaboration with the UN Economic Commission for Europe and UN Statistical Division, Geneva, Switzerland, October 8–10. http:// www.un.org/womenwatch/daw/vaw/v-egms-ind2007.htm.

UN Economic and Social Commission for Asia and the Pacific. 2011. *Report on the Work of the Secretariat on Gender Statistics*. Room document, United Nations Statistical Commission, 42nd session, February 22–25. http://unstats.un.org/unsd/statcom/doc11/BG -GenderStats-ESCAP.pdf.

UN Economic and Social Commission for Western Asia. 2010. *Training of Trainers on Violence against Women and Adaptation*. Workshop for Arab Countries, Beirut, May 3–7. E/ ESCWA/SD/2010/WG.3/Report. http://www.escwa.un.org/information/publications /edit/upload/E_ESCWA_SD_10_WG-3_Report_e.pdf.

UN Economic and Social Council. 2011. *Report of the United Nations High Commission for Human Rights: Social and Human Rights Questions*. July 4–29. E/2011/90.

UN Economic Commission for Europe. 2009. *Report of the Expert Group Meeting on Measur-

ing Violence against Women. Conference of European Statisticians. ESA/STAT/AC.193/ Item12. http:/unstats.un.org/unsd/demographic/meetings/vaw/docs/Item12.pdf.

UN General Assembly. 1966. *International Covenant on Economic, Social and Cultural Rights.* United Nations Treaty Series, vol. 993, December 16. http://www.ohchr.org/EN /ProfessionalInterest/Pages/CESCR.aspx.

———. 2003. *In-Depth Study on All Forms of Violence against Women.* Resolution adopted by the General Assembly on December 22. A/RES/58/185.

———. 2006. *In-Depth Study on All Forms of Violence against Women: Report of the Secretary-General.* 61st session, July 6. A/61/122/Add.1.

———. 2007. *Intensification of Efforts to Eliminate All Forms of Violence against Women.* Resolution adopted by the General Assembly on December 19. A/RES/61/143.

———. 2010. *Intensification of Efforts to Eliminate All Forms of Violence against Women: Report of the Secretary-General.* 65th session, August 2. A/65/208.

———. 2011. *Report of the Special Rapporteur on Trafficking in Persons, Especially Women and Children.* 66th session, August 9. A/66/283.

———. 2014. *Strengthening and Enhancing the Effective Functioning of the Human Rights Treaty Body System.* Resolution adopted by the General Assembly on April 9. A/RES/68/268.

UN Global Compact and Global Reporting Initiative. 2006. "Making the Connection: The GRI Guidelines and the UNGC Communication on Progress." http://www .unglobalcompact.org.

UN Human Rights Council. 2010. *Guidelines for the Treaty-Specific Document to Be Submitted by States Parties under Article 40 of the International Covenant on Civil and Political Rights.* November 22. CCPR/C/2009/1. http://www2.ohchr.org/english/bodies/hrc/docs/CCPR .C.2009.1.doc.

———. 2011. "Guiding Principles for the Implementation of the United Nations' 'Protect, Respect and Remedy' Framework." In *Report of the Special Representative of the Secretary General on the Issue of Human Rights and Transnational Corporations and other Business Enterprises, John Ruggie.* 17th session, March 21. A/HRC/17/31.

———. 2012a. *Report of the Special Rapporteur on Trafficking in Persons, Especially Women and Children, Joy Ngozi Ezielo.* June 5. A/HRC/20/18.

———. 2012b. *Trafficking in Persons, Especially Women and Children: Access to Effective Remedies for Trafficked Persons and Their Right to an Effective Remedy for Human Rights Violations.* Resolution adopted by the Human Rights Council on July 18. A/HRC/RES/20/1.

UN Human Rights Council and Commission on the Status of Women. 2008. *Report of the United Nations Development Fund for Women on the Activities of the Fund to Eliminate Violence against Women: Note by the Secretary-General.* December 18. A/HRC/10/43-E/ CN.6/2009/10.

UN Human Rights Treaty Bodies. 2001. *Review of Recent Developments to the Work of the Treaty Bodies.* Report to the 13th meeting of chairpersons of the UN human rights treaty bodies, Geneva, Switzerland, August 6. HRI/MC/2001/2.

UN International Human Rights Instruments. 2000. *Establishment of Indicators/Benchmarks to assess the Realization of Human Rights.* Report of the secretariat to the 12th meeting of chairpersons of the UN human rights treaty bodies, Geneva, Switzerland, June 16. HRI/ MC/2000/3.

———. 2009. *Compilation of Guidelines on the Form and Content of Reports to be Submitted by States Parties to the International Human Rights Treaties: Report of the Secretary-General.* Annex 3, June 3. HRI/GEN/2/Rev.6.

UN International Human Rights Instruments and Office of the High Commissioner for Human Rights. 2006. *Report on Indicators for Monitoring Compliance with International*

Human Rights Instruments. Report to the 18th meeting of chairpersons of the UN human rights treaty bodies, Geneva, Switzerland, June 22–23. HRI/MC/2006/7.

———. 2008. *Report on Indicators for Promoting and Monitoring the Implementation of Human Rights.* Report to the 20th meeting of chairpersons of the UN human rights treaty bodies, Geneva, Switzerland, June 26–27. HRI/MC/2008/3.

UN International Labour Organization. 2005. *A Global Alliance against Forced Labor: Global Report under the Follow-Up to the ILO Declaration on Fundamental Principles and Rights at Work.* Report of the director general to the International Labor Conference, 93rd session, Geneva, Switzerland. http://www.ilo.org/global/publications/books/WCMS_081882/lang--en/index.htm.

———. 2008. *ILO Action against Trafficking in Human Beings.* Geneva, Switzerland: International Labour Office. http://www.ilo.org/wcmsp5/groups/public/@ed_norm/@declaration/documents/publication/wcms_090356.pdf.

UN International Labour Organization (ILO), Office of the High Commissioner for Human Rights (OHCHR), and Secretariat of the Permanent Forum on Indigenous Issues (SPFII). 2010. *Using Indicators to Advance the Rights of Indigenous Peoples.* Concept note, Technical Expert Workshop, Geneva, Switzerland, September 20–21.

UN Office in Geneva. 2009. "Human Rights Committee Discusses Human Rights Indicators and the Influence of Parliamentarians on the Implementation of Human Rights." July 27. Document on file with author.

UN Office of Drugs and Crime. 2013. *Current Status of Victim Service Providers and Criminal Justice Actors in India on Anti-Trafficking.* India Country Assessment Report. http://www.unodc.org/documents/southasia//reports/Human_Trafficking-10-05-13.pdf.

UN Office of the High Commissioner for Human Rights. 2002. *Recommended Principles and Guidelines on Human Rights and Human Trafficking.* May 20. E/2002/68/Add.1.

———. 2007. "Criteria for Identifying Indicators on VAW." Supporting paper 3, October 5. http://www.un.org/womenwatch/daw/egm/vaw_indicators_2007/papers/Supporting%20Paper%20OHCHR.pdf.

———. 2009. *Report of the High Commissioner for Human Rights on Implementation of Economic, Social, and Cultural Rights.* UN Economic and Social Council. June 8. E/2009/90.

———. 2012a. *Human Rights Indicators: A Guide to Measurement and Implementation.* New York: Office of the High Commissioner for Human Rights. HR/PUB/12/5. http://www.ohchr.org/Documents/Publications/Human_rights_indicators_en.pdf.

———. 2012b. "Indicators: Essential Tools in the Realization of Human Rights." http://www.ohchr.org/EN/NewsEvents/Pages/IndicatorsessentialtoolsinrealizationofHR.aspx.

UN Secretariat. 1993. *Report of the Seminar on Appropriate Indicators to Measure Achievements in the Progressive Realization of Economic, Social, and Cultural Rights.* Report of the secretariat to the World Conference on Human Rights preparatory committee, 4th session, Geneva, Switzerland, April 20. A/CONF.157/PC/73.

———. 2006. "Concept Paper on the High Commissioner's Proposal for a Unified Standing Treaty Body." Paper delivered at the 4th intercommittee meeting of the human rights bodies, Geneva, Switzerland, March 22. HRI/MC/2006/2.

UN Secretary General. 2005. *In Larger Freedom: Towards Development, Security and Human Rights for All: Report of the Secretary-General.* March 21. A/59/2005.

———. 2011. "Unite to End Violence against Women." http://endviolence.un.org/index.shtml.

UN Statistical Commission. 1994. *Report on the Special Session.* April 11–15. E/1994/29.

———. 2008. *Report on the Thirty-Ninth Session.* February 26–29. E/CN.3/2008/34.

———. 2009. *Friends of the Chair of the United Nations Statistical Commission on the Indicators on Violence against Women: Note by the Secretary-General.* UN Economic and Social Council,

40th session, December 11. E/CN.3/2009/13. http://unstats.un.org/unsd/demographic/meetings/vaw/reports/E_CN-3_2009-13-en.pdf.

———. 2011a. *Implementation of the Fundamental Principles of Official Statistics.* 43rd session, December 20. E/CN.3/2012/14.

———. 2011b. *Report of Brazil, Morocco and South Africa on Member States' Concerns with Indicators Released by the United Nations Agencies.* December 7. E/CN.3/2011/16.

———. 2011c. *Report of the Bureau of the Statistical Commission on Statistics of Human Development.* December 7. E/CN.3/2011/14.

———. 2011d. *Report on the Implementation of the Fundamental Principles of Official Statistics.* 42nd session, February 22–25. E/CN.3/2011/17. http://unstats.un.org/unsd/statcom/doc11/2011-17-FundamentalPrinciples-E.pdf.

———. 2012a. *Draft Revised Preamble for the Fundamental Principles of Official Statistics.* 43rd session, February 28–March 2. http://unstats.un.org/unsd/statcom/doc12/BG-FPOS.pdf.

———. 2012b. *Report of the Friends of the Chair on the Implementation of the Fundamental Principles of Official Statistics.* December 18. E/CN.3/2013/3.

———. 2014a. "Friends of the Chair group for Indicators on Violence against Women." http://unstats.un.org/unsd/demographic/meetings/vaw/default.htm.

———. 2014b. "UN Statistical Commission" (homepage). http://unstats.un.org/unsd/statcom/commission.htm.

UN Statistics Division. 2009. *Proposed Draft Outline for the Guidelines for Producing Statistics on Violence against Women, Part I: Statistical Survey.* Instituto Nacional de Estadística y Geografía de México, Aguascalientes, Mexico, December 9–11. ESA/STAT/AC.193/Item13. http://UNstats.un.org/unsd/demographic/meetings/vaw/docs/Item13.pdf.

———. 2010. *Report on the Meeting of the Friends of the Chair of the United Nations Statistical Commission on Statistical Indicators on Violence against Women.* Instituto Nacional de Estadística y Geografía de México, Aguascalientes, Mexico, December 9–11. ESA/STAT/AC.193/L.3. http://UNstats.un.org/unsd/demographic/meetings/vaw/docs/finalreport.pdf.

———. 2013. *Guidelines for Producing Statistics on Violence against Women: Statistical Surveys.* September 9. ST/ESA/STAT/SER.F/110. http://unstats.un.org/unsd/gender/docs/Guidelines_Statistics_VAW.pdf.

———. 2014. *Fundamental Principles of National Official Statistics.* January 29. A/RES/68/261. http://unstats.un.org/unsd/dnss/gp/fundprinciples.aspx.

UN Working Group on the Harmonization of Working Methods of the Treaty Bodies. 2006. *Report of the Working Group on the Harmonization of Working Methods of Treaty Bodies.* Report to the 19th meeting of chairpersons of the UN human rights treaty bodies, Geneva, Switzerland, June 18–22. HRI/MC/2007/2.

UN Working Group on the Right to Development. 2010. "Right to Development Criteria and Operational Sub-Criteria" (addendum). In *Report of the High-Level Task Force on the Implementation of the Right to Development at Its Sixth Session.* Human Rights Council, Geneva, Switzerland, January 14–22. A/HRC/15/WG.2/TF/2/Add.2.

UNICEF. 2014. "Multiple Indicator Cluster Survey (MICS)." http://www.unicef.org/statistics/index_24302.html.

———. 2015. "MICS" (homepage). http://mics.unicef.org.

United Nations. 1961. "Statistical Questions." In *Yearbook of the United Nations, 1961*, pp. 290–91. New York: Department of Public Information.

———. 1995. *Beijing Declaration and Platform of Action.* Adopted at the Fourth World Conference on Women on October 27. A/CONF.177/20.

———. 2000. "Protocol to Prevent, Suppress and Punish Trafficking in Persons, Especially Women and Children, Supplementing the United Nations Convention against Transnational Organized Crime." November 15. https://treaties.un.org/pages/viewdetails.aspx ?src=ind&mtdsg_no=xviii-12-a&chapter=18&lang=en.

——. 2008a. "Millennium Development Goals Indicators." http://mdgs.un.org/unsd/mdg /Host.aspx?Content=Indicators/OfficialList.htm.

——. 2008b. "News on Millennium Development Goals." http://www.un.org /millenniumgoals.

US Congress. 2011. *Trafficking in Persons Report Improvement Act.* 1st session of the 112th US Congress. S. 1362.

US Department of State. 2001. *Trafficking in Persons Report.* Washington, DC: US Department of State.

——. 2002. *Trafficking in Persons Report.* Washington, DC: US Department of State.

——. 2003. *Trafficking in Persons Report.* Washington, DC: US Department of State.

——. 2004. *Trafficking in Persons Report.* Washington, DC: US Department of State.

——. 2005. *Trafficking in Persons Report.* Washington, DC: US Department of State.

——. 2006. "Introduction." In *Country Reports on Human Rights Practices.* Washington, DC: US Government Printing Office.

——. 2010. *Trafficking in Persons Report.* Washington, DC: US Department of State.

——. 2011. *Trafficking in Persons Report.* Washington, DC: US Department of State.

——. 2012. "Office to Monitor and Combat Trafficking in Persons: Programs Funded During Fiscal Year 2012." http://www.state.gov/j/tip/rls/other/2012/201451.htm.

——. 2013a. "Request for Information for the 2014 Trafficking in Persons Report." In *Federal Register*, vol. 78, no. 241. December 16. Public notice 8548. pp. 76183–86, federal register document no. 2013-29860. http://www.gpo.gov/fdsys/pkg/FR-2013-12-16/html /2013-29860.htm.

——. 2013b. "Request for Statements of Interest: G/TIP FY 2014 International Programs to Combat Trafficking in Persons." http://www.state.gov/j/tip/rls/other/2013/215006.htm.

——. 2013c. "Technology as a Tool in the Fight against Human Trafficking." http://www .state.gov/r/pa/pl/cwa/212411.htm.

——. 2013d. *Trafficking in Persons Report.* Washington, DC: US Department of State.

US Government Accountability Office. 2006. *Human Trafficking: Better Data, Strategy, and Reporting Needed to Enhance U.S. Anti-trafficking Efforts Abroad.* Washington, DC: US Government Accountability Office. http://www.gao.gov/new.items/d06825.pdf.

Vaghri, Ziba, Adem Arkadas, and Early Childhood Rights Indicators Group. 2009. *Manual for Early Childhood Rights Indicators: A Guide for State Parties Reporting to the Committee on the Rights of the Child.* New York: UNICEF.

Vaghri, Ziba, Adem Arkadas, Sami Kruse, and Clyde Hertzman. 2011. "CRC General Comment 7 Indicators Framework: A Tool for Monitoring the Implementation of Child Rights in Early Childhood." *Journal of Human Rights* 10(2): 178–88.

Vance, Carole S. 2011. "States of Contradiction: Twelve Ways to Do Nothing about Trafficking While Pretending To." *Social Research* 78(3): 933–48.

——. 2012. "Innocence and Experience: Melodramatic Narratives of Sex Trafficking and Their Consequences for Law and Policy." *History of the Present* 2(2): 200–218.

Van Hoof, G. J. H. 1984. "The Legal Nature of Economic, Social, and Cultural Rights: A Rebuttal of Some Traditional View." In *The Right to Food*, pp. 97–110. Philip Alston and Katerina Tomaševski, eds. Leiden, Netherlands: Martinus Nijhoff.

Venezuela. 2013. *Concluding Observations on the Combined Nineteenth to Twenty-First Periodic Reports of the Bolivarian Republic of Venezuela.* Country report to the Committee on the Elimination of Racial Discrimination, September 23. CERD/C/VEN/19–21.

Vizard, Polly. 2012. "Evaluating Compliance Using Quantitative Methods and Indicators:

Lessons from the Human Rights Measurement Framework." *Nordic Journal of Human Rights* 30(3): 239–78.

Voices of Women Organizing Project. 2008. "Justice Denied: How Family Courts in NYC Endanger Battered Women and Children." http://www.leadershipcouncil.org/docs/VOW _JusticeDenied_sum.pdf.

Walby, Sylvia. 2007. "Indicators to Measure Violence against Women: Invited Paper." Paper presented at the expert group meeting on indicators to measure violence against women, UN Statistical Commission and Economic Commission for Europe, UN Division for the Advancement of Women, and UN Statistics Division, Geneva, Switzerland, October 8–10. Working paper 1.

Waldmueller, Johannes M. 2014. *From Natural Rights to Rights of Nature? Human Rights Indicators and Buen Vivir in Ecuador: A Decolonial Actor-Network Study*. PhD dissertation, Graduate Institute of International and Development Studies, Geneva, Switzerland.

Walk Free Foundation. 2013. "The Global Slavery Index" (homepage). http://www .globalslaveryindex.org.

Ward, Michael. 2004. *Quantifying the World: UN Ideas and Statistics*. United Nations Intellectual History Project Series. Bloomington: Indiana University Press.

Warren, Kay B. 2007. "The 2000 UN Human Trafficking Protocol: Rights, Enforcement, Vulnerabilities." In *The Practice of Human Rights: Tracking Law between the Global and the Local*, pp. 242–70. Mark Goodale and Sally Engle Merry, eds. Cambridge: Cambridge University Press.

———. 2010. "The Illusiveness of Counting Victims and the Concreteness of Ranking Countries: Trafficking in Persons from Columbia to Japan." In *Sex, Drugs, and Body Counts: The Politics of Numbers in Global Crime and Conflict*, pp. 110–26. Peter Andreas and Kelly M. Greenhill, eds. Ithaca, NY: Cornell University Press.

———. 2012. "Troubling the Victim/Trafficker Dichotomy in Efforts to Combat Human Trafficking: The Unintended Consequences of Moralizing Labor Migration." *Indiana Journal of Global Legal Studies* 19(1): 105–20.

Weiner, Neil, and Nicole Hala. 2008. *Measuring Human Trafficking: Lessons from New York City*. New York: Vera Institute.

Weiss, Ayla. 2012. "Ten Years of Fighting Trafficking: Critiquing the Trafficking in Persons Report through the Case of South Korea." *Asian-Pacific Law and Policy Journal* 13: 304–39.

Weitzer, Ronald. 2007. "The Social Construction of Sex Trafficking: Ideology and Institutionalization of a Moral Crusade." *Politics and Society* 35: 447–75.

Welling, Judith V. 2008. "International Indicators and Economic, Social, and Cultural Rights." *Human Rights Quarterly* 30: 933–58.

Winkler, Inga T., Margaret L. Satterthwaite, and Catarina de Albuquerque. 2015. "Treasuring What We Measure, and Measuring What We Treasure: Post-2015 Monitoring for the Promotion of Equality in the Water, Sanitation, and Hygiene Sector." *Wisconsin International Law Journal* 32(3): 547–94.

Wood, Reed M., and Mark Gibney. 2010. "The Political Terror Scale (PTS): A Re-Introduction and a Comparison to CIRI." *Human Rights Quarterly* 32(2): 367–400.

World Health Organization. 2005. *Multi-Country Study on Women's Health and Domestic Violence against Women and Initial Results on Prevalence, Health Outcomes and Women's Responses*. Geneva, Switzerland: World Health Organization.

Yamin, Alicia Ely, and Katherine L. Falb. 2012. "Counting What We Know; Knowing What to Count: Sexual Reproductive Health, Maternal Health, and the Millennium Development Goals." *Nordic Journal of Human Rights* 30(3): 350–71.

Index

THE CHICAGO SERIES IN LAW AND SOCIETY

Edited by John M. Conley and Lynn Mather

Series titles, continued from front matter: